Best Hikes Near
New York City

BEN KEENE

FALCONGUIDES

GUILFORD, CONNECTICUT
HELENA, MONTANA
AN IMPRINT OF GLOBE PEQUOT PRESS

To buy books in quantity for corporate use
or incentives, call **(800) 962–0973**
or e-mail **premiums@GlobePequot.com.**

FALCONGUIDES®

FalconGuides is an imprint of Globe Pequot Press.
Falcon, FalconGuides, and Outfit Your Mind are registered trademarks of Morris Book Publishing, LLC.

All interior photos by Ben Keene
Maps by Mapping Specialists Ltd © Morris Book Publishing, LLC

Text Design: Sheryl P. Kober
Layout: Maggie Peterson
Project Editor: Gregory Hyman

TOPO! Explorer software and SuperQuad source maps courtesy of National Geographic Maps. For information about TOPO! Explorer, TOPO!, and Nat Geo Maps products, go to www.topo.com or www.natgeomaps.com.

Library of Congress Cataloging-in-Publication Data is available on file.

ISBN 978-0-7627-6121-0

Printed in the United States of America

10 9 8 7 6 5 4 3 2 1

The author and Globe Pequot Press assume no liability for accidents happening to, or injuries sustained by, readers who engage in the activities described in this book.

Contents

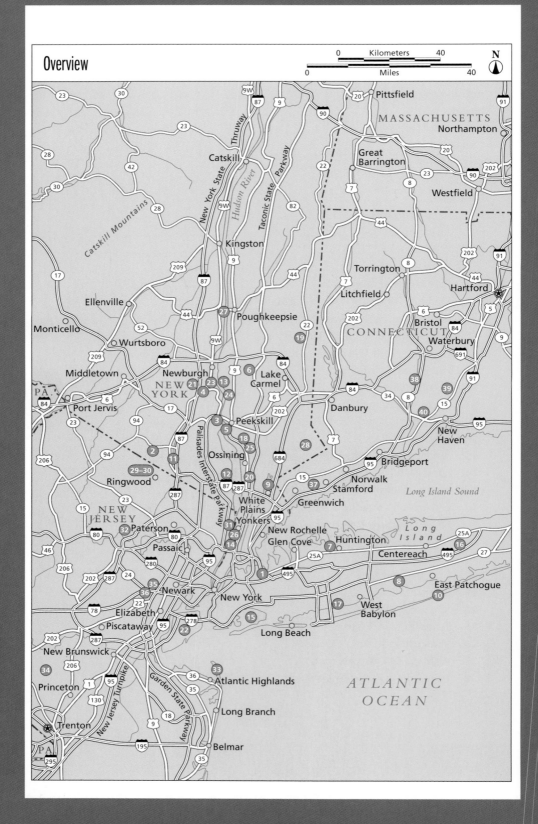

Overview

Kilometers 40

Miles 40

N

New Jersey

Connecticut

Acknowledgments

I would like to thank my family—Mom, Dad, and Becky; Ali Rohrs; Bill Elliston; Stephanie Jelliffe; Melissa Markle; Jeb, Neela, and Finn Woodard; Chris Bertram; Christina and Conor McNamara; Rob Tempio and Erin Graham; Peter Bruland and Minona Heaviland; Lindsay Tuthill and Tim Maidment; Gwen and Richard Petronzio; Mike Wei; Bill and Mary Burnham; and my devoted assistant, Caledonia. Without your advice, encouragement, and generosity, I never would have been able to finish my first book.

As diurnal lizards, five-lined skinks like to bask in the sun during the day. See Hike 23.

Introduction

Introduce yourself as a New Yorker and few people will imagine that you have a dresser drawer full of hiking socks, a small library of trail maps, and an informed if somewhat stubborn opinion about the appropriate ratio of nuts, dried fruit, and chocolate pieces in a serving of trail mix. And yet there are those of us who fit that description. I can trace my own love of the outdoors back to childhood, when my dad would overload the Ford station wagon (in Clark Griswold–esque fashion) with sleeping bags, a camp stove, an enormous tent, and a cooler full of perishables and drive the family to a nearby park for a short summer escape from suburbia. Wherever we ended up—coastal Maine, upstate New York, or western Maryland—my sister and I always had fun exploring the woods and trying to memorize the names of the birds, reptiles, and mammals pictured in our Audubon Society guidebooks.

As I got older, the hiking bug I caught in my youth never really went away, and I've since tested several pairs of boots on the slopes of hills and mountains in Europe, Asia, and Central America. Never did I imagine this would become anything more than a hobby. Which made the offer to write this book especially exciting, because it allowed for a certain rededication to an activity that I've enjoyed off and on for the majority of my life. It also gave me the chance to learn more about the natural and man-made characteristics of a region I have called home for more than a decade.

In gathering information for the guide, I gained an appreciation for places I hadn't known of before and I increased my understanding of local history and geography. Van Cortlandt Park is one such spot—an extensive public property that, while physically distant from Manhattan's ceaseless activity, has a past that relates to both the earliest days of the city and the origins of the United States. Research projects are by their very nature educational opportunities, and setting out to become an expert on outdoor New York certainly taught me a lot about the surrounding area. I learned, for instance, just how many New York–area hiking trails are accessible by public transportation. In fact, more than half of the hikes in this book can be reached by train or bus.

I'm not much for choosing favorites—for different reasons, any one of the treks within these pages is worth trying. But in making my selections, I did attempt to offer a variety of destinations in terms of scenery, accessibility, and level of difficulty. Hopefully I've been successful. I also tried to bring these parks and preserves to life, and sought to add context wherever possible. So whether you decide to systematically hike this book in its entirety or just cherry-pick a selection of trails, I am optimistic that you'll find it to be a useful tool and an enjoyable read. Because I certainly had fun putting it together.

Weather

While generally agreeable, New York's climate can be more variable than that in the other mid-Atlantic states. Winters are cold—sometimes severely so—and typically include a moderate amount of snow along with the occasional storm bringing sleet or freezing rain. Wintry precipitation well into March is not uncommon. For hikers who enjoy a brisk day out to shake off cabin fever, note that snow accumulation outside of the five boroughs (and particularly in the Lower Hudson Valley) will be greater than it is in the city.

Spring is often a relatively short season characterized by rain and unexpected temperature fluctuations. The region might experience a warm snap in early March, with highs approaching 80 degrees, only to endure a stretch of chilly, overcast days in late April where the thermometer seems stuck in the 50s. For this reason, it's wise to dress in layers and to bring waterproof outerwear if there's a chance of rain in the forecast.

Summer often arrives suddenly in New York, turning otherwise pleasant, sunny afternoons into scorchers and transforming the cement and steel environment of the city into a pressure cooker. Temperatures usually range in the 80s and 90s during July and August, with an infrequent spike into the triple digits. But it's the humidity, not the heat, that causes so many New Yorkers to flee for the Hamptons

Fossilized hedgehog or American chestnut burr?

or the Jersey Shore on summer weekends. If you're planning on visiting a park during this season, carry plenty of drinking water.

That leaves autumn, a span of eight to ten weeks from mid-September until late November when the skies are generally clear, the temperature remains well suited for outdoor activity, and the foliage brightens the forests with shades of red, yellow, and orange. Bring a camera and prepare for the trails to be busier on weekends.

Flora and Fauna

New York is a city of many cultures, faiths, and lifestyles. In a similar way, the natural habitats that can be found in and around the metro area are anything but monolithic. Mixed hardwood forests occur throughout New York, New Jersey, and Connecticut; pine barrens, while less extensive today than they were in the past, still exist at the eastern end of Long Island; and pockets of maritime forest survive on Fire Island and Sandy Hook in New Jersey. Look for oaks (and their telltale acorns), chestnuts (with spiny yellow-green fruit), and even flowering crab apple trees on hikes in this book. These plants, to name but a very few, are common in the Northeast. Birch, with their pale, papery bark, are easy to identify as well, and tend to occur in higher elevations such as on the slopes of Bellvale Mountain on the Appalachian Trail. Meanwhile, in Inwood Hill Park, grand sycamore trees share real estate with handsome American elms and ginkos, recognizable by their fan-shaped leaves.

Providing color and fragrance to parks and preserves across all three states, wildflowers such as violets, goldenrod, Queen Anne's lace, black-eyed Susans, and Indian paintbrush appear in sunny open meadows, along trail edges, and around bodies of water. These are some of the most photogenic flora, and attract moths, butterflies, bees, and other pollen collectors. Clumps of tiny white saxifrage are often the first flowers to appear in early spring—frequently sprouting from cracks and crevices in outcroppings of stone. Many flowers, however, including the bright white-and-yellow heads of the common fleabane, appear throughout the spring and summer months, while others, like the soft pink or white petals of the mild water pepper, can bloom into September. Some species, the deep blue or violet-colored downy gentian in particular, can flower as late as November.

The chances of seeing more than a few of the animals native to the region on a single hike are not as great however. That said, some of the larger parks, such as Clarence Fahnestock Memorial State Park and Black Rock Forest, do protect a wider range of fauna than you might imagine. The eastern chipmunk, the gray squirrel, and the white-tailed deer are the most ubiquitous mammals in the tristate area, but muskrats, woodchucks, opossum, and beaver occur with some frequency. And even if you never have a face-to-face encounter, it's likely that you'll catch a whiff of striped skunk by spending enough time in the woods. In terms of predators, both red and gray fox, raccoon, eastern coyote, black bear, and less commonly, bobcat hunt in the hills and valleys of the Hudson Highlands. Near bodies of water it is not unusual to see wood, green, and pickerel frogs, along with painted, snapping, and box turtles.

More impressive, perhaps, is the tremendous diversity of birdlife that either nests in or migrates through greater New York. Wading birds are typical in places such as Jamaica Bay, Alley Pond Park, and the Massapequa Preserve, as are swans, geese, and ducks. Raptors such as American kestrels, broad-winged hawks, red-tailed hawks, northern harriers, and increasingly, bald eagles, have been spotted and counted by birders at places like Hook Mountain State Park. Once endangered in New York, the osprey, which uses its long talons to fish, has returned to the rivers and lakes of Long Island. And the list of songbirds that call the area home is lengthy—but with some practice you'll eventually begin to hear the calls of dozens of feathered creatures on the next hike you take. Listen for the chatty northern mockingbird, try to identify the red-winged blackbird's call in marshlands, and let sparrows and warblers enliven your walking.

Getting Around

Area Codes

The area codes in New York City are 212, 347, 646, 718, and 917. Long Island has two area codes: 516 (Nassau County) and 631 (Suffolk County). In Westchester County the area code is 914; 845 covers the rest of southeastern New York. Area codes for New Jersey areas covered in this book are 201, 551, 862, 973, 908, 609, 732, and 848. In southwestern Connecticut the area codes are 203 and 475.

Roads

For current information on New York road conditions, weather, and closures, contact the New York State Department of Transportation Travel Center at (888) GO5-11NY (888-465-1169; 511 within New York) or visit www.nysdot.gov/travel, where you can subscribe to TransAlert to get short e-mails or text messages about major incidents affecting transportation for particular regions or routes you specify. For New Jersey conditions, contact the New Jersey Department of Transportation at (866) 511-NJDT (6538), (511 within New Jersey) or visit www.511nj .org. For conditions in Connecticut, consult the department of transportation's Interactive Travel Information Map at www.dotdata.ct.gov/iti/master_iti.html or follow eTraffic incidents on Twitter.

By Air

Located in the borough of Queens, LaGuardia Airport (LAG) is just 9 miles from midtown Manhattan, while John F. Kennedy International Airport (JFK) is 15 miles away. Newark Liberty International Airport (EWR) is 15 miles west of the city in New Jersey. The Port Authority of New York and New Jersey's website has information on all three: www.panynj.gov/airports.

Visit your favorite airline's website to book reservations online or search an aggregator such as www.kayak.com, www.cheaptickets.com, www.expedia.com, www.orbitz.com, www.priceline.com, www.farecompare.com, www.travelocity .com, http://travel.yahoo.com/flights, or www.bing.com/travel.

By Rail

The Metropolitan Transportation Authority (MTA) operates New York's subway system, along with the Long Island Railroad and the Metro North Railroad, which services New Haven as well as both sides of the Hudson Valley. To plan a trip by rail, visit www.mta.info. Schedule, ticketing, and fare information about train (and bus) service to New Jersey can be found at www.njtransit.com.

By Bus

Twenty different carriers operate out of the Port Authority Bus Terminal in Manhattan; call (800) 221-9903 or visit www.panynj.gov/bus-terminals/port-authority-bus-terminal.html for more information. The buses used to reach the hikes in this book are primarily run by Coach USA. Visit www.coachusa.com for sales office contact information.

Looking south over Fox Island and Greenwood Lake from the Appalachian Trail in New York. See Hike 2.

How to Use This Guide

Take a close enough look, and you'll find that this guide contains just about everything you'll ever need to choose, plan for, enjoy, and survive a hike near New York. Stuffed with useful area information, *Best Hikes Near New York City* features forty mapped and cued hikes. What follows is an outline of the book's major components.

Each hike begins with a short **summary** of the hike's highlights. These quick overviews give you a sense of the kind of adventure to expect. You'll learn about the terrain and what surprises each route has to offer.

Following the overview you'll find the **hike specs:** quick, nitty-gritty details of the hike. Most are self-explanatory, but here are some details on others:

Distance: The total distance of the recommended route—one way for loop hikes, round-trip for an out-and-back or lollipop hike, point-to-point for a shuttle. Options are additional.

Approximate hiking time: The average time it will take to cover the route. It is based on the total distance, elevation gain, and condition and difficulty of the trail. Your fitness level will also affect your time.

Difficulty: Each hike has been assigned a level of difficulty, with the majority of the trails earning an **easy** or **moderate** rating. The rating system was developed from several sources and personal experience. These levels are meant to be a guideline only and may prove easier or harder for different people depending on ability and physical fitness.

- **Easy:** 5 miles or less total trip distance in one day, with minimal elevation gain and a paved or essentially smooth-surfaced dirt trail.
- **Moderate:** Up to about 7 miles total trip distance in one day, with moderate elevation gain and potentially rough terrain.
- **Difficult:** More than 7 miles total trip distance in one day, with numerous strenuous elevation gains and rough and/or rocky terrain.

Trail surface: Provides general information about what to expect underfoot.

Seasons: Offers general information on the best time of year to hike.

Other trail users: Other users may include horseback riders, mountain bikers, cross-country skiers, etc.

Wheelchair accessibility: When available, a description of the features that make a park or a trail accessible to people with disabilities is given.

Canine compatibility: Know the trail regulations before you take your dog hiking with you. Dogs are not allowed on several trails in this book.

Land status: Lists whether the trail is in a state forest, county park, nature preserve, etc.

Fees and permits: Lets you know whether you need to carry any money with you for park entrance fees and permits.

Maps: This is a list of other maps to supplement the maps in this book. USGS maps are the best source for accurate topographical information, but the local park map may show more recent trails. Use both.

Trail contacts: This is the location, phone number, and website URL for the local land manager(s) in charge of all the trails within the selected hike. Call before you head out to get trail access information, or contact the land manager after your visit if you see problems with trail erosion, damage, or misuse.

Other: Includes other information that will enhance your hike.

Special considerations: This section calls your attention to specific trail hazards, such as a lack of water or hunting seasons.

The **Finding the trailhead** section gives you the best public transportation route to the trailhead and/or dependable driving directions to where you'll want to park.

The Hike is the meat of the chapter. Detailed and honest, it's a carefully researched impression of the trail. It also often includes lots of area history, both natural and human.

Under **Miles and Directions,** mileage cues identify all turns and trail name changes, as well as points of interest. **Options** are also given for many hikes to make your journey longer, depending on the amount of time you have.

Finally, the **Hike Information** section provides information on local events and attractions, restaurants, hiking tours, and hiking organizations.

Don't feel restricted to the routes and trails that are mapped here. Be adventurous and use this guide as a platform to discover new routes for yourself. One of the simplest ways to begin is to just turn the map upside down and hike the route in reverse. The change in perspective is often fantastic, and the hike should feel quite different. With this in mind, it'll be like getting two distinctly different hikes on each map. For your own purposes, you may wish to copy the route directions onto a small sheet of paper to help you while hiking, or photocopy the map and cue sheet to take with you. Otherwise, just slip the whole book in your backpack and take it along. Enjoy your time in the outdoors and remember to pack out what you pack in.

How to Use the Maps

Overview map: This map shows the location of each hike in the area by hike number.

Route maps: These are your primary guides to each hike. Each shows all of the accessible roads and trails, points of interest, water, landmarks, and geographical features. Each also distinguishes trails from roads, and paved roads from unpaved roads. The selected route is highlighted, and directional arrows point the way.

Trail Finder

Hike No.	Hike Name	Best Hikes for Children	Best Hikes for Great Views	Best Hikes for Water Lovers	Best Hikes for Birders	Best Hikes for Backpackers	Best Hikes for History Lovers	Best Hikes for Non-drivers	Best Hikes for Nature Lovers	Best Hikes for Dogs	Best Hikes for Wheelchair Accessibility
1	Alley Pond Park	●									
2	Appalachian Trail		●			●		●	●		
3	Bear Mountain State Park		●					●			
4	Black Rock Forest						●				
5	Blue Mountain Reservation							●	●		
6	Clarence Fahnestock Memorial State Park					●					
7	Cold Spring Harbor State Park	●		●				●			
8	Connetquot River State Park Preserve				●		●	●			
9	Cranberry Lake Preserve				●			●	●		
10	Fire Island National Seashore			●							
11	Harriman State Park					●		●			
12	Hook Mountain State Park		●					●			
13	Hudson Highlands State Park		●					●			
14	Inwood Hill Park	●					●	●		●	
15	Jamaica Bay Wildlife Refuge			●	●			●	●		●
16	Long Island Pine Barrens	●									●
17	Nassau–Suffolk Trail					●		●			
18	Old Croton Aqueduct						●	●		●	●
19	Pawling Nature Preserve							●			
20	Rockefeller State Park Preserve				●					●	

Trail Finder

Hike No.	Hike Name	Best Hikes for Children	Best Hikes for Great Views	Best Hikes for Water Lovers	Best Hikes for Birders	Best Hikes for Backpackers	Best Hikes for History Lovers	Best Hikes for Non-drivers	Best Hikes for Nature Lovers	Best Hikes for Dogs	Best Hikes for Wheelchair Accessibility
21	Schunemunk Mountain State Park		●								
22	Staten Island Greenbelt							●	●		
23	Storm King State Park		●								
24	Sugarloaf Hill		●								
25	Teatown Lake Reservation								●		
26	Van Cortlandt Park						●				●
27	Walkway Over the Hudson	●	●					●			●
28	Ward Pound Ridge Reservation	●							●		
29	Long Pond Ironworks					●	●				
30	Monks Mountain									●	
31	Palisades Interstate Park	●	●	●				●			
32	Pyramid Mountain Natural Historic Area	●							●		
33	Sandy Hook			●				●			
34	Sourland Mountain Nature Preserve				●					●	
35	South Mountain Reservation		●				●	●			
36	Watchung Reservation						●				●
37	Mianus River Park	●		●							
38	Naugatuck State Forest		●					●			
39	Sleeping Giant State Park		●								
40	West Rock Ridge State Park		●								

Map Legend

Transportation

Symbol	Description
80	Freeway/Interstate Highway
101	U.S. Highway
1	State Highway
1431	Minor Road
———	Local Road
= = = =	Unpaved Road
⊢—⊢—⊢	Railroad

Trails

-------	Selected Route
- - - - -	Trail or Fire Road
→	Direction of Travel

Water Features

	Body of Water
～	River or Creek

Land Management

	Local & State Parks

Symbols

Symbol	Description
⌣	Bridge
■	Building/Point of Interest
Λ	Campground
∩	Cave
⫯	Gate
▲	Mountain Peak
P	Parking
×	Physical Feature
🛆	Picnic Area
🛈	Ranger Station
🚻	Restroom
🖼	Scenic View
🐎	Stable
🗼	Tower
○	Towns and Cities
20	Trailhead
❓	Visitor/Information Center
≋	Waterfalls

New York

Perkins Tower at the summit of Bear Mountain. See Hike 3.

Black Rock Forest's connection to the history of New York State can be traced back to the American Revolution, when George Washington's army used Continental Road to travel from West Point to Newburgh and watched the river for British warships from Spy Rock. See Hike 4.

Alley Pond Park

Home to the Alley Pond Giant, the oldest known tree in New York City, this park is the second largest in the borough but considerably less well known. Visit the site of New York's first nature trail and explore the meadows in the northern part of this undeveloped terminal moraine alongside Little Neck Bay.

Start: The parking lot of Alley Pond Environmental Center

Nearest town: Douglaston, NY

Distance: 3.2 miles out and back

Approximate hiking time: 1.5 to 2 hours

Difficulty: Easy

Trail surface: Mulch, grass, and plank tracks

Seasons: Year-round

Other users: School groups, birders

Wheelchair accessibility: The 1-mile nature trail offers limited access for disabled visitors.

Canine compatibility: Dogs permitted if on a leash 10 feet or less

Land status: City park

Fees and permits: None

Schedule: Daily from sunrise to sunset

Facilities: Restrooms, water fountain, gift shop, classrooms, natural history exhibit with live animal specimens

Maps: USGS Flushing and Sea Cliff, NY. A black-and-white interpretive map is available at the environmental center, and a smaller-scale printable PDF of trails in the Alley Wetlands and the Alley Woodlands can be found at www.runyourcity.com/state/ny/new-york-city/running-map-of-new-york-city/queens/running-map-alley-pond-park.

Trail contacts: New York City Department of Parks & Recreation, The Arsenal, Central Park, 830 Fifth Ave., New York, NY 10065; (212) NEW-YORK; www.nycgovparks.org Alley Pond Environmental Center, 228-06 Northern Blvd., Douglaston, NY 11362; (718) 229-4000; www.alleypond.com

Finding the trailhead: From the city, take the Long Island Expressway/495 west. Take exit 32 onto Little Neck Parkway and drive north for 1.1 miles to reach Northern Boulevard/Route 25A. Turn left and drive an additional 1.1 miles. The Alley Pond Environmental Center will be on the left. **By public transportation:** Ride the Long Island Railroad to the Douglaston stop, which is walking distance from the northern park entrance. Head south from the station on 235th Street/Douglaston Parkway and make a right (west) turn on Northern Boulevard. Look for the environmental center on the left after walking about 0.5 mile. GPS: N40 45.756' / W73 45.221'

THE HIKE

In a city as populous and built-up as New York, the idea that something resembling wilderness might exist anywhere within its boundaries seems counterintuitive. And yet at the fringes of the five boroughs, wild places such as Alley Pond Park do exist, wedged between expressways and shopping plazas, quietly providing habitats for plants and animals that manage to carve out niches for themselves in a much larger urban environment.

Like many of the waterways around New York, Alley Creek powered mills that processed locally grown grain in the eighteenth and nineteenth centuries. In 1788 the first post office in Flushing appeared in Bayside, not far from the present site of the environmental center. As the city expanded east into Queens from the island of Manhattan in the early twentieth century, officials began to set aside property for public use, and in 1935 opened the then smaller Alley Pond Park.

Setting out from the parking area just off Northern Boulevard, it's possible to circumnavigate "The Alley," a marshy strip of land bordering the tidal creek in the northern section of the park. Representing a fraction of the wetlands that were here before concerns about mosquitoes provoked a short campaign to fill them in during the early 1960s, the marshes nonetheless support a diverse if somewhat smaller range of flora and fauna today. The boardwalk that charts a southward course through the cordgrass and cattails is easy to find from the parking lot, and soon widens into a path thickly layered with mulch. Keep your eyes open for a diamondback terrapin, an eastern bluebird, or an eastern box turtle.

Tulip trees can reach 150 feet in height and can live to be 600 years old, making them among the largest and longest-living organisms on the planet. At 133.8 feet tall, the Alley Pond Giant is approximately 400 years old.

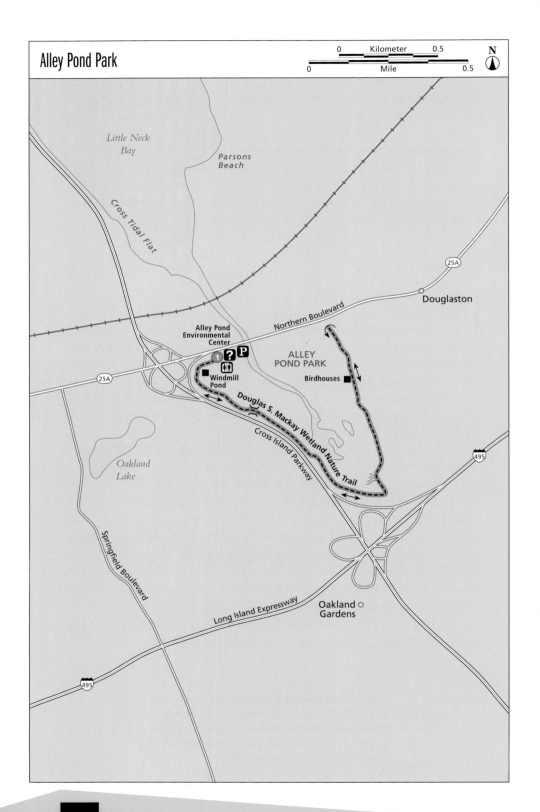

0   Kilometer   0.5

0   Mile   0.5

N

Little Neck Bay

Parsons Beach

Cross Tidal Flat

25A

Douglaston

Northern Boulevard

Alley Pond Environmental Center

? P

Windmill Pond

ALLEY POND PARK

Birdhouses

25A

Douglas S. Mackay Wetland Nature Trail

Cross Island Parkway

Oakland Lake

495

Springfield Boulevard

Long Island Expressway

Oakland Gardens

495

Weeping willow, black locust, and red oak grow near the low-lying trail, which must complete the difficult task of finding a narrow passageway of dry soil between the Cross Island Parkway and the edge of the marsh. Approaching the road, vehicular noise can drown out the melodic sounds of songbirds, and roadside trash creeping under the guardrail at the top of the embankment on your right (south) mars the effect of venturing farther away from civilization, but after about 0.5 mile the trail curves east and then north on the other side of the swiftly flowing creek that gives the park its name.

Square white markers that lie flush with the ground guide hikers through a healthy meadow where curlycup gumweed, bright yellow goldenrod, and sweet-smelling honeysuckle thrive. Climbing over almost everything it can get its tendrils on, the fast-growing, invasive woody vine called porcelain berry is another plant that dominates the sunny areas on the banks of the stream. Amidst the tall grasses

Hidden from the road, an old windmill stands behind the Alley Pond Environmental Center.

just after mile 1, a collection of birdhouses on slender wooden poles appears suddenly, standing in a cluster like a tiny, elevated subdevelopment. Red-winged blackbirds and tree swallows are two of the many types of bird that make their homes on the margins of the ponds in the park.

Beyond the birdhouses, the trail heads up and over an incline before dipping down into a thick stand of tall phragmites, otherwise known as the common reed. Another invasive species, the phragmites often outcompete native plants for territory and are less nutritious for herbivores. But they actually remove more contaminants from polluted wetlands and as such can be a beneficial presence in polluted habitats. The tan and green stalks of these reeds end at a chain-link fence at the rear of an auto dealership. Turn around here and walk back the way you came in order to return to your car.

MILES AND DIRECTIONS

0.0 Start behind the Alley Pond Environmental Center, where a green sign indicates the entrance to a wetland garden. Pass alongside Windmill Pond (and its operational replica of a windmill dating to 1870), where wading birds such as herons fish for their lunch.

0.25 The mulch trail angles left into a marshy area. Look for a small sign at ground level reading 6 REUSE. Continue straight ahead (south) on the dirt track at the fork.

0.4 Use a small arched wooden bridge to cross a murky stream. Follow the white markers of the Douglas S. Mackay Wetland Nature Trail as it curves to the east alongside the Cross Island Parkway.

0.7 Walk over a culvert that carries Alley Creek under the multilane road. You may be lucky enough to spot a family of mallards swimming with the current in the spring.

0.9 Take the left fork (to the north) where the trail forks again and proceed toward the open meadows that border Alley Creek. Turn right after a short distance to stay on the now grassy corridor leading to Northern Boulevard.

1.4 Traverse a particularly open section of meadow where a number of birdhouses have been erected. Duck under low branches and thorny vines here and there as you cross another mowed clearing in the otherwise overgrown tall grasses and shrubs.

1.6 After getting over a miniature hill and passing between two thick walls of purple-topped phragmites, arrive at a chain-link fence and the halfway point of your hike. Retrace your steps around Alley Creek to the environmental center.

3.2 Arrive back at the parking lot and trailhead on Northern Boulevard.

HIKE INFORMATION

Local information: Queens Tourism Council, Queens Borough Hall, 120-55 Queens Blvd., Room 309, Kew Gardens, NY 11424; (718) 263-0546; www.discover queens.info

Local events/attractions: Queens County Farm Museum, 7350 Little Neck Parkway, Glen Oaks, NY 11004; (718) 347-3276; www.queensfarm.org. New York's only working historical farm and the longest continuously farmed site in the state.
National Art League, 44-21 Douglaston Parkway, Douglaston, NY 11363; (718) 224-3957; www.nationalartleague.org

Good eats: Grimaldi's, 242-02 61st Ave., Douglaston, NY 11362; (718) 819-2133; www.grimaldis.com. Coal-fired, brick oven pizza at its best.
Press 195, 40-11 Bell Blvd., Flushing, NY 11361-2062; (718) 281-1950; www.press195 .com. Soups, sandwiches, wine, and beer—try them in the backyard garden.

Organizations: Queens County Bird Club, c/o Alley Pond Environmental Center, 228-06 Northern Blvd., Douglaston, NY 11363; http://qcbirdclub.org

A great blue heron hunts for prey.

Appalachian Trail

Trade the concrete canyons of Manhattan for the lush slopes around Greenwood Lake. As one of the most spectacular and challenging treks in the greater New York area, this short but demanding piece of the Appalachian Trail is ideally suited for seasoned hikers who crave views.

Start: At the trailhead in the Village of Greenwood Lake Recreation Park
Nearest town: Greenwood Lake, NY
Distance: 10.0 miles out and back
Approximate hiking time: 6 to 7 hours
Difficulty: Difficult
Trail surface: Steep forest paths and lots of exposed rock
Seasons: May through Oct
Other users: None
Wheelchair accessibility: None
Canine compatibility: Leashed dogs permitted
Land status: National scenic trail
Fees and permits: None
Schedule: Daily from sunrise to sunset
Facilities: None
Maps: USGS Greenwood Lake, NY; New York-New Jersey Trail Conference Sterling Forest Trails Map 100
Special considerations: Overnight stays must be limited to shelters and established tenting areas.
Trail contacts: Appalachian Trail Conservancy, 799 Washington St./P.O. Box 807, Harpers Ferry, WV 25425; (304) 535-6331; www.appalachiantrail.org.
National Park Service, Appalachian Trail Park Office, P.O. Box 50, Harpers Ferry, WV 25425; (304) 535-6278; www.nps.gov/appa
Abram S. Hewitt State Forest, c/o Wawayanda State Forest, 885 Warwick Turnpike, Hewitt, NJ 07421; (973) 853-4462; www.state.nj.us/dep/parksandforests/parks/abram.html

Finding the trailhead: By car, take I-87 north to the Tappan Zee and then drive west on I-87/I-287, over the bridge, to exit 15A. Continue north on Route 17/Orange Turnpike, turning left (west) on Route 17A, toward Warwick. Drive 7.5 miles and then turn left (south) on Windermere Avenue/Route 210. Make the fifth right (west) onto Elm Street to reach the park and the trailhead. **By public transportation:** Coach USA's Short Line buses stop at Greenwood Lake several times a day (about two hours from Port Authority). From the bus stop at the Park-n-Ride on Jersey Avenue, walk west 0.1 mile to Vine Street and turn right. Cover two short blocks and then turn left (west) on Elm Street. Enter the village park at the end of the road and look for the trailhead in the northwest corner, behind the picnic pavilion. GPS: N41 13.580' / W74 17.828'

THE HIKE

P lenty of hikes in the highland region of New York and New Jersey culminate in breathtaking vistas of the natural landscape, a distant town or city, or both. To find one that offers views from at least a half dozen spots in just 5 miles, then, would make it an especially attractive destination. Yet, to describe the part of the Appalachian Trail (AT) that runs atop Bearfort Mountain and Bellvale Mountain as essentially one long ridge stretching from Passaic County, New Jersey, into Orange County, New York, would be fair and accurate. On a bright, clear day in the early summer, or better yet, in the colorful early autumn, the sight of Greenwood Lake against the backdrop of Sterling Ridge is a simply stunning image.

The drawback of this hike—if it can be called a drawback at all—is that its terrain will challenge you over and over, from the bookend climbs at the start and the midway point, to the repeated ups and downs over knobs, ledges, and ragged stone. In short, the AT as it approaches the New Jersey state line is a lot of fun, but count on getting a workout.

The exercise begins at the bottom of the blue-blazed Village Vista Trail in Greenwood Lake. Climbing through mixed hardwood forest, you'll gain approximately 600 feet in 0.7 mile. Charging up this slope will leave both experienced and novice hikers out of breath by the time they reach the first overlook.

Pack plenty of supplies if you're planning to hike to Georgia.

The scenery from 1,250 feet up, however, is worth the effort. Look down on the rooftops of the town, marvel at the tininess of the baseball field from this vantage point, and admire the deep blue-green hue of the 7-mile-long body of water originally called Long Pond by early European arrivals to the area. Continue northwest from this vista and meet the AT just before mile 1. Turn left, and let the bright white blazes guide you 4 miles southwest into Abram S. Hewitt State Forest. To get there, you'll scramble over rugged outcroppings of lichen-covered rock and pass through groups of rhododendron and stands of pitch pine that seem to spring directly from the rock they've rooted themselves to.

Another outstanding view, after the 2.5-mile mark, enables you to look back on Bellvale Mountain and Dutch Hollow beyond. On the other side of Greenwood Lake, Big Beech Mountain stands out at the southern end of Sterling Ridge. Partially descend the west side of the ridge (with the help of a ladder at one point), cross a stream that plunges over the side of the mountain, and enter a little ravine that feels something like a tunnel. Emerge from the vegetation and pick your way to the top of another bald knob of granite for a view of Warwick Mountain to the northwest. From here it's only a few steps until you pass a blue-blazed trail on the right that leads into Cascade Lake Park and then a blunt peak labeled on maps as Prospect Rock.

At mile 4.4 the abbreviations NJ/NY are painted on the rock in white paint, and the AT logo is painted on a box hanging from a nearby tree. Walk through this invisible boundary and enter Abram S. Hewitt State Forest. You'll be standing in New Jersey when you turn left (southeast) on the blue State Line Trail and walk across Bearfort Mountain, a ridge formed during the last glacial retreat. This trail slopes downhill for about 1 mile (ending at a parking area on Route 511), and can pose difficulties for tired legs. Turn right (south) on the yellow Ernest Walker Trail and climb close to 200 feet to your final view. The treetops rustle in the wind, recalling the sound of waves crashing on a distant beach. Slender Fox Island is visible at the southern end of the lake. Tiny white boats etch faint lines on its glassy surface with their wakes. Savor this, then retrace your steps to the trailhead.

MILES AND DIRECTIONS

0.0   Start at the trailhead in the Village of Greenwood Lake Recreation Park. Begin climbing the eastern face of Bellvale Mountain, moving in the direction of the light blue blazes on the Village Vista Trail.

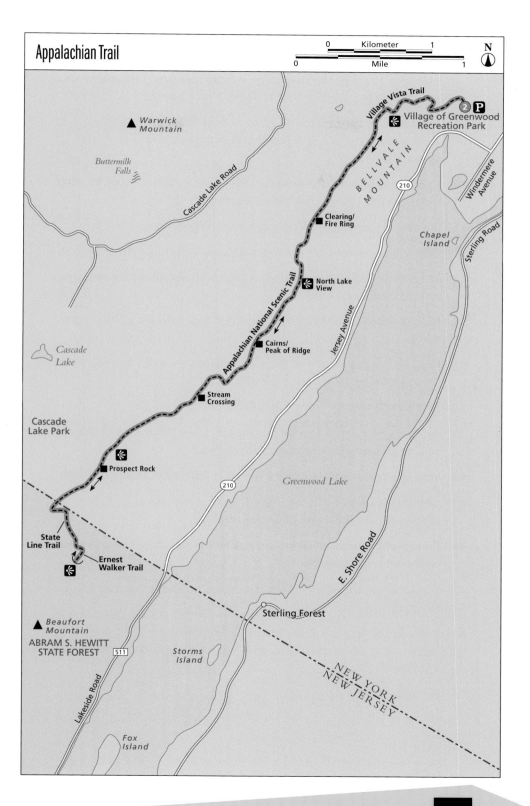

Appalachian Trail

| 0 | Kilometer | 1 |
| 0 | Mile | 1 |

N

Warwick Mountain

Buttermilk Falls

Cascade Lake Road

Village Vista Trail

Village of Greenwood
Recreation Park

BELLVALE MOUNTAIN

210

Windermere Avenue

Chapel Island

Sterling Road

Clearing/
Fire Ring

North Lake
View

Appalachian National Scenic Trail

Jersey Avenue

Cairns/
Peak of Ridge

Cascade
Lake

Stream
Crossing

Cascade
Lake Park

Prospect Rock

210

Greenwood Lake

State
Line Trail

Ernest
Walker Trail

E. Shore Road

Beaufort
Mountain

ABRAM S. HEWITT
STATE FOREST

511

Storms
Island

Sterling Forest

NEW YORK
NEW JERSEY

Lakeside Road

Fox
Island

0.3 After crossing a maintenance road, make a sharp right on the trail to continue your ascent up the steep slope. A lesser trail crosses the main path a few hundred feet later; ignore it and keep heading west.

0.7 Arrive at 1,250 feet and the village vista. Look down on the baseball field where you started, across the north end of the lake, and to Sterling Ridge on the other side.

0.8 Meet the Appalachian Trail and veer left, to the southwest. Look for white rectangles and cairns to guide you hereafter.

1.1 Use care descending a short but treacherous 50-foot drop.

1.6 Walk across a clearing in the woods with a small fire ring in the center of it.

2.0 Stand on the bare, lichen-covered rock at this viewpoint to look back at the town of Greenwood Lake.

2.6 Reach an open summit of bare stone (1,320 feet) crowned by two sizeable cairns.

2.9 Arrive at another viewpoint and then make a very steep descent, where the trail loses nearly 150 feet in elevation.

3.2 Ford a small stream.

3.8 Pass through a narrow, shady little ravine and then climb up to a knob with commanding views to the north, east, and west.

4.0 Walk by a blue-blazed trail on the right that leads into Cascade Lake Park.

4.1 Climb up Prospect Rock, the highest point on the hike at 1,430 feet. You will have a panoramic view of Greenwood Lake.

4.4 Cross the New Jersey state line and look for the blue-blazed State Line Trail on the left soon thereafter.

4.8 Turn right on the yellow-blazed Ernest Walker Trail to ascend Bearfort Mountain.

5.0 Arrive at the final overlook—another peak with a romantic view of the serene water. Finish the hike by retracing your steps north to the Village Vista Trail.

10.0 Arrive back at the village park.

Local information: Orange County Tourism, 124 Main St., Goshen, NY 10924; (845) 615-3860; www.orangetourism.org

Passaic County, Passaic County Administration Building, Freeholder's Office, 401 Grand St., Paterson, NJ 07505; (973) 881-4402; www.passaiccountynj.org

Local events/attractions: Franklin Mineral Museum, 32 Evans St., Franklin, NJ 07416; (973) 827-3481; http://franklinmineralmuseum.com. Open weekends in Mar, daily from Apr through Nov.

The Sterling Hill Mining Museum, 30 Plant St., Ogdensburg, NJ 07439; (973) 209-7212; http://sterlinghillminingmuseum.org. Step into an underground mine, visit Thomas S. Warren Museum of Fluorescence, study rocks and fossils, and stop by the gift shop before you go.

Good eats: Huckleberry's BBQ, 37 Oak St., Greenwood Lake, NY 10925; (845) 477-4737; www.huckleberrys bbq.com. Country breakfast on weekend mornings, and a dinner menu that includes squirrel-less Brunswick stew, broiled catfish, and smoked, shredded, and spice-rubbed beef brisket.

Planet Pizza, 120 Windermere Ave., Greenwood Lake, NY 10925; (845) 477-2404; http://planetpizzany.com

Organizations: Appalachian Mountain Club, 5 Joy St., Boston, MA 02108; (617) 523-0636; www.outdoors.org. The nation's oldest outdoor recreation and conservation organization.

American Hiking Society, 1422 Fenwick Lane, Silver Spring, MD 20910; (301) 565-6704; www.americanhiking.org. Working to ensure that hiking trails and natural places are cherished and preserved for future generations.

Not only is Sterling Hill one of the oldest mining sites in the country, but when it closed in 1986, this business became the last underground mine in New Jersey to cease operations.

Bear Mountain State Park

Tackle a popular hike in New York's second largest state park for views of Bear Mountain Bridge, Brooks Lake, and Popolopen Torne. Cover one of the first sections of the Appalachian Trail and see how volunteers have made major improvements to ensure the enjoyment of future generations of walkers and backpackers.

Start: Just behind the historic inn on the edge of the lake

Nearest town: Fort Montgomery, NY

Distance: 5.2-mile lollipop

Approximate hiking time: 2.5 to 3.5 hours

Difficulty: Moderate to difficult

Trail surface: Paved multiuse path, dirt footpath, grass, exposed rock faces, stone steps

Seasons: Spring, summer, and fall

Other users: None

Wheelchair accessibility: The paved multiuse path around Hessian Lake makes for a pleasant 1.5-mile loop. Perkins Memorial Tower and the views from the summit of Bear Mountain can also be reached by car via Perkins Memorial Drive.

Canine compatibility: Dogs permitted if muzzled and on leashes 6 feet or less

Land status: State park

Fees and permits: A small vehicle fee; no fee for arrivals by bus

Schedule: Daily from 8 a.m. until dusk

Facilities: Restrooms, water fountains, picnic area, gift shop, boat rentals, zoo

Maps: USGS Peekskill and Popolopen Lake, NY; New York-New Jersey Trail Conference Northern Harriman Bear Mountain Trail Map 119. A hiking guide can be downloaded from the Palisades Park Commission website (see below) or picked up at the park administration building.

Special considerations: This popular park is often crowded on nice weekends.

Trail contacts: New York State Office of Parks, Recreation & Historic Preservation, Palisades Interstate Park Commission, Bear Mountain, NY 10911; (845) 786-2701; http://nysparks.state.ny.us/

Finding the trailhead: If driving from New York, take I-87 north to the Taconic State Parkway. Exit onto Route 35/US 202/Crompond Road and continue west for 2.7 miles. Keep right (northwest) at the fork onto Bear Mountain Beacon Highway. Drive about 7.8 miles more to the Bear Mountain Bridge, merging with Highland Avenue outside of Peekskill. Go around the traffic circle on the other side of the bridge, and immediately look for signs for Bear Mountain State Park. The distance to the inn is approximately one-quarter of a mile. **By public transportation:** Coach USA's Short Line buses drop off passengers in front of the Bear Mountain Inn on US 9W/202. To reach the Major Welch trailhead (white blazes with red circles), walk west around the inn on the paved multiuse path to the southwestern corner of Hessian Lake. GPS: N41 18.753' / W73 59.501'

THE HIKE

While it's not the only Bear Mountain in the Empire State, Orange County's peak is the best known, and its proximity to Manhattan has long made it a favorite destination for hikers. In fact, one of the first sections of the Appalachian Trail was built here in 1923. Predictably, the ease of access to this protected landscape has contributed to the popularity of the park, and its trail network (which extends into the adjacent Harriman State Park) can often seem too conveniently located for anyone seeking solitude. After more than eighty years of heavy traffic, the New York-New Jersey Trail Conference harnessed the energy of some 700 volunteers to restore the piece of America's oldest hiking trail that leads down to Hessian Lake. The project, which was completed in 2010, involved cutting and placing 800 granite steps on the eastern face of the mountain.

From the lakeshore, proceed north on the multiuse path, slowly leaving the picnic area, with its smoky grills and gleeful shouts of children, behind. On sunny days the surface of the lake will be dotted with rowboats and paddleboats. A few steps before reaching the 0.4-mile mark, look for red-on-white plastic tags indicating a sharp left and prepare for uneven terrain during the next 0.5 mile on the Major Welch Trail. Heading up the mountainside, you'll step over the gnarled roots of elm and maple trees. Wear sturdy hiking boots to protect your feet from the many stony obstacles that stubbornly occupy the route.

At 0.9 mile, the real work begins. For about the next 1,000 feet, the Major Welch Trail leads nearly straight up to the park's main feature, and you'll have to contend with small toeholds and a couple of scrambles on the smooth surface of exposed bedrock. If you don't mind the huffing and puffing, it's a thrilling passage topped off with breathtaking views. You'll be able to see Bear Mountain Bridge and Canada Hill to the east across the Hudson River from your vantage point, and just to the north, Brooks Lake and Popolopen Torne. One more short, steep section and you'll run into Perkins Memorial Drive. Ascend a little farther on the other side of the road and you're nearly to the summit, where grasses and highbush blueberry take the place of tall trees. Then, approximately 1,305 feet above the river, Perkins Memorial Tower provides an even better opportunity to enjoy the scenery—four states and the skyline of Manhattan can be seen from its observation deck. The autumn is a particularly ideal time to visit.

Inside the tower, learn about the Palisades Interstate Parks Commission, an organization that George W. Perkins helped to create in 1900, and then look for an Appalachian Trail (AT) signpost outside—its large, solid white blazes will guide you back to the inn and trailhead. A large arrow painted on the rock at the top of the mountain directs hikers east, and as crickets chirp from either side of the trail, you'll pass through more blueberry, crossing Perkins Memorial Drive twice in the span of a tenth of a mile. When you meet the road for the third time, make a sharp right (south) and follow it for 0.3 mile until it ends in a roundabout. This is where the new section of the AT begins.

Back at the start of the hike, walk through the small playground, turn right on the multiuse path again, and walk north around Hessian Lake. Turn right (east) again before you get to the zoo, walk under US 9W/202, go past the swimming pool, and follow the path downhill to reach Bear Mountain Dock, where you can look up Anthony's Nose across the water.

Boaters on Hessian Lake, with Anthony's Nose in the background

MILES AND DIRECTIONS

0.0 Start behind the Bear Mountain Inn, where buses from New York drop off and pick up passengers. Three white blazes with red circles denoting the Major Welch trailhead are painted on a tree on the southwest corner of Hessian Lake.

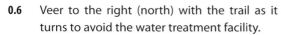

0.4 Turn left (west) into the woods from the paved multiuse path and proceed uphill on the Major Welch Trail.

0.6 Veer to the right (north) with the trail as it turns to avoid the water treatment facility.

0.9 Begin the steepest part of the hike, picking your way over loose stones and up the exposed rock while heading toward the summit, southwest of your current position.

1.1 Reach the scenic overlook on Bear Mountain's northern face.

1.3 Scramble up a stony slope to Perkins Memorial Drive and look for the continuation of the Major Welch Trail on the other side of the road.

1.6 The trail briefly merges with the scenic drive as you proceed toward Perkins Memorial Tower. Vending machines and portable restrooms are available for those in need.

1.7 Reach the summit. Stop to catch your breath, admire the views, and learn a little about the history of the Palisades Interstate Park Commission by reading the narrative tile mosaics inside Perkins Memorial Tower.

1.8 Turn left (east) just beyond the parking lot and picnic area onto the Appalachian Trail. A large white arrow indicating the direction of travel has been painted on a boulder.

2.0 Cross Perkins Memorial Drive and continue downhill on the AT.

2.1 Make your second road crossing.

2.3 Still following the white rectangular AT blazes, turn right onto the road and follow it for 0.3 mile until it ends in a small roundabout. Look for newly constructed stone steps just past a large dumpster.

3.1 Pause at the rock shelf just off the trail to watch boats on the river as they cruise by Iona Island to the south.

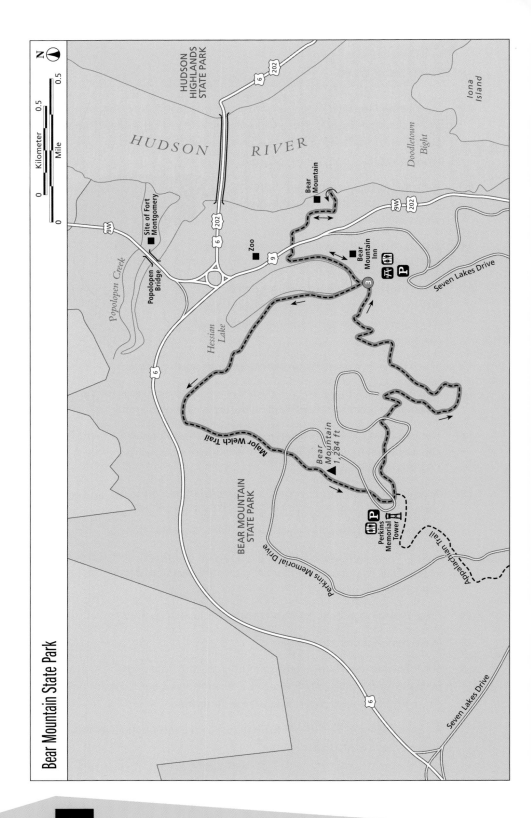

3.4 The AT joins with a paved road behind the inn. Follow this northeast to the edge of Hessian Lake, crossing a small playground.

3.8 Take the staircase underneath US 9W and stay on the paved path past the swimming pool, the elk's head statue, and then under the railroad tracks.

4.4 Arrive at the Bear Mountain Dock. Return toward the trailhead.

5.2 Arrive back at the trailhead.

> **🌿 Green Tip:**
> *Carry a reusable water container that you fill at the tap. Bottled water is expensive; lots of petroleum is used to make the plastic bottles; and they're a disposal nightmare.*

The Appalachian Trail uses Bear Mountain Bridge to cross the Hudson River.

Local information: Orange County Tourism, 124 Main St., Goshen, NY 10924; (845) 615-3860; www.orangetourism.org

Local events/attractions: Fort Montgomery State Historic Site, P.O. Box 213, Fort Montgomery, NY 10922; (845) 446-2134; http://nysparks.state.ny.us/historic-sites/28/details.aspx. The visitor center is open Wed through Sun from 9 a.m. to 5 p.m.

Stony Point Battlefield State Historic Site, P.O. Box 182, Stony Point, NY 10980; (845) 786-2521; http://nysparks.state.ny.us/historic-sites/8/details.aspx. Visit a Revolutionary War battlefield, as well as the oldest lighthouse on the Hudson.

Good eats: The Bagel Cafe, 1048 Rte. 9W, Fort Montgomery, NY 10922; (845) 446-4638. It's all in the name: bagels, muffins, donuts, coffee—and ice cream.

Barnstormer Barbeque, 1076 Rte. 9W, Fort Montgomery, NY 10922; (845) 446-0912; www.barnstormerbbq.com

Local outdoor stores: Eastern Mountain Sports, 66 Rockland Plaza, Nanuet, NY 10954; (845) 623-5282; www.ems.com

Hike tours: Urban Escapes New York (national headquarters), 150 East 58th St., Suite 1802A, New York, NY 10155; (212) 609-2547; www.urbanescapesnyc.com

Organizations: Palisades Parks Conservancy, Administration Building, Bear Mountain, NY 10911; (845) 786-2701; www.palisadesparksconservancy.org

Parks & Trails New York, 29 Elk St., Albany, NY 12207; (518) 434-1583; www.ptny.org

School or Fortress?

West Point—one of five US Service Academies—is no ordinary college campus. Although President Thomas Jefferson established the United States Military Academy in 1802, this site north of New York City had already served another important purpose during the latter part of the American Revolution: guarding the river. Perched on a cliff overlooking a tight bend in the Hudson, West Point actually began its tenure as the oldest continuously occupied military post in the country by defending an infant nation against an empire's navy. At the outset of the war in 1776, Thaddeus Kosciuszko, a Polish officer and military engineer, traveled to America to offer his services to the Continental army. Two short years later, he became the chief engineer for the fortifications that were called Fort Arnold until Benedict Arnold defected to the British in 1780. Its name was then changed to Fort Clinton. Along with gun batteries and redoubts, this location also served as the western end of The Great Chain, a massive, 65-ton iron cable that floated between the base of the fortifications and Constitution Island. Thirteen links of the original chain can still be seen today at the West Point Museum.

Black Rock Forest

Explore an underappreciated part of the Hudson Highlands named for the magnetite that was found here and in the surrounding area in the eighteenth century. Choose to wander along woods roads (some of which follow historic routes) or test your fitness and endurance on one of the many hills that rise to over 1,000 feet.

Start: Parking lot on US 9W southbound (at the sign for Pecks Road)
Nearest town: Cornwall, NY
Distance: 6.0-mile lollipop
Approximate hiking time: 4 to 5 hours
Difficulty: Moderate
Trail surface: Gravel roads, grassy tracks, and exposed rock
Seasons: May through Oct
Other trail users: Mountain bikers, equestrians; cross-country skiers (seasonally)
Wheelchair accessibility: None
Canine compatibility: Leashed dogs permitted
Land status: Not-for-profit preserve/educational and research institution
Fees and permits: None
Schedule: Daily from dawn until dusk

Facilities: None
Maps: USGS Cornwall-on-Hudson, NY; New York-New Jersey Trail Conference West Hudson Trails Map 113. Forest maps can be accessed through the consortium's website (see below), and a map of the Highlands Trail can be downloaded at www.highlands-trail.org.
Special considerations: Boating, fishing, and swimming (with the exception of Sutherland Pond), are not permitted in Black Rock Forest, and hikers should take care to avoid study areas and any scientific equipment they may see.
Trail contacts: Black Rock Forest Consortium, 129 Continental Rd., Cornwall, NY 12518; (845) 534-4517; www.blackrockforest.org

Finding the trailhead: Take exit 17 off the New York State Thruway and then take the next right onto Route 300/Union Avenue. Drive south to Vails Gate, where Route 300 intersects Route 32. Follow Route 32 for about 1.7 miles and then turn left onto Quaker Avenue, toward Cornwall. Make your next right on US 9W and head south 1.6 miles until you see a parking area large enough for several vehicles to the right. Begin at the gate; this is the trailhead. GPS: N41 25.216' / W74 01.655'

Across US 9W from Storm King State Park and bordered by the United States Military Academy to the south, Black Rock Forest stretches west, encompassing close to 4,000 acres of hills, ponds, meadows, and swampland. And although its role as a scientific research station dates to the late 1920s, Black Rock's connection to the history of New York State can be traced back to the American Revolution, when George Washington's army used Continental Road to travel from West Point to Newburgh and watched the river for British warships from Spy Rock. This might seem surprising given Spy Rock's inland location, but at 1,461 feet it's actually the highest point in the Highlands region.

Briefly owned by Harvard University (Dr. Ernest Stillman's alma mater), this forest is now managed by a consortium of public and private institutions and also protects several reservoirs that supply water to the nearby towns of Cornwall and Highland Falls. When Dr. Stillman designated the land as a research forest in 1928, it was only beginning to return to health after 200 years of damaging human activity. But because Storm King, Black Rock's neighbor to the east, tends to attract most of the hikers that venture up to this part of Orange County today, the likelihood that a visit to this sanctuary will involve running into more than a few fellow outdoors enthusiasts is relatively small.

Pointing like an arrow toward the Science Center and Forest Lodge that sit just inside the eastern border of Black Rock, this mid-length lollipop, described in a counterclockwise direction, begins by following Idlewild Creek for approximately 0.5 mile. From here (next to a water filtration plant), the white blazes of the Black Rock Hollow Trail lead steadily uphill over the moss-covered gneiss and granite that litter dry streambeds. This trail segment runs into the yellow Stillman Trail after 1.3 miles, and a right turn (northeast) leads up to the forest's namesake Black Rock. A shelf at 1,400 feet offers views of Frog Hill, Schunemunk, and in the distance, Stewart International Airport's runway. The unmistakable sound of artillery fire and machine gun strafing from the firing ranges at West Point can be clearly heard above the tree line.

Climb down the other side of this dark geologic mass, cross Hulse Road and Continental Road in short succession, and then continue west on the Stillman Trail, weaving around scarlet oaks, red maples, black walnuts, and green ash trees. At mile 2.5, turn left (southeast) on the White Oak Trail, cross Sutherland Road, and skirt around the shore of Sphagnum Pond, where brilliant purple bull thistle flowers bloom in late summer. Half a mile later, the white blazes lead to the right (south), down Continental Road. In the opposite direction stands an enormous white oak, while farther down the gravel road stands the Chatfield Stone House, the oldest building in the forest.

Navigate around the north end of Arthurs Pond (which may require fording after heavy rains) and head downhill once more, through a boulder field, until you meet White Oak Road again, curving in from the north. Stay on the road, and after passing the Aleck Meadow Reservoir on your left, look for the Stillman Trail (yellow). Follow the Stillman Trail around and eventually over the top of the intimidatingly named Mount Misery. Black Rock dominates the skyline from the summit. Note that the climb on both sides is strenuous, and in some places the trail is badly eroded.

Cross White Oak Road for the final time, watching for the Reservoir Trail's blue blazes on the left (northwest). This last part of the route runs along the foot of Honey Hill, crosses the waterway leading to the Upper Reservoir via Ben's Bridge, and terminates at the water filtration plant and the Black Rock Hollow Trail, which you took into the forest from US 9W.

The invasive bull thistle blooms from July to September.

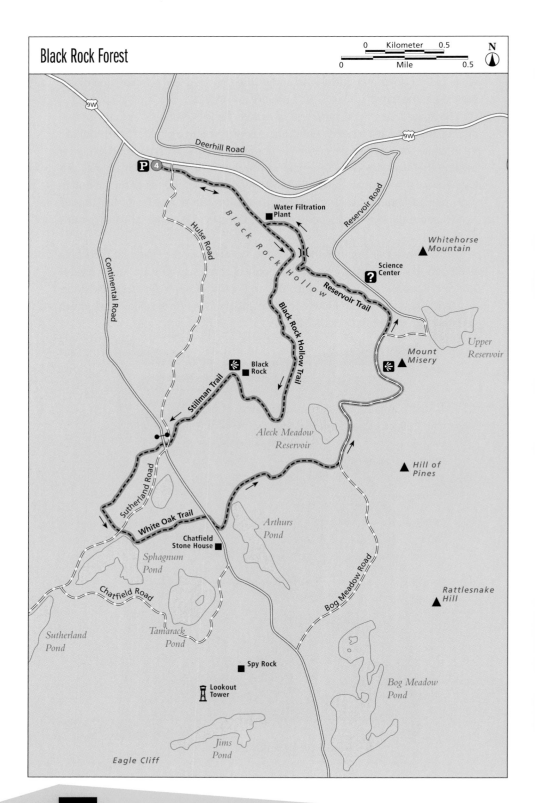

Black Rock Forest

0   Kilometer   0.5
0   Mile   0.5

9W

Deerhill Road

9W

P 4

Water Filtration
Plant

Reservoir Road

Whitehorse
Mountain

Black Rock Hollow

Science
Center

Reservoir Trail

Hulse Road

Continental Road

Black Rock Hollow Trail

Upper
Reservoir

Mount
Misery

Black
Rock

Stillman Trail

Aleck Meadow
Reservoir

Hill of
Pines

Sutherland Road

White Oak Trail

Arthurs
Pond

Bog Meadow Road

Chatfield
Stone House

Sphagnum
Pond

Rattlesnake
Hill

Chatfield Road

Sutherland
Pond

Tamarack
Pond

Spy Rock

Bog Meadow
Pond

Lookout
Tower

Eagle Cliff

Jims
Pond

MILES AND DIRECTIONS

0.0 Start from the gate on US 9W, walking southeast on the gravel woods road alongside Idlewild Creek.

0.1 A kiosk displays a map of Black Rock Forest and lists emergency contact telephone numbers. Pass Hulse Road on the right.

0.5 Approach a water filtration plant to the left of the trail. Turn right (south) in the direction of the white blazes.

1.3 Turn right (west) onto the Stillman Trail/Highlands Trail, marked with a yellow blaze and a teal diamond. Follow this path to the summit of Black Rock.

1.7 Arrive at the top of Black Rock. Admire the view to the west and take a few minutes to catch your breath and replenish lost calories with a granola bar or a piece of fruit.

2.1 Turn left (south) onto Hulse Road, make an immediate right onto Continental Road, and then turn left again to stay with the Stillman Trail. You will pass two gates in the process.

2.5 At the cairn, turn left (southeast) onto the White Oak Trail, cross Sutherland Road (gravel), and walk past Sphagnum Pond. A trail appears to head northeast alongside a swampy area, but stay close to the pond for a few hundred feet and watch for white blazes.

3.0 Turn right (south) on Continental Road and then take the next left down another woods road that leads to Arthurs Pond.

3.3 At the junction with the yellow Tower View Trail on the east side of the pond, turn left at the top of a small slope and stick to the White Oak Trail. After 0.2 mile, follow a seam of granite downhill into a field of boulders.

3.7 The white blazes end. Turn right (east) onto the gravel White Oak Road and stay with it for 0.4 mile, passing Meadow Road and then the blue-blazed Swamp Trail on the right.

4.1 Rejoin the Stillman Trail by turning right (east) and follow it up the steep flank of Mount Misery.

4.5 From the top of the hill, gaze across the forest to Black Rock, your first climb of the day. Take a water break and prepare for the descent back to the trailhead.

4.7 Turn left (northwest) onto the Reservoir Trail (blue).

5.2 Cross over Ben's Bridge, continue for another 0.3 mile, then circle around the water filtration plant. Pick up the white-blazed Black Rock Hollow Trail and follow it back to the start of the hike.

6.0 Arrive back at the parking area on US 9W.

Options: The network of maintained trails and woods roads in Black Rock allows for a great deal of customization. Hikers who crave more climbing can explore the southern ledges by taking the white Scenic Trail from the Upper Reservoir area. And individuals looking to add a few more miles, as well as a refreshing dip, should stay on the Stillman Trail past the White Oak Trail junction. It eventually intersects with Sutherland Road, from which the swimming pond of the same name can be accessed.

HIKE INFORMATION

Local information: Orange County Tourism, 124 Main St., Goshen, NY 10924; (845) 615-3860; www.orangetourism.org

Local events/attractions: Knox's Headquarters State Historic Site, P.O. Box 207, Vails Gate, NY 12584; (845) 561-5498; www.nysparks.com. Open between Memorial Day and Labor Day, Wed through Sun.

Washington's Headquarters State Historic Site, P.O. Box 1783, Corner of Liberty and Washington Streets, Newburgh, NY 12551; (845) 562-1195; www.nysparks .com. The museum is open from mid-Apr to the end of Oct, Wed through Sun.

Good eats: Woody's, 30 Quaker Dr., Cornwall, NY 12520; (845) 534-1111; www .woodysallnatural.com. Arguably the best burger in the Hudson Valley. (The milkshakes aren't bad, either.)

Hudson Street Cafe, 237 Hudson St., Cornwall-on-Hudson, NY 12520; (845) 534-2450; www.hudsonstreetcafe.com

Organizations: The Highlands Coalition, 520 Long St., Bethlehem, PA 18018; (610) 868-6915; www.highlandscoalition.org. A four-state alliance of organizations working to protect the natural resources in this region.

New York-New Jersey Trail Conference, 156 Ramapo Valley Rd., Mahwah, NJ 07430-1199; (201) 512-9348; www.nynjtc.org

Blue Mountain Reservation

Tour the second largest park in Westchester County and test your stamina on a climb to its highest point. Notice an old trail lodge, a pair of comfort stations built by the Civilian Conservation Corps in the early 1930s, and relax on the banks of Lounsbury Pond, a man-made body of water that once provided ice for the surrounding communities.

Start: Near the north end of the large pond inside the park entrance

Nearest town: Peekskill, NY

Distance: 4.5-mile loop

Approximate hiking time: 3 hours

Difficulty: Moderate, with one small climb

Trail surface: Multiuse woods roads and rocky tracks

Seasons: Year-round

Other trail users: Mountain bikers, equestrians

Wheelchair accessibility: Although the woods trails aren't suited for disabled visitors, Lounsbury Pond can be circled with relative ease.

Canine compatibility: Leashed dogs permitted; pets not allowed in picnic areas

Land status: County park

Fees and permits: A small parking fee for Westchester County Park Pass holders; a higher fee for those without. No charge for walk-ins.

Schedule: Daily from 8 a.m. until dusk

Facilities: Restrooms, water fountain, picnic area, playground. There is no swimming in Lounsbury Pond.

Maps: USGS Peekskill, NY. Copies of the Westchester Mountain Bike Association (WMBA) trail map are available at the entrance to the park as well as at www.wmba.org.

Special considerations: Be aware of the fact that you will likely be sharing the trails—even the narrower singletracks—with mountain bikers.

Trail contacts: Westchester County Department of Parks, Recreation, and Conservation, 25 Moore Ave., Mount Kisco, NY 10549; (914) 864-PARK; http://parks.westchester gov.com

Finding the trailhead: From New York by car, take the Bronx River Parkway north toward White Plains. Continue on the Sprain Brook Parkway for 12.5 miles and then merge with the Taconic State Parkway. In Briarcliff Manor, exit onto Route 9A north/Saw Mill River Road. Merge onto US 9 north via the ramp to Peekskill. After 7.2 miles, take the right-hand exit to Welcher Avenue and drive east 0.5 mile to the park entrance. **By public transportation:** The train ride on Metro North from Grand Central to Peekskill takes about one hour. From the station it's about a 1.5-mile walk (uphill for several blocks) to the park, or short bus ride on Bee Line Route 14, which drops off passengers at Washington Street and Welcher Avenue. Once inside the park, keep to the left on the road and head toward the trail lodge. GPS: N41 16.341' / W73 55.362'

THE HIKE

The Kitchawanks, members of the Mahican tribe—who were themselves part of the much larger Algonquin nation—hunted and fished in the area around Peekskill when English explorer Henry Hudson sailed up the river that now bears his name in 1609. Four hundred years later, the 1,538 acres within the boundaries of Blue Mountain Reservation shelter much of the same native flora and fauna that early colonists would have encountered near the settlement of Peeck's Kil, so-called because of a Dutch fur trader, Jan Peeck, who did business with the Kitchawanks here. To see this park with fewer modern distractions, consider visiting on a weekday—on Saturdays and Sundays you're likely to share the trail with mountain bikers.

Stepping into the woods from the park road, you'll follow a gently undulating trail northeast, bypassing several smaller footpaths on your left and traveling in a clockwise direction. Dickey Brook will be on your right. Deer are numerous in the park, and the chances of coming across a trio browsing for food or even a single animal meandering through a clearing is not uncommon. Listen carefully to hear chipmunks foraging in the leaf litter, or gray squirrels racing skyward up the thick trunk of an oak or an eastern hemlock. In the distance you may detect a faint popping noise every so often. The Sportsman Center occupies the southeastern corner of the reservation and is off-limits to hikers and bikers.

After 0.6 mile you'll make a right (south) turn across the brook via a weathered plank bridge, and then a quick left (east). From this point on, the trail branches frequently, and conflicting markers and blazes can be confusing for first-time visitors. Keep your map and GPS handy. Approximately one-tenth of a mile beyond the bridge, veer right at the fork and begin to slowly gain elevation en route to the top of Blue Mountain.

For the sake of variety and a bit of a challenge, take both of the small footpaths that veer to the left of the main trail as you proceed eastward into the park. Both of them wind up and over some of the rocky outcroppings that appear with more frequency at this stage of the hike, offering a few views that are arguably more interesting than the wide, stony corridor you've followed thus far. The termite-eaten skeletons of trees stand like sentinels alongside the trail, and by the middle of the day, several mosquitoes will probably be shadowing you as you push yourself forward up a slope that grows noticeably steeper by about mile 2.

Following this short spurt of exercise you'll find yourself standing among spiky clumps of grass at the highest point in the park, possibly admiring the sliver of river that's visible between the branches that partially obstruct the scenic overlook. Enjoy the cool breeze that blows across Blue Mountain's low peak and head up the summit a bit beyond the yellow sign directing hikers to the end of the trail to discover an old mountain hut or lean-to, long abandoned to the elements. Turn left (south) at the base of Blue Mountain and continue along in this direction until you descend into a shallow swampy gully that has been cleared for a utility line. Keep to the right here to avoid the firing range.

You'll be momentarily at the mercy of the sun as the Blue Mountain Summit Trail guides you over a hill, but it will soon curve west again, into the cooler shade

Sunset on the Hudson River in Peekskill

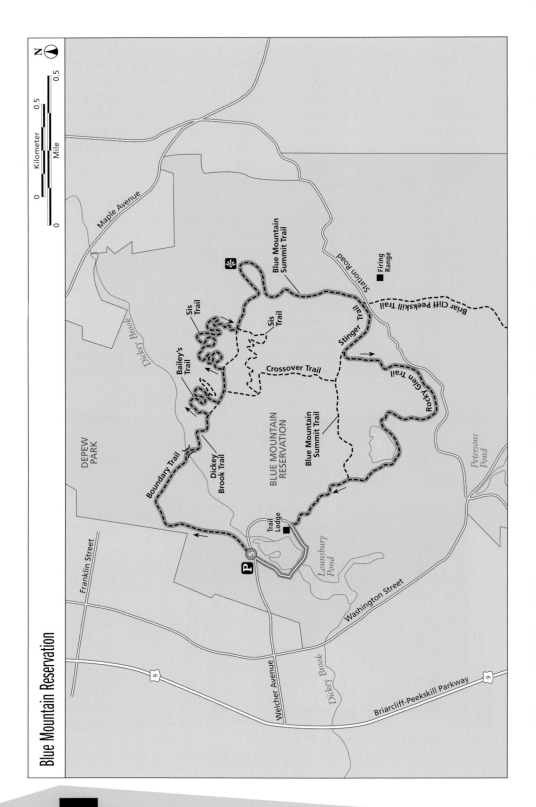

Blue Mountain Reservation

of the forest. Make a sharp left (south) roughly 0.3 mile after the fork, and allow this footpath to lead you to the Rocky Glen Trail, which circles around a secluded pond and then rejoins the Summit Trail to end on the other side of Lounsbury Pond from where the hike began. A small bridge across the water will carry you into the picnic area. The park entrance is just beyond, to the west.

MILES AND DIRECTIONS

0.0   Start at the trailhead just north of Lounsbury Pond. Keep left where the road forks at the entrance and look for a sign on the left before you reach the lodge.

0.1   A yellow trail enters from the left. Stay on the main path as it curves to the northeast.

0.3   Make a right (east) turn onto the yellow Boundary Trail at the T intersection. Do not follow the green blazes leading west.

0.6   Traverse a small, ordinary bridge over Dickey Brook and take an immediate left (east) on the other side of the crossing onto the Dickey Brook Trail. (**NOTE:** At various points along the route, numbered signs have been tacked to trees. Ignore them and don't let these markers confuse you. While the WMBA trail map shows them as trail junctions, many are missing and they don't appear in consecutive order.)

0.7   Turn right (southeast) at the fork and head uphill on the Crossover Trail.

0.8   Turn left (north) onto the narrow Bailey's Trail and let it circuitously lead you through the woods for two-tenths of a mile.

1.0   Rejoin the main path (the Limbo Trail), traveling in the same eastward direction.

1.1   Keep left at the next fork, watching for red trail blazes now. After several hundred feet you'll again take a left (north) turn off the wider main path onto the Sis Trail, marked with green and white.

2.0   Sis winds over the terrain for a good distance until it rejoins the red-blazed Limbo Trail.

2.1   Make a right turn (southeast) onto the Blue Mountain Summit Trail and then a quick left (east) to reach the top of this landform. The track becomes somewhat steeper here.

2.3   Arrive at the summit and a view of the Hudson River. (**NOTE:** Just before the top of Blue Mountain you'll notice a sign with a yellow arrow tacked to a tree. It points left to the top, but by heading right a little farther you'll reach a higher elevation, where the remains of a small stone building or lean-to can be seen.

2.5 Back at the intersection with the summit trail, turn left (south) to begin circling back toward the park entrance.

2.8 Keep right at the next fork to skirt the shooting range in the southeast corner of the park. Emerge from the tree cover and walk up a small hill, vaguely following the right-of-way created by the presence of an underground utility line.

3.1 Turn left (southwest) on the Stinger Trail. You'll cross several intermittent streams as well as the same utility line before meeting the wider Rocky Glen Trail (white blazes).

3.8 When a small, secluded pond comes into view, make a sharp left (west), keeping the body of water on your right.

4.2 Rejoin the Blue Mountain Summit Trail, which enters from the east. Keep to the left.

4.5 After reaching the parking lot facing the pond, follow a path that leads over the water on a bridge. Keeping to the right, continue on the path to arrive back at the trailhead.

HIKE INFORMATION

Local information: Westchester County Tourism & Film, 222 Mamaroneck Ave., White Plains, NY 10605; (914) 995-8500; www.westchestertourism.com

Local events/attractions: Paramount Center for the Arts, 1008 Brown St., Peekskill, NY 10566; (914) 739-2333; www.paramountcenter.org. A historic theater with art, film, stage, and music events year-round.

Hudson Valley Center for Contemporary Art, 1701 Main St./P.O. Box 209, Peekskill, NY 10566; (914) 788-0100; www.hvcca.org

Good eats: The Peekskill Brewery, 55 Hudson Ave., Peekskill, NY 10566-2025; (914) 734-2337; www.thepeekskillbrewery.com. A restaurant, bar, and microbrewery that's open for lunch and dinner.

Mercado Azteca & Deli, 1101 Main St., Peekskill, NY 10566; (914) 737-5513. Authentic, inexpensive Mexican cuisine.

Local outdoor stores: Kelloggs & Lawrence, 26 Parkway, Katonah, NY 10536; (914) 232-3351; www.kelloggsandlawrence.com

Organizations: Westchester Trails Association (c/o Herbert Hochberg), 112 Carthage Rd., Scarsdale, NY 10583; www.westhike.org

Hudson River Audubon Society, P.O. Box 616, Yonkers, NY 10703; (914) 237-9331; www.hras.org

Clarence Fahnestock Memorial State Park

Complete a circuit in the center of the Taconic region's largest park—a place that could just as easily have been named Hiker's Heaven. Ramble between several lakes and ponds, exploring an area that was mined for iron ore in the eighteenth and nineteenth centuries before it became a haven for outdoor recreation.

Start: The small parking area at the south end of Canopus Lake
Nearest town: Carmel, NY
Distance: 6.0-mile loop
Approximate hiking time: 3 to 4 hours
Difficulty: Moderate
Trail surface: Steep forest paths and lots of exposed rock
Seasons: May through Oct
Other trail users: Equestrians, mountain bikers, anglers; hunters and cross-country skiers (seasonally)
Wheelchair accessibility: None
Canine compatibility: Dogs permitted on leashes 10 feet or less, except at the beach and in picnic areas
Land status: State park
Fees and permits: A vehicle entry fee; additional charges for equipment rental and camping

Schedule: Daily from sunrise to sunset
Facilities: Restrooms and showers, campsites, pavilions and picnic areas, nature center, snack bar, boat rental
Maps: USGS West Point and Oscawana Lake, NY; New York-New Jersey Trail Conference East Hudson Trails Map 103. A black-and-white map and brochure is also available at the park office on Route 301 or as a PDF on the parks department website (see below).
Special considerations: Swimming is permitted at Canopus Lake from May 29 to Sept 6.
Trail contacts: Clarence Fahnestock Memorial State Park, 1498 Rte. 301, Carmel, NY 10512; (845) 225-7207; http://nysparks.state.ny.us/

Finding the trailhead: Drive north from New York City on the Taconic State Parkway and then take Route 301/Cold Spring Turnpike west into the park. The ranger station is on the right after about 1 mile, and the parking area is at the south end of Canopus Lake. GPS: N41 27.161' / W73 50.278'

Clarence Fahnestock wanted his own hunting preserve. And so, in 1900, this Manhattan physician began buying abandoned farms and claims to land that the iron industry had heavily mined until 1876. His biggest acquisition occurred in 1915, when he purchased the former property of the Reading Coal and Iron Company. But Major Fahnestock's dream of a personal game park would elude him; three years later he died in France during the First World War. Private property became public park when his brother Ernest donated 2,400 acres to the state in 1929. Clarence Fahnestock Memorial State Park has grown tremendously in the intervening years, adding nearly 10,000 acres to its footprint.

The loop in the center of this forested landscape doesn't include a mountain summit such as those on the southern and western margins of the park, but it instead guides hikers through an area with a rich history. Beginning on the Appalachian Trail (AT), take this long-distance footpath north and then access the blue-blazed Fahnestock Trail by scrambling up a rocky section that angles west once you've emerged from the tree cover. Pushing across the ridgetop, the sun beats down on spring and summer afternoons, causing chipmunks and squirrels to scamper for shade while songbirds such as the eastern bluebird and the black-capped chickadee chirp, twitter, and squeak.

Stick with the blue trail blazes until you meet the red-blazed Charcoal Burners Trail, just before the 1.5-mile mark. In the mid-1800s, most of the slopes in the region had been stripped bare to supply furnaces and forges with fuel. Turn left and walk south on the red trail, and then follow the white Cabot Trail west again, where you might catch a glimpse of a drab swamp sparrow or a brightly colored dragonfly darting around the edges of Jordan Pond. Gradually climbing uphill from the small body of water, you might pass through wispy strands of web strung across the trail by industrious spiders. Don't let these flimsy obstacles deter you from pressing on however—there's still a lot of hiking left.

Turn left where the Cabot Trail meets the yellow-blazed Perkins Trail, avoiding the private property in the other direction and then rejoining the Charcoal Burners Trail. Taking this trail across Cold Spring Turnpike, you'll be entering the place with the highest concentration of old mines: Denny Mine, Hamilton Mine, and Sunk Mine are clustered close together here, suggesting the existence of a valuable seam of magnetite, the ore used for smelting by the West Point Foundry in Cold Spring. Patches of moss are plentiful along this section of trail, forming a pale green runway leading south into the mixed hardwood forest. The red blazes terminate eventually, but before they do, walk over the route of an old narrow gauge railroad that enabled mule-drawn cars full of iron ore to be pulled from Sunk Mine to Dump Hill and the Philipstown Turnpike (now Route 301).

Turn left on the blue Three Lakes Trail at mile 4 and walk around Hidden Lake, one of several bodies of water in the park (including Canopus Lake) that were artificially created in the 1930s. One mile later, turn left again at a giant cairn and let the AT guide you north along Canopus Creek back to your car and civilization. If the sections of elevated trail bed seem unusual to you, they should: They were originally an extension of the mining railroad that led up to the Canada Mines, now underneath Canopus Lake.

As you prepare to drive back to the city, consider one more thing: Clarence Fahnestock is plenty big enough to warrant repeat visits.

The pale blue chicory flower frequently appears on the sides of roads such as Route 301, which cuts through the park.

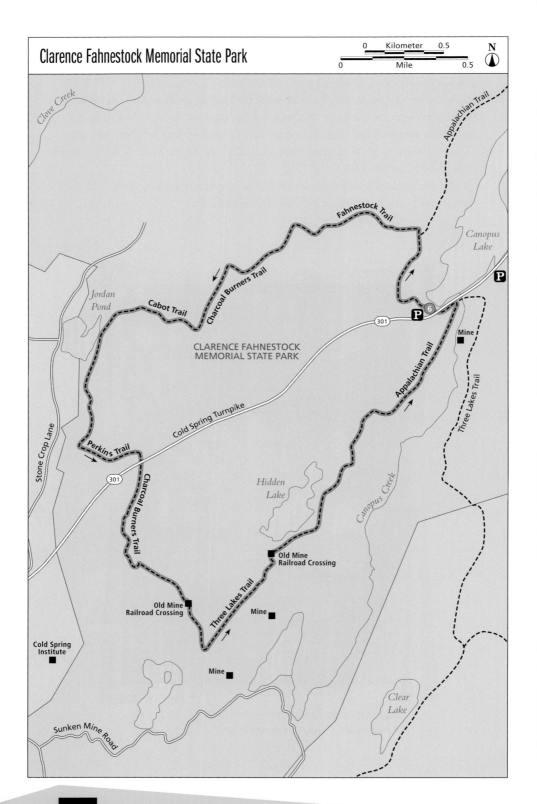

Clarence Fahnestock Memorial State Park

CLARENCE FAHNESTOCK
MEMORIAL STATE PARK

Fahnestock Trail

Charcoal Burners Trail

Cabot Trail

Jordan Pond

Clove Creek

Appalachian Trail

Canopus Lake

301

Cold Spring Turnpike

Perkins Trail

Stone Crop Lane

Charcoal Burners Trail

Hidden Lake

Three Lakes Trail

Appalachian Trail

Canopus Creek

Mine

Old Mine Railroad Crossing

Old Mine Railroad Crossing

Mine

Cold Spring Institute

Mine

Clear Lake

Sunken Mine Road

0.0 Start at the small parking area at the south end of Canopus Lake. Follow the white Appalachian Trail blazes over jumbled piles of stone, gaining elevation as you go.

0.2 Walk by an AT sign-in box mounted on a tree.

0.4 Turn left onto the blue Fahnestock Trail, heading north up a hill and then running west. Push through brush and over rock outcroppings, steadily gaining altitude.

1.0 Curve to the left (south) and descend about 100 feet. Step across an intermittent creek.

1.4 At a T intersection, after a switchback leads you over a small ledge, turn left (south) on the red-blazed Charcoal Burners Trail.

1.7 Make a sharp right (west) turn at the cairn onto the white-blazed Cabot Trail.

2.1 Follow the Cabot Trail south as it drops down under 1,000 feet and passes by Jordan Pond.

2.7 The white blazes dead-end at the yellow Perkins Trail. Turn left (east) at the cairn and head up a small ridge.

3.0 Meet the red Charcoal Burners Trail once more and turn right (south). Cross Route 301 and then a little brook on the other side of the road. Listen for the kerplunk of a frog hopping into the water.

3.5 After a series of ups and downs, follow a bumpy ridge of exposed rock that points southeast.

3.8 Cross the yellow Old Mine Railroad Trail (closed).

4.0 Turn left on the blue Three Lakes Trail, heading northeast.

4.5 A yellow-blazed trail enters from the left, but don't alter your course. Circle around the eastern shore of Hidden Lake.

5.0 Turn left at the huge cairn to take the narrower AT north. The final mile is a generally flat section that clings to the side of a ridge.

5.8 Turn left (west) to reach the road. An unmarked trail to the east links with the Three Lakes Trail.

6.0 Arrive back on Route 301, across from the small parking area and the trailhead.

Local information: Putnam County Visitors Bureau, 110 Old Rte. 6, Bldg. 3, Carmel, NY 10512; (800) 470-4854; www.visitputnam.org

Local events/attractions: Dia:Beacon Riggio Galleries, 3 Beekman St., Beacon, NY 12508; (845) 440-0100; www.diabeacon.org. An old Nabisco box printing factory serves as a museum housing a major collection of artworks from the 1960s to the present.

The Chuang Yen Monastery at the Buddhist Association of the United States, 2020 Rte. 301, Carmel, NY 10512; (845) 225-1819; www.baus.org/en/. Visit Great Buddha Hall, Thousand Lotus Terrace, Seven Jewel Lakes, and the Garden.

Good eats: Cacciatore's, 1116 Rte. 52, Kent Center, Carmel, NY 10512; (845) 225-4695; www.cacciatorestrattoria.com. Pizza, pasta, calzones, and three kinds of cheesecake (including fried).

Creme de la Creme Bakery, 509 Rte. 312, Brewster, NY 10509; (845) 278-4979; www.cremedelacreme.spruz.com. Make a quick stop to pick up something sweet before or after your hike.

Local outdoor stores: Hudson Valley Outfitters, 63 Main St., Cold Spring, NY 10516; (845) 265-0221; www.hudsonvalleyoutfitters.com

Organizations: Friends of Fahnestock and Hudson Highlands State Parks, P.O. Box 194, Cold Spring, NY 10516; www.fofhh.org. Founded in 2007 to preserve, protect, and improve these historic and natural resources.

Hudson River Valley Greenway, Capitol Building, Room 254, Albany, NY 12224; (518) 473-3835; www.hudsongreenway.state.ny.us

Hudson Highlands Land Trust, P.O. Box 226, Garrison, NY 10524; (845) 424-3358; www.hhlt.org

Dennytown Road once ran through the middle of a mining community that was able to support a blacksmith shop, a school, and two stores.

Cold Spring Harbor State Park

Get a workout hiking the last few miles of a long-distance trail that cuts across Long Island's glacial moraine deposits, and end up in a hamlet with a past that's linked to the history of science, music, and maritime life in the nineteenth century.

Start: Access from the shoulder of Route 108

Nearest town: Cold Spring Harbor, NY

Distance: 4.2 miles out and back

Approximate hiking time: 2 to 3 hours

Difficulty: Easy to moderate

Trail surface: Woodland dirt footpath, gravel, and somewhat steep, uneven terrain

Seasons: Year-round

Other trail users: Joggers; snowshoers and cross-country skiers (seasonally)

Wheelchair accessibility: The Daniel P. Davidson Trail at the Uplands Farm Sanctuary in Cold Spring Harbor is a short loop with very little terrain change.

Canine compatibility: Dogs not permitted

Land status: State park

Fees and permits: None

Schedule: Daily from dawn to dusk

Facilities: There is a public restroom just off the trail at the Cold Spring Harbor Library and Environmental Center

Maps: USGS Huntington, NY. A trail map is available for free download from the New York State Office of Parks, Recreation & Historic Preservation website (see below).

Trail contacts: New York State Office of Parks, Recreation & Historic Preservation, Care of Caumsett State Historic Park, 25 Lloyd Harbor Road, Huntington, NY 11743; (631) 423-1770; www.nysparks.state.ny.us
Long Island Greenbelt Trail Conference, Inc., P.O. Box 5636, Hauppauge, NY 11788; (631) 360-0753; www.ligreenbelt.org

Finding the trailhead: From the Cold Spring Harbor Long Island Railroad station, walk downhill to the stoplight on Woodbury Road. Turn left and then make an immediate right (north) turn onto Route 108/Harbor Road. Continue north on the shoulder of Route 108 for roughly 0.9 mile, taking care to watch for oncoming traffic. The trailhead is on your left shortly after Stillwell Lane. Enter here and follow the white blazes north. GPS: N40 50.677′ / W73 27.375′

THE HIKE

The northernmost section of the 20-mile Nassau–Suffolk Trail can be either a relatively short afternoon outing, or extended into a longer tour of Long Island's varied terrain. Charting a meandering course along a low ridgeline, this hike ends at a scenic waterfront park in the town of Cold Spring Harbor. Beginning about 0.9 mile from the train station and just off a somewhat busy north-south artery, the track twists and turns through a marshy zone just below the roadbed on your right. Here, close to the asphalt, bright orange jewelweed flowers stand out against a natural canvas painted in shades of green. Watching your feet as you step over gnarled roots, swaths of ivy, and patches of moss, it's likely that you'll spot a dragonfly or two, a black-and-yellow eastern garter snake sunning itself on the path, or a chipmunk watching you from a fallen log.

Carefully cross back over Route 108 after approximately one-tenth of a mile and prepare for more of a challenge as the path heads up a wooded slope. Proceeding northward, you'll pass through white pine and rhododendron, gaining and losing as much as 200 feet in elevation as the route dips and climbs up and down the hillside on its way toward the Long Island Sound. To either side of the blazed trail, life flitters and scurries in the undergrowth. Blue jays may tussle in the branches above, and an attentive ear will hear the call of a warbler, or maybe a mockingbird.

Avoiding an unmarked spur at about mile 0.6, the trail next takes a sharp left (northwest) turn on an old road—notice the weathered fence posts on your left—then curves back to the north up a gravel incline. It then veers west again where it intersects the yellow-blazed Nature Conservancy path. From here you'll parallel a chain-link fence for a short distance, cross Lawrence Hill Road, enter Cold Spring Harbor State Park, and climb the south side of Lawrence Hill. The Nassau–Suffolk Trail will test your knees in the remaining mile, but on warm summer days, the breeze blowing from the inner harbor will keep you from overheating too quickly.

Another steep downhill after mile 1.5 is followed by a long east-to-west switchback that leads to a final scramble and then the payoff: a scenic overlook just behind the Cold Spring Harbor Library. From this vantage point, the boats anchored in the water below appear to be toys, and the southern coast of Connecticut looks closer than it is—roughly a dozen miles away on the other side of the sound. Push on between the tall oaks and maples to the northern terminus of the trail and a parking area.

A picnic area on the other side of the road presents hikers with an opportunity to rest their feet and refuel with a piece of fruit or a granola bar. Music fans may also take note of a large rock in the park that bears a plaque commemorating a popular American pianist and composer. In 1971 a young Billy Joel, who had grown up in nearby Hicksville, named his first solo album Cold Spring Harbor.

When you have enjoyed the sights at trail's end, retrace your steps to the trailhead.

MILES AND DIRECTIONS

0.0 Start from the shoulder of Route 108/Harbor Road. Immediately turn right and walk north in the direction of the white blazes. Don't cross the small bridge directly ahead of you.

0.1 Climb a few steps up to the road and cross to the other side.

0.5 Walk across a dirt access road for the telephone line.

0.6 Pass by an unmarked trail on the left; keep to the right. At the top of a tiny rise, turn left (northwest) onto a wider gravel woods road that curves back down toward Route 108.

0.8 Veer left at a fork and continue up an incline. Stick with the white blazes as they turn and descend slightly alongside a chain-link fence.

1.2 Climb up to Lawrence Hill Road and cross into Cold Spring Harbor State Park. Climb a small but steep slope up Lawrence Hill. Now that you're inside the park, the trail will gain and lose small amounts of elevation for the remainder of the hike.

1.5 Still heading north, make the steepest descent of the hike and then use a switchback to reach the top of another small hill.

Looking across Cold Spring Harbor toward Long Island Sound

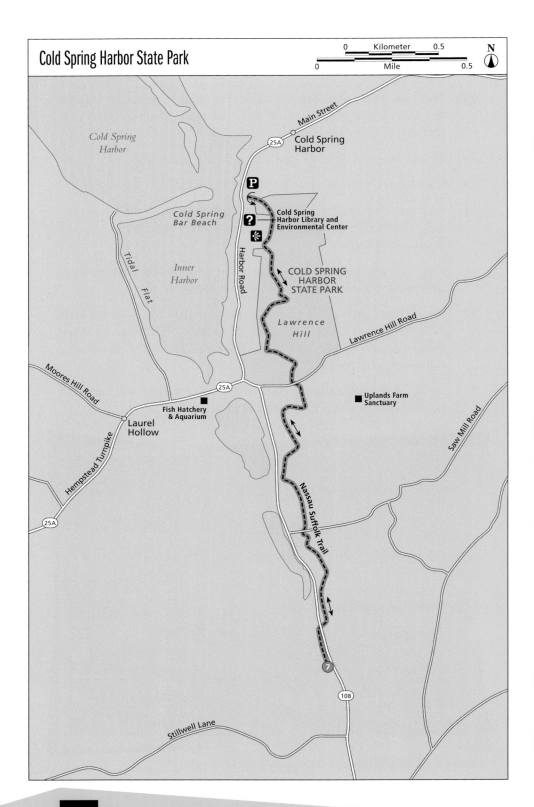

Cold Spring Harbor State Park

0   Kilometer   0.5

0   Mile   0.5

N

Cold Spring Harbor

Main Street

25A

Cold Spring Harbor

Cold Spring Bar Beach

P

Cold Spring Harbor Library and Environmental Center

COLD SPRING HARBOR STATE PARK

Tidal Flat

Inner Harbor

Harbor Road

Lawrence Hill

Lawrence Hill Road

Moores Hill Road

25A

Fish Hatchery & Aquarium

Uplands Farm Sanctuary

Laurel Hollow

Saw Mill Road

Hempstead Turnpike

25A

Nassau Suffolk Trail

7

108

Stillwell Lane

1.9 Reach a partially obstructed overlook above Cold Spring's Inner Harbor. Pass a spur trail that leads to the bathroom in the library a few hundred feet farther on.

2.1 Arrive at the north end of the Nassau–Suffolk Trail and a small parking area on Harbor Road. Cross to the small green space overlooking the water—a great spot for a picnic or a break. Follow the same trail south to complete the hike.

4.2 Arrive back at the trail entry point on Route 108.

Options: Tack on up to 2 additional miles by exploring the Uplands Farm Sanctuary, headquarters of the Long Island Chapter of The Nature Conservancy. The generally flat trails on this 97-acre property were once part of a dairy farm, and today the fields and vernal pools shelter animals such as wood frogs, downy woodpeckers, and spotted salamanders.

HIKE INFORMATION

Local information: Long Island Convention & Visitors Bureau and Sports Commission, 330 Motor Parkway, Suite 203, Hauppauge, NY 11788; (877) FUN-ON-LI; www.discoverlongisland.com

Local events/attractions: Cold Spring Harbor Whaling Museum, 279 Main St., Cold Spring Harbor, NY 11724; (631) 367-3418; www.cshwhalingmuseum.org Dolan DNA Learning Center, 334 Main St., Cold Spring Harbor, NY 11724; (516) 367-5170; www.dnalc.org

Good eats: Harbor Mist Restaurant, 105 Harbor Road, Cold Spring Harbor, NY 11724; (631) 659-3888; http://harbormistrestaurant.com

Local outdoor stores: Eastern Mountain Sports, 204 Glen Cove Rd., Carle Place, NY 11514; (516) 747-7360; www.ems.com

Organizations: Long Island Trail Lovers Coalition, P.O. Box 1466, Sayville NY 11782; (631) 563-4354; www.litlc.org

🌿 Green Tip:
On the trail eat grains and veggies instead of meat, which has a higher energy cost.

What in the Blazes?

Set out on any well-maintained trail in the New York area (or elsewhere for that matter) and you'll notice two things. First, any blown-down trees, brush, and other obstacles have typically been cleared from the trail, and in some cases, structures such as bridges or informational kiosks have been added to the landscape. And second, these wilderness routes have been mapped and blazed with bright squares of paint and/or plastic tags of a matching color. Look for them every few hundred feet on large rocks or the trunks of trees, several feet off the ground. Marked trails are important for a few reasons: They limit the erosion and damage caused by shortcuts, spur trails, and tangents that often dead-end before they really get anywhere. They're also helpful when you haven't hiked in a particular park before and need reassurance that you're heading in the right direction. Blazes indicate where a trail begins and ends (three squares in a triangle shape), that a trail continues (a single square), and that a turn should be expected (stacked squares with the uppermost square set to the right or the left depending on which way the trail turns). Equally important, trail blazes designate detours, where paths have been rerouted to avoid a hazard or to spare an area from damage caused by excessive traffic. In other words, pay close attention to these colorful codes as you hike and don't just rely on the packed earth under your boots to show you the way.

🌿 **Green Tip:**
Don't take souvenirs home with you. This means natural materials such as plants, rocks, shells, and driftwood, as well as historic artifacts such as fossils and arrowheads.

Connetquot River State Park Preserve

Spend some time in New York State's first preserve, formerly the South Side Sports-men's Club. Learn about the three trout hatcheries established along the Connetquot ("Great River" in the native Secatogue tongue) in the late nineteenth century and the three types of trout that inhabit the waterway to this day. Go on a wildlife safari in any season and test your knowledge of the flora and fauna native to Long Island.

Start: At the compass rose painted on the pavement at the south end of the Main Pond

Nearest town: Islip, NY

Distance: 4.1-mile loop

Approximate hiking time: 2.5 to 3 hours

Difficulty: Easy

Trail surface: Gravel bridle trails, dirt footpaths, and pavement

Seasons: Year-round

Other trail users: Equestrians, fly fishermen; cross-country skiers (seasonally)

Wheelchair accessibility: Paved multiuse trails near the park entrance allow for limited exploration of the preserve. All of the grades on the bridle paths are very minimal.

Canine compatibility: Dogs not permitted

Land status: State park preserve

Fees and permits: A vehicle entry fee

Schedule: Wed through Sun from dawn until dusk

Facilities: Restrooms, gift shop, natural history museum at the trailhead

Maps: USGS Central Islip, NY. Black-and-white maps of the preserve are available at the park entrance and in the museum.

Trail contacts: Connetquot River State Park Preserve, Box 505, Oakdale, NY 11769; (631) 581-1005; www.nysparks.com

Finding the trailhead: By car, follow I-495/Long Island Expressway to exit 56/Route 111. Head south on Route 111 to the Sunrise Highway/Route 27 east (approximately 5 miles). From the Sunrise Highway, take exit 47A and follow signs for the preserve. Turn left on Oakdale-Bohemia Road, cross Route 27, turn left onto the westbound service road, and look for the park entrance on the right after 1.5 miles. **By public transportation:** Take the Long Island Railroad to the Great River station in East Islip. Walk north on Connetquot Avenue for about 0.7 mile, cross over Route 27, and turn right onto the paved bike path heading east alongside the highway. Look for the park entrance on the left after 1.1 miles. GPS: N40 45.005' / W 73 08.979'

Teeming with fish and birdlife, the territory that adds up to Connetquot River State Park Preserve also attracted wealthy sportsmen (hunters and fishermen) in the late nineteenth century. This group of citizens went on to found a club on 879 acres of property around a tavern and stagecoach stop called Snedecor's. They created hatcheries to keep the river stocked, and gradually expanded the property until it reached its present size, becoming one of the largest undeveloped areas on Long Island. Following its purchase of the land in 1973, New York designated it as a state park preserve five years later.

Mallard ducks, mute swans, and American robins—birds frequently spotted throughout the state—are also abundant within Connetquot's boundaries, but numerous other species, such as the green heron, the yellow-bellied sapsucker, the red-breasted nuthatch, and the wood duck, are often present or are likely to be seen. Many more birds, from owls to warblers, appear occasionally or rarely, depending on the season. Endangered or threatened species like the osprey, the pied-billed grebe, and the whip-poor-will nest in the park. Since 2006, over 3,000 bobwhite quail and 250 ring-necked pheasants have been released in an effort to control the tick population and add to the park's biodiversity.

Begin by strolling by the Oakdale Grist Mill, a structure built by the Nicoll family in the early 1700s to grind corn and wheat. Skirt the southern edge of the Main Pond and then proceed north, traveling the loop in a counterclockwise direction. Watch for red blazes as you move through the understory of fern and huckleberry, pausing (perhaps) should you notice the uncommon pyxie moss or trailing arbutus (mayflower). As you get closer to the water, dense, spiky spartina grass and the nearly ubiquitous phragmites cloak the shoreline. About a mile into the hike the trail leads into pitch pine, where a red-capped (and poisonous) fly agaric might poke up through the leaf litter to break the monochromatic brown of the forest floor.

Instead of staying with the blue trail all the way to the northern border of the preserve, turn back to the southwest after mile 2 and use a modern bridge to get to the other side of the Connetquot Brook at a historic crossing known as Bunces. Linger by the river if you want to try to glimpse the streamlined shape of a brook trout or a brown trout; otherwise, keep going in the direction of the green blazes.

With about 1 mile remaining you'll maintain a straight line to the south/ southeast, getting closer to the sound of traffic on the Sunrise Highway with every step. To the right and left of the trail, a large field and thick brush hide some of the preserve's other residents from curious visitors. The historic two- and three-storey shingled buildings clustered around the park gate come into view at mile 4, as the green trail runs into the yellow trail leading to the fish hatchery.

MILES AND DIRECTIONS

0.0 Start at the compass rose on the multiuse path just south of the Main Pond. Walk east toward the gristmill on the red trail and keep the museum behind you.

0.1 Turn left (north) on Brook Road, passing through two old wooden gate-posts and remaining on the red trail.

0.3 Keep to the left at the fork in the broad, sandy bridle trail. Some of the trees will have rectangular bat boxes affixed to their trunks. Follow the red blazes to the left (west) again after 0.1 mile.

0.6 Walk out onto a small dock that extends into the river.

0.7 Once again turn left on the red trail. The sandy route narrows briefly here, beneath the conifers and mixed hardwood forest.

0.9 Arrive at a small clearing with a sign reading ANGLER'S AREA. Note that fishing in the preserve is only permitted at designated sites by licensed anglers. Veer away from the Connetquot by choosing the red trail to the right (northeast).

1.3 At the junction, follow the wide, blue-blazed trail north, deeper into the preserve, where deer are commonly sighted. The red trail continues west toward the hatchery complex.

A small toadstool bears evidence of a hungry passerby.

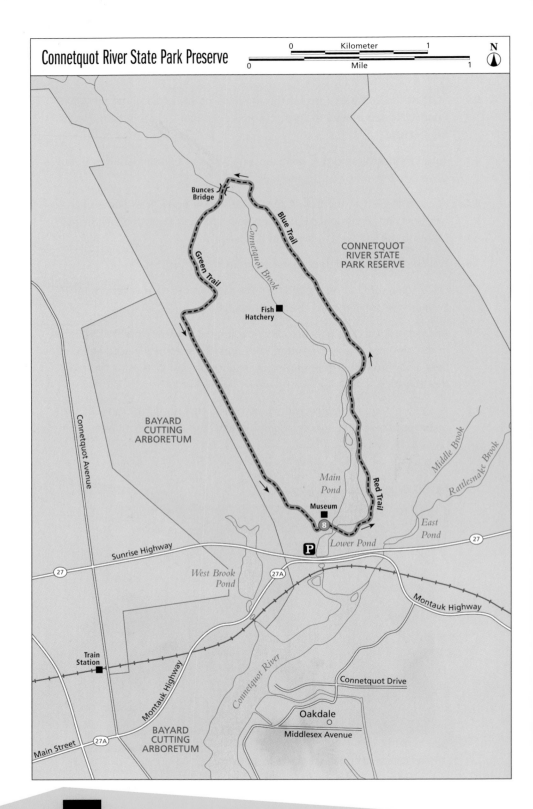

Connetquot River State Park Preserve

1.7 Pass Poacher's Path, one of several fire lanes that divide the park into an irregular-shaped grid.

2.1 The blue trail meets the green trail at a four-way intersection. Turn left and walk southwest on the green trail.

2.2 Cross Bunces Bridge, a popular fishing location since the days of the Sportsmen's Club in the 1860s. The river runs shallow at this point, which was originally known as Bunces Crossing. An earlier vehicular bridge made of locust is still visible beneath the water.

2.7 Turn right (west) to remain on the green trail. Let the flat gravel path guide you past large open meadows where butterflies and moths flit between wildflower blossoms.

4.0 Pass a small barn and the yellow trail (West Club Road), which leads to the hatchery complex.

4.1 Arrive back at the parking area and trailhead, just inside the park entrance.

Options: Fifty miles of bridle paths and nature trails crisscross the preserve, permitting a variety of different routes within the 3,473-acre property. This hike uses part of the red, blue, and green trails to create a loop. At 8.4 miles, the blue trail—which stretches north to Veterans Memorial Highway—is the longest.

HIKE INFORMATION

Local information: Long Island Convention & Visitors Bureau and Sports Commission, 330 Motor Parkway, Suite 203, Hauppauge, NY 11788; (877) FUN-ON-LI; www.discoverlongisland.com

Local events/attractions: Islip Art Museum, 50 Irish Lane, East Islip, NY 11730-2003; (631) 224-5402; www.islipartmuseum.org

Good eats: Coliseum Pizza & Pasta, 142 Connetquot Ave., East Islip, NY 11730-1418; (631) 224-2699

Long Island's Beachtree Restaurant, 166 W. Main St., East Islip, NY 11730; (631) 277-4800; www.beachtreerestaurant.com

Organizations: Long Island Trail Lovers Coalition, P.O. Box 1466, Sayville NY; (631) 563-4354; www.litlc.org

Friends of Connetquot River State Park Preserve, P.O. Box 472, Oakdale, NY 11769; www.friendsof connetquot.org. Committed to conservation, this group has also dedicated itself to restoring the gristmill, reopening the hatchery, and converting the ice house into a research library.

Cranberry Lake Preserve

Tucked between Rye Lake and the Kensico Reservoir, Cranberry Lake Preserve includes a variety of sights within its relatively small footprint: A nature lodge, a bird observation tower, an old quarry, and the namesake lake itself share space within the 190-acre park.

Start: At the map kiosk just inside the park entrance

Nearest town: Valhalla, NY

Distance: 2.2-mile double loop

Approximate hiking time: 1 to 1.5 hours

Difficulty: Easy to moderate

Trail surface: Dirt and gravel footpaths with a few rocky sections and several stretches of boardwalk

Seasons: Year-round

Other trail users: Joggers; cross-country skiers (seasonally)

Wheelchair accessibility: None

Canine compatibility: Dogs not permitted

Land status: County park

Fees and permits: None

Schedule: Daily from sunrise to sunset. The nature lodge and front gate are open Tues through Sun from 9 a.m. to 4 p.m.

Facilities: Restrooms and a drinking fountain at the nature lodge

Maps: USGS White Plains, NY. A map of the hiking trails is available at the trailhead or online at the parks department website (see below).

Trail contacts: Westchester County Department of Parks, Recreation and Conservation, 25 Moore Ave., Mount Kisco, NY 10549; (914) 864-PARK; http://parks.westchestergov.com/

Finding the trailhead: Take the New York State Thruway/I-87 north from New York, heading east on I-287 toward White Plains at exit 8. Drive 3.9 miles and then take exit 6 north on Route 22. Keep left to remain on Route 22. Make a right at the stoplight on Old Orchard Street after 3 miles and look for a large sign marking the park entrance on the right.

By public transportation: Metro North train service from Grand Central delivers passengers to Valhalla, a short cab ride or about a forty-minute walk (1.7 miles) through Kensico Dam Plaza and along busy Route 22/Mount Kisco Road. The signed entrance is on Old Orchard Street, no more than 150 feet from the stoplight on Route 22. GPS: N41 04.912′ / W73 45.352′

Bordered by three different highways and only about 2 miles from Westchester County Airport, this sliver of green named for the lake at its center is a small but attractive park that offers more peace and quiet than 190 acres might seem capable of. Plus, with four trails to choose from, it's possible to design a handful of interesting hikes that encompass scrubland and hardwood forest, swamp and low cliffs. Although Cranberry Lake Preserve doesn't have the name recognition of Rockefeller State Park Preserve to the northwest, or the immensity of Ward Pound Ridge Reservation to the northeast, a visit to this preserve on Valhalla's doorstep can be a charming experience nonetheless. Stop by the nature lodge to check out the educational displays and maybe pick up a bird checklist before you start exploring.

At sunset the woods glow with an orange light.

Stepping into the woods from the park road that bears south from Old Orchard Street, traveling the loop in a clockwise direction, you may interrupt black squirrels busily chattering to each other from treetop perches. However, even if eavesdropping on rodents causes a slight delay in your progress to Cranberry Lake, this small remnant of the last ice age is less than 0.5 mile from the trailhead and doesn't take long to reach on foot. Proceed around its eastern edge and let the Red/Yellow/Purple Trail lead you up and over a rocky slope to an old granite quarry. From 1912 to 1917, building material blasted from the hillside here (holes drilled for sticks of dynamite are still visible in places) was shaped by stonemasons in a large shed nearby, and then carried by rail to the construction site for a taller, stronger Kensico Dam.

The engineering feat that is the Kensico Dam was completed to supply more water to a thirsty population. The first dam, finished in 1885, was capable of capturing 18 million gallons of water from the Bronx and Bryam Rivers, but twenty years on, it became clear to the state legislature that demand would soon exceed capacity. By contrast, the new reservoir held back by a 1,843-foot-long dam contains a staggering 30 billion gallons of clean water at any given time. It is part of the larger Croton System.

Once you've tired of scaling the quarry's cliffs, work your way around the pit to the Red/Purple Trail and proceed south through slender beeches and stout sycamore trees.

Walking on what seems like an old railroad bed, cross a little brook and pass a cascade to the left of the trail. In dry years the show at this point of interest might be rather lackluster, while the bird observation tower slightly farther along is definitely worth stopping for, especially in the spring. Veery, wood thrush, green herons, belted kingfishers, and pileated woodpeckers are just a few of the species that breed within the park.

Descend the steps from the tower back down to the Blue Trail and walk west on the boardwalk at the southern end of South Pond. It soon curves north around the shoreline, running parallel to a wall of neatly stacked stone before splitting off at the 1.6-mile mark. An orange connecting trail enters from the east here, and curious hikers can follow it a short distance over Bent Bridge to reach a prehistoric-looking stone chamber.

Skip this short detour or dash out and back, and then head up a modest rise on a trail with both red and purple blazes. Late in the day the sun will set through the conifers between you and the Kensico Reservoir, warming the woods with an orangey glow.

Instead of taking the Purple Trail to the nature lodge (which is another option), stroll over a carpet of pine needles to the conclusion of the Red Trail, listening to the boughs above you creak in the wind.

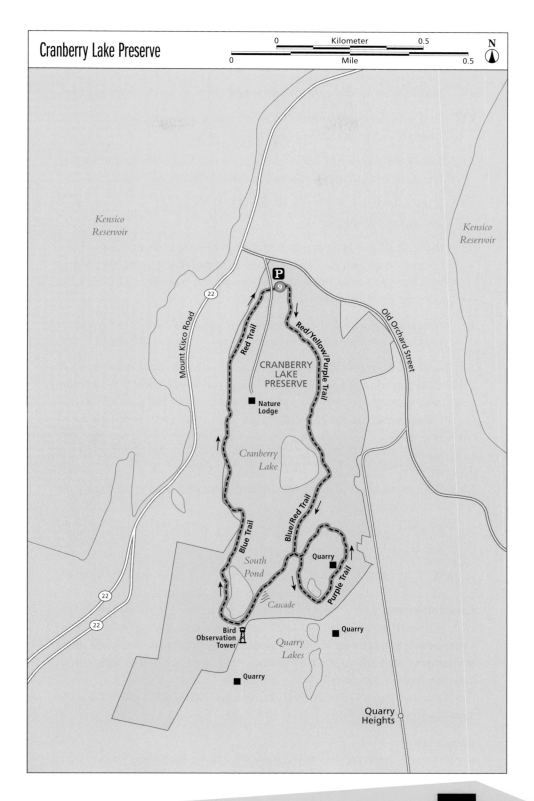

Cranberry Lake Preserve

0   Kilometer   0.5

0   Mile   0.5

N

Kensico
Reservoir

Kensico
Reservoir

Mount Kisco Road

22

Old Orchard Street

P
9

Red Trail

Red/Yellow/Purple Trail

CRANBERRY
LAKE
PRESERVE

Nature
Lodge

Cranberry
Lake

Blue Trail

Blue/Red Trail

Purple Trail

Quarry

South
Pond

22

22

Cascade

Bird
Observation
Tower

Quarry Lakes

Quarry

Quarry

Quarry

Quarry
Heights

0.0   Start at the map kiosk just inside the park entrance on Old Orchard Street.

0.1   Turn left on the Red/Yellow/Purple Trail and continue walking southeast, traveling along the loop in a clockwise direction.

0.3   Follow the yellow trail blazes almost due south at the next intersection. The surface of Cranberry Lake will shimmer through the trees ahead.

0.4   Make another left (east) turn on the Blue Trail, passing over several short sections of boardwalk.

0.5   Pause at an overlook, sitting in the large Adirondack-style bench if you choose. Afterwards, stay on the Blue Trail for another 0.1 mile, then merge with the Red/Purple Trail and work your way up a small rise. Turn left and then make a right to circle the quarry.

1.1   With the quarry behind you now, turn left (west) to head back toward the red-blazed perimeter trail. Make a left (south) on the Red Trail after 0.1 mile.

1.3   Arrive at a tiny cascade, just past the point where the Purple Trail splits off to the left and right. A few hundred feet beyond this intersection a wooden bird observation tower rises above South Pond to the right of the trail. Continue west on the Blue Trail.

1.5   The Blue Trail rejoins the Red and Purple Trails and proceeds north. Keep to the left when the Red and Purple Trails veer to the left (west).

1.8   Keep to the left on the Red Trail when the Purple Trail splits off toward the nature lodge.

2.2   Arrive back at the park entrance, slightly south of the red trailhead where you started, inside of the main gate.

HIKE INFORMATION

Local information: Westchester County Tourism & Film, 222 Mamaroneck Ave., White Plains, NY 10605; (914) 995-8500; www.westchestertourism.com

Local events/attractions: Neuberger Museum of Art, Purchase College, State University of New York, 735 Anderson Hill Rd., Purchase, NY 10577; (914) 251-6100; www.neuberger.org

Rye Nature Center, 873 Boston Post Rd., Rye, NY 10580; (914) 967-5150; www .ryenaturecenter.org

Good eats: Valhalla Crossing, 2 Cleveland St., Valhalla, NY 10595; (914) 682-4076; www.valhallacrossing.com. A self-described "fun pub with style," open seven days a week.

Riverfront Deli, 6 Broadway, Valhalla, NY 10595; (914) 684-2161; www.riverfront deli.com. Breakfast, lunch, and if you're still hungry, Hershey's ice cream.

So Dam Hot, 10 Broadway, Valhalla, NY 10595; (914) 328-6051; www.sodamhot .com. Hot dogs, fries, burgers, chili, and of course, plenty of wings.

Local outdoor stores: American Terrain Outdoors, 175 East Post Rd., White Plains, NY 10601; (914) 682-3971; www.americanterrain.com

Eastern Mountain Sports, 693 White Plains Post Rd., Eastchester Shopping Center, Scarsdale, NY 10583; (914) 725-0024; www.ems.com

Organizations: Friends of Westchester County Parks, 25 Moore Ave., Mount Kisco, NY 10549; (914) 864-7032; www.friendsofwestchesterparks.com

Hudson River Audubon Society, P.O. Box 616, Yonkers, NY 10703; (914) 237-9331; www.hras.org

Like people, insects are drawn to colorful flora.

Fire Island National Seashore

Venture east—almost to the end of this thin 32-mile-long barrier island—to discover a small but still thriving salt marsh, once a flourishing part of the Atlantic coastline. Miles from the city and yet a breeze to reach by train, Fire Island shelters endangered animals like piping plovers, and provides intrepid visitors with family and group campsites near the only federal wilderness area in New York.

Start: Near the mouth of the Watch Hill channel
Nearest town: Patchogue, NY
Distance: 1.1-mile loop
Approximate hiking time: 45 min.
Difficulty: Easy
Trail surface: Sand and boardwalk
Seasons: Mid-May to Oct
Other trail users: Birders
Wheelchair accessibility: None
Canine compatibility: Leashed dogs permitted
Land status: National park/federal wilderness area
Fees and permits: None
Schedule: Daily from sunrise to sunset
Facilities: Restrooms, showers, campground, picnic area, snack bar. Small interpretive displays on beach ecology are located in the visitor center.
Maps: USGS Howells Point, NY. A detailed black-and-white map of the Watch Hill Nature Trail is available at the visitor center, as is a larger map of the entire national seashore.
Special considerations: Be sure to bring plenty of sunscreen for this hike—you'll find little to no shade on the island.
Trail contacts: Fire Island National Seashore, 120 Laurel St., Patchogue, NY 11772; (631) 687-4750; www.nps.gov/fiis

Finding the trailhead: To reach the Fire Island ferry terminal by car, drive east on I-495 and then take exit 63 toward Patchogue on North Ocean Avenue/CR 83. After 4.2 miles turn right (west) on Baker Street (which becomes Division Street) and then take the second left (south) turn on West Avenue. The parking area for the ferry terminal will be on the right. Ride across Great South Bay, disembark, and walk south (toward the beach) from the visitor center, following signs for the nature trail and the campground. Next to the ranger station at the edge of the marina, take a left on the boardwalk and continue about 0.2 mile to the entrance into the salt marsh. **By public transportation:** The Long Island Railroad stops in Patchogue, and from the station it's only a ten-minute walk to the ferry terminal. GPS: N40 41.599' / W72 59.355'

THE HIKE

For people whose idea of going to the beach is a ride on the N train to Coney Island, Fire Island National Seashore might seem like it's a long way from the city. Which is part of the point of visiting. But the good news for travelers is that every year Fire Island gets a little closer. With ocean tides ceaselessly pounding against its sandy shape, this barrier island has no hope of staying put. And so, the Fire Island Lighthouse, which in 1858 stood at Democrat Point on the edge of this slender landmass, now shines its beacon a full 5 miles from that westernmost extreme.

In other words, a visit to Fire Island is a chance to observe change slowly taking place all around you. Migrating birds cruise by overhead, beachgoers arrive and depart by boat, and the dunes themselves shrink and grow with storms and seasons. For a microcosm of the various environments to be found here, take a short nature walk around the salt marsh at Watch Hill. In the span of just over 1 mile, you'll move between the Great South Bay and the Atlantic, passing through freshwater bog, maritime forest, swale, and if you plan to spend time on the beach, primary dune.

Setting out from the marina area, you'll stroll by sailboats and powerboats anchored in numbered slips as their owners seek entertainment and relaxation on the island. The faint crash of waves will be your soundtrack on this leisurely loop, as

Across the Great South Bay, Long Island is visible on the horizon.

Fire Island National Seashore

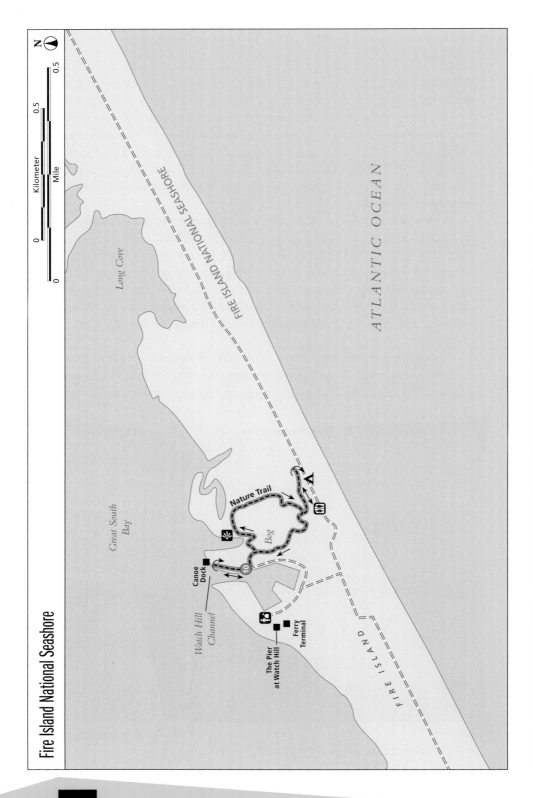

will the squeaks and peeps of swallows darting back and forth across the salt marsh. Progressing north toward the open water of the bay, it's impossible to ignore the pungent odor of decaying plant matter. Unpleasant though it may be, this smell is simply the result of sulfur compounds that allow tiny organisms living in the soil to perform their basic life functions. Fortunately Fire Island is a breezy place.

Pause at one of the benches and let your eyes wander across the south shore of Long Island. Then try to count the dragonflies flitting here and there in the hardy marsh grasses below the boardwalk. Once you've soaked up enough sun and scenery, turn south and step into the shade offered by the patch of sunken forest that tenaciously clings to life in spite of the wind and salt spray that constantly blows across the island. You'll likely notice stunted trees and woody shrubs at first, but here and there taller hollies and a few other temperate hardwoods dare to grow to greater heights.

Make a left (east) turn just before the 0.5-mile mark to explore the swale zone between the dunes, and then backtrack to the main trail, following the steps up the side of a tiny hill. From the zenith you can look down at the ground you've already covered, or scan the southern horizon for the silhouette of a ship moving along the coast.

Continue down the stairs on the other side of the hilltop platform and look for red-winged blackbirds or an alabaster egret in the freshwater bog. For a final detour, turn right (north) just before the trailhead and walk out to the mouth of the Watch Hill channel. Poke around for a horseshoe crab shell or watch seagulls lunch on the dock before heading back to the marina and the trailhead.

MILES AND DIRECTIONS

0.0 Start at the nature trail entrance northeast of the visitor center and the marina. Make a sharp left (north) after traveling 330 feet on the boardwalk.

0.2 Stop at the bench for a view across the Great South Bay.

0.3 Head south toward the thicket growing on the margins of the freshwater bog.

0.5 Turn left (east) at the spur that leads into the camping area. Follow the boardwalk into the swale, turn around, and walk back to the spur junction.

0.8 Reach the top of a small hill with expansive views of the Great South Bay and the Atlantic Ocean across the dunes.

0.9 Circle around the other side of the freshwater bog and listen to the diverse variety of birdsong.

1.0 Turn right (north) where you started and walk out to the point where you can observe waterfowl as well as the many boats coming and leaving Watch Hill.

1.1 Arrive back at the dock at the mouth of the channel.

HIKE INFORMATION

Local information: Long Island Convention & Visitors Bureau and Sports Commission, 330 Motor Parkway, Suite 203, Hauppauge, NY 11788; 877-FUN-ON-LI; www.discoverlongisland.com

Local events/attractions: The General William Floyd House, 245 Park Dr., Mastic Beach, NY 11951; (631) 399-2030; www.nps.gov/fiis/planyourvisit/williamfloyd estate.htm. This former home of a signer of the Declaration of Independence is also a national landmark.

The Long Island Maritime Museum, P.O. Box 184, 86 West Ave., West Sayville, NY 11796; (631) HISTORY; www.limaritime.org

Good eats: The Pier at Watch Hill, P.O. Box 4, Sayville, NY 11782; (631) 597-9060; www.thepieratwatchhill.com. The only place to quell your hunger at Watch Hill.

The BrickHouse Brewery, 67 West Main St., Patchogue, NY 11772; (631) 447-BEER (2337); www.brickhousebrewery.com. A short walk from the ferry terminal, this popular brewpub pours six to eight local beers and serves everything from steak to raw bar seafood.

Blue Point Brewing Company, 161 River Ave., Patchogue, NY 11772; (631) 475-6944; http://bluepointbrewing.com. Try one of their award-winning beers in the tasting room, open Thurs through Sat.

Local outdoor stores: Tent City, 236 Front St., Hempstead, NY 11550; (516) 486-0960; www.tentcityoutdoor.com

Eastern Mountain Sports, Smith Haven Mall, Lake Grove, NY 11755; (631) 724-1933; www.ems.com

Hike tours: Ranger-led walks and canoe tours leave from the visitor center between July and Sept.

Organizations: Friends of Watch Hill, P.O. Box 60, Oakdale, NY 11769; friendsof watchhill.org

Friends of Fire Island National Seashore, P.O. Box 504, Patchogue, NY 11772; http://ffins.org

> 🌿 **Green Tip:**
> *When hiking at the beach, stay off dunes*
> *and away from nesting areas.*

Harriman State Park

Outstanding views, an old mine, and the former den of an eighteenth-century outlaw are just a few of the rewards on this intermediate hike that straddles two counties. Complete the circuit in an afternoon or push on to a shelter on Tom Jones Mountain or Car Pond Mountain and extend your visit with an overnight stay.

Start: Across the railroad tracks near the end of Grove Drive on the Ramapo-Dunderberg Trail (follow red blazes from the Tuxedo train station)
Nearest town: Tuxedo, NY
Distance: 6.8-mile lollipop
Approximate hiking time: 3.5 to 4 hours
Difficulty: Moderate, with several challenging climbs
Trail surface: Rocky forest trails, gravel road
Seasons: Year-round
Other trail users: Mountain bikers, skiers, and equestrians (only on designated trails)
Wheelchair accessibility: None
Canine compatibility: Dogs permitted on leashes 10 feet or less

Land status: State park
Fees and permits: None
Schedule: Daily from sunrise to sunset
Facilities: None
Maps: USGS Monroe and Sloatsburg, NY; New York-New Jersey Trail Conference Southern Harriman Bear Mountain Trail Map 118
Special considerations: Some of the park roads are closed in winter; a small number of camping shelters are available on a first-come, first-served basis.
Trail contacts: New York State Office of Parks, Recreation & Historic Preservation, Palisades Interstate Park Commission, Bear Mountain, NY 10911; (845) 786-2701; http://nysparks.state.ny.us/

Finding the trailhead: By car, take I-87 north to the Tappan Zee and then drive west on I-87/I-287 over the bridge to exit 15A. Continue north on NY 17/Orange Turnpike. Drive 5 miles and look for parking in Tuxedo, just past the train station to the right of Route 17. From here, walk east on East Village Road for approximately 0.4 mile, following it underneath the New York State Thruway. Then turn left on Grove Drive and walk 0.1 mile to the trailhead. **By public transportation:** Short Line buses from Port Authority stop in Tuxedo, as does the New Jersey Transit rail service. Leave from Hoboken or connect from New York's Penn Station at Seacaucus. GPS: N41 11.707' / W74 10.820'

THE HIKE

Considerably more people flock to the river views, picnic areas, and facilities clustered at the northeastern corner of neighboring Bear Mountain State Park, making the relative isolation of Harriman's network of hiking trails that much more appealing for those in search of solitude. Totaling 200 miles altogether, these forest tracks lead to lakes, reservoirs, campsites, abandoned mines, and the occasional old cemetery. Created in large part by the gift of 10,000 acres of land and $1 million from Mary Harriman, the state park named for this philanthropic family began to take shape in 1910 and has since become a beloved destination for outdoor enthusiasts throughout the Northeast. To explore a relatively small area of Harriman, take the bus or the train to Tuxedo and then let East Village Road guide you under the New York State Thruway to Grove Drive and the trailhead.

The Kakiat Trail also leads south from this same location, so look for white blazes with a red bull's-eye as you work your way up the stone staircase set into the hillside on the Ramapo-Dunderberg Trail. An overlook 0.5 mile in offers a photo opportunity for day-trippers carrying cameras, but until the midpoint of the hike, most of the travel will be up and down the numerous high hills along the border between Orange and Rockland Counties. You may not run into other people during your time in the park, but you won't be alone either: Wild turkeys are encountered quite commonly, and the noise of a small group moving through the woods might startle a northern flicker, recognizable by the black-scalloped pattern on its brown or buff-colored plumage.

Moving on, you'll pass what once was the Black Ash Mine, followed soon thereafter by Black Ash Mountain, the first serious climb of the day. Press onward over huge chunks of ancient metamorphic and sedimentary rock that thrust up from beneath the Ramapo-Dunderberg Trail. Near the top, the dark, aerodynamic shapes of raptors swoop low, searching the ground for a meal.

Don't stop to celebrate reaching this summit though—less than 1 mile away Parker Cabin Mountain rises still higher from the surrounding landscape. Besides, the views from this topographic feature are objectively better, and its rounder form allows plenty of room for spreading out to eat lunch, or to simply soak up the sun's rays.

Use the yellow Triangle Trail to descend from Parker Cabin Mountain, and head southeast to a sliver of cerulean called Lake Skemonto. Clouds drifting by overhead will cast their shadows on exposed parts of this undeveloped corridor, and your ears will fill with the sound of snapping twigs and dry leaves crackling under your thick rubber boot soles. Chipmunks that hear you coming will issue their loud chirps before dashing to safety along a fallen log, or ducking into a crevice in a pile of rocks. Although it isn't included in this hike, a beach at the northern end of nearby Lake Sebago is accessible by following the blue-blazed trail north from this junction and then picking up a woods road that leads to a parking area under Good Spring Mountain.

From here, the return trip is easier, initially keeping to a wide gravel road that runs west and then cuts south on the Blue Disc Trail. The blue blazes chart a course over one last low peak, dodging the grayish trunks of elm trees and the white trunks of birches. When your energy begins to flag, let the crickets cheer you to higher elevations, and savor one more view before hurrying to catch a train or a bus back to the city. A final point of interest is Claudius Smith's Den, a shallow cave located at the base of the cliff near the spot where the red Tuxedo-Mount Ivy Trail crosses the Blue Disc Trail.

MILES AND DIRECTIONS

0.0 Start near the end of Grove Drive on the Ramapo-Dunderberg Trail (follow red blazes from the Tuxedo train station).

0.5 Arrive at a shelf overlooking the town of Tuxedo.

0.7 Turn left (northeast) to remain on the Ramapo-Dunderberg (white blazes with red bull's-eyes), traveling in a clockwise direction. The red-blazed Tuxedo-Mount Ivy Trail continues due east.

0.9 Pass a large, square mine shaft on the left. After heavy rain, standing water—and perhaps even a solitary frog—might be visible at the bottom.

1.2 Continue past an old trail on the left and ford a small intermittent stream.

1.4 Keep to the left (north) at the intersection with the blue-blazed Victory Trail. Begin climbing Black Ash Mountain.

Instead of simply trusting the cairns to lead you through the park, bring a GPS and a map.

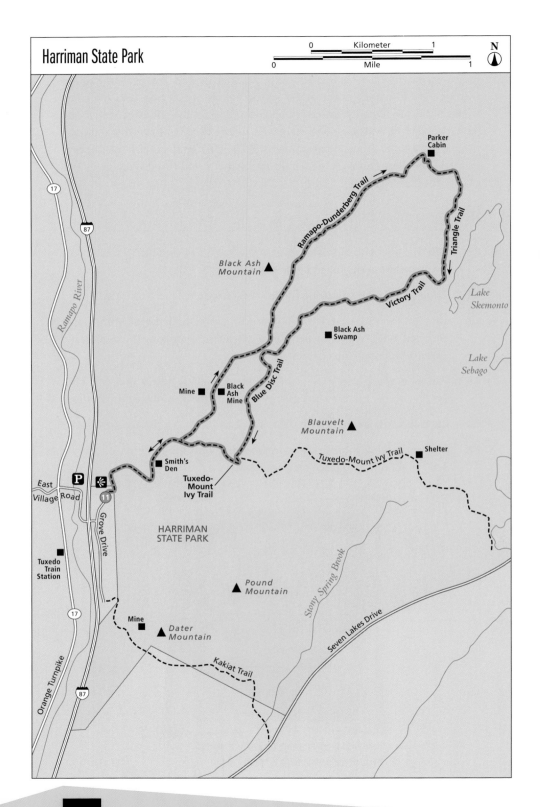

Kilometer

Mile

N

Parker
Cabin

Ramapo-Dunderberg Trail

Triangle Trail

Black Ash
Mountain

Lake
Skemonto

Victory Trail

Black Ash
Swamp

Lake
Sebago

Mine

Black
Ash
Mine

Blue Disc Trail

Blauvelt
Mountain

Shelter

Tuxedo-Mount Ivy Trail

Smith's
Den

Tuxedo-
Mount
Ivy Trail

East
Village Road

P

11

Grove Drive

HARRIMAN
STATE PARK

Pound
Mountain

Stony Spring Brook

Tuxedo
Train
Station

Mine

Dater
Mountain

Seven Lakes Drive

Orange Turnpike

Kakiat Trail

Ramapo River

1.8 Arrive at the top of the ridge, where your elevation will be about 1,130 feet.

2.3 Walk through the intersection with the White Bar Trail, which runs north to south, and start the ascent up Parker Cabin Mountain.

2.7 Stop to enjoy the panoramic view of the park from an opening on the summit. To the southeast, Lake Skemonto and the much larger Lake Sebago will stand out, while Blauvelt Mountain, Black Ash Mountain, Fox Mountain, and Poor Fawn Mountain dominate the sight lines south and west.

2.9 Turn right (southeast) on the yellow-blazed Triangle Trail—the highest point on this hike at 1,269 feet above sea level. Use caution on the initial descent, which drops off rather precipitously.

3.7 Take a short detour to walk to the shore of Lake Skemonto, and then turn left (west) onto the Victory Trail.

4.1 Pass the White Bar Trail and the White Cross Trail (which loosely form an "X" on the map) in quick succession, and stay with the blue blazes.

5.0 Back at the intersection with the Ramapo-Dunderberg Trail, make a left (south) on the Blue Disc Trail, following a seam of stone on the edge of Black Ash Swamp.

5.3 A cairn indicates that you've reached the top of a knob after steadily gaining about 300 feet in elevation. Pound Mountain and Dater Mountain share the horizon.

5.7 Turn right (west) on the Tuxedo-Mount Ivy Trail after hopping down a few large rocks at the bottom of a cliff. During the Revolutionary War, Loyalist Claudius Smith used the cave at this spot as a hideout.

6.1 Arrive at the intersection with the Ramapo-Dunderberg Trail and continue west, using the same route you followed into the park to return to the trailhead.

6.8 Arrive back at the trailhead on Grove Drive, within easy range of the train station/bus stop.

HIKE INFORMATION

Local information: Orange County Tourism, 124 Main St., Goshen, NY 10924; (845) 615-3860; www.orangetourism.org
Rockland County Tourism, 18 New Hempstead Rd., New City, NY 10956; (845) 708-7300; http://rockland.org

Local events/attractions: Lafayette Theater, 97 Lafayette Ave., Suffern, NY 10901; (845) 369-8234; www.bigscreenclassics.com. Go to this historic movie palace to see a classic film and hear the Mighty Wurlitzer Theatre Pipe Organ on Friday and Saturday nights.

Good eats: Bentley's Deli, 233 Rte. 17, Tuxedo Park, NY 10987; (845) 351-2050. Fuel up with an inexpensive Bentley's Zebra: eggs, cheese, bacon, and a hash brown on a roll.

Orange Top Diner, 192 Rte. 17, Tuxedo Park, NY 10987; (845) 351-3316

Local outdoor stores: Ramsey Outdoor, 835 Rte. 17 South, Ramsey, NJ 07446; (201) 327-8141; www.ramseyoutdoor.com

Eastern Mountain Sports, 66 Rockland Plaza, Nanuet, NY 10954; (845) 623-5282; www.ems.com

Hike tours: Outdoor Bound Adventures, Inc., 154 Grand St., Suite 610, New York, NY 10013; (212) 579-4568; www.outdoorbound.com

Urban Escapes New York (national headquarters), 150 East 58th St., Suite 1802A, New York, NY 10155; (212) 609-2547; www.urbanescapesnyc.com

Organizations: Palisades Parks Conservancy, Administration Building, Bear Mountain, NY 10911; (845) 786-2701; www.palisadesparksconservancy.org

Parks & Trails New York, 29 Elk St., Albany, NY 12207; (518) 434-1583; www.ptny.org

The Cowboy of the Ramapos

On January 22, 1779, five years before the Continental Congress formally ended the American Revolution by ratifying the Treaty of Paris, a notorious outlaw and Loyalist was publicly hanged in the town of Goshen, New York. For years Claudius Smith and his gang of "Cow-boys" menaced the population of Orange County by robbing local farms, ambushing travelers, stealing livestock, and even hijacking the wagon supply trains of the Continental Army. Between heists, they retreated into the Ramapo Mountains, using places like the cave on the Blue Disc Trail as hideouts. They avoided capture until the murder of a prominent citizen prompted Governor George Clinton to offer a hefty reward of $1,200 for the apprehension of the infamously large man, and another $600 for his sons. In November 1778, a group of men from Connecticut seized Smith in his sleep while he was on Long Island, and delivered him to the authorities in Fishkill. After his death, legends arose about the spoils of his exploits. According to an article published in the *New York Times* on November 23, 1879, "Many believe to this day that there is gold and silver coin and plate still lying in the hidden recesses of the mountains mentioned, and not a year passes but much time and labor is expended by searchers after the legendary wealth." Smith and his band also allegedly used Horse Stable Rock, near the western end of Lime Kiln Road, as a lookout.

Hook Mountain State Park

Soak in the views of the Hudson at its widest point on this short Rockland County out-and-back hike. Linger on the summit with a pair of binoculars and watch for raptors such as broad-winged hawks, American kestrels, red-tailed hawks, and the rare bald eagle.

Start: At the gas station on the corner of Christian Herald Road and US 9W

Nearest town: Upper Nyack, NY

Distance: 3.0 miles out and back

Approximate hiking time: 2 hours

Difficulty: Moderate

Trail surface: Dirt footpath, exposed rock faces, highway shoulder

Seasons: Spring, summer, and fall

Other users: Birders

Wheelchair accessibility: None

Canine compatibility: Leashed dogs allowed on hiking trails but not permitted in Rockland Lake State Park from May 1 to Sept 30

Land status: State park

Fees and permits: None

Schedule: Daily from 8 a.m. until dusk

Facilities: Restrooms and other amenities at Rockland Lake State Park

Maps: USGS Nyack, NY; New York-New Jersey Trail Conference Hudson Palisades Trail Map 110

Special considerations: Take care on US 9W and use caution near the two overlooks as the cliff drops off sharply to the river below.

Trail contacts: Rockland Lake State Park, P.O. Box 217, Congers, NY 10920; (845) 268-3020; www.nys parks.com/parks/81/details.aspx

Finding the trailhead: To access the park by car from New York, take I-87 north to the Tappan Zee and then drive west on I-87/I-287 over the bridge to exit 11 in Nyack. From there, head north on US 9W/North Highland Avenue and look for parking on the left, just past the intersection with Christian Herald Road. Another small parking area can be found on the right, within the park boundaries.

By public transportation: Coach USA's Short Line buses drop off passengers at the corner of US 9W and Christian Herald Road. Aqua-colored Long Path blazes appear on the east side of 9W and head north for about 0.4 mile until you reach the edge of the park property. GPS: N41 06.555' / W73 55.625'

Along the Palisades ridge, only High Tor surpasses Hook Mountain, which rises to 728 feet above the Hudson shoreline. Dutch sailors called this menacing feature Verdrietige Hoogte, or Troublesome Point, because the winds that whip around its jagged shape made navigating up the river that much more difficult. Although fewer sailors ply the river currents today than in the past, a short but strenuous climb to the bare summit of Hook Mountain only confirms the aptness of this rather unflattering name.

Such a trek also grants determined hikers the single best view of the Tappan Zee, New York State's longest automobile bridge. Completed in 1955, the Tappan Zee carries I-87/I-287 over the second widest point in the Hudson River—slightly more than 3 miles in all.

Before this land was set aside as a park, Hook Mountain, and Rockland Lake specifically, served as an important source of employment for the surrounding area. Beginning in the eighteenth century, and continuing until the early 1920s, this body of water supplied hundreds of thousands of tons of ice to New York City, less than 30 miles away. At its peak, the Knickerbocker Ice Company had four thousand men on its payroll. Even as the ice business was slowly being replaced by mechanical refrigeration, quarries sprung up and began to methodically strip the mountain of stone in order to keep the city to the south supplied with building materials.

Setting out from the trailhead at the bus stop and parking area, the first section of this hike can be unpleasant, with rumbling trucks and other vehicles speeding by as you march along the shoulder of US 9W. Once you've entered the woods and, a bit farther on, the park itself, the experience improves dramatically. Aqua blazes initially run along the side of the slope, gradually dipping below the roadway, but the trail doesn't remain flat for long. Climbing the southeast flank of the massif, the Long Path leads steadily north toward Haverstraw Beach, with three connecting paths offering opportunities to loop back south on a bike trail that hugs the base of the cliffs. The swimming and boating areas at Rockland Lake State Park can also be accessed from the Long Path.

The narrowest sections of the trail can be treacherous, particularly after heavy rain, so it is wise to tread with care. Approaching the 1-mile mark, glimpses of Upper Nyack will appear through the trees, and if you can resist the urge to hurry to the summit, there's a chance that you'll be lucky enough to observe a deer or two wandering amidst the vegetation downslope. When you've tired of scanning the terrain for wildlife, charge up the last 0.1 mile to reach the top of Hook Mountain.

Look down on big waterfront homes with docks and swimming pools, stare at Tarrytown and Sleepy Hollow across the river, and spot Nyack High School's football field to the southwest. Venture north along the escarpment for 0.4 mile to another transfixing view, and then turn around and retrace your path to catch a bus back to Port Authority.

MILES AND DIRECTIONS

0.0 Start walking north on the shoulder of US 9W from the gas station on Christian Herald Road.

0.4 Look for aqua-colored Long Path blazes to continue into the woods on the right, behind the guardrail. Just off the road, white blazes marking the Upper Nyack Trail will enter from the right (east), but stay on the Long Path.

0.7 Begin to ascend the southern flank of the mountain, gradually curving away from 9W. The terrain becomes steeper and more rugged.

0.9 The real views are still to come, but catch a glimpse of Upper Nyack through the trees.

Sometimes you make new friends while on the trail.

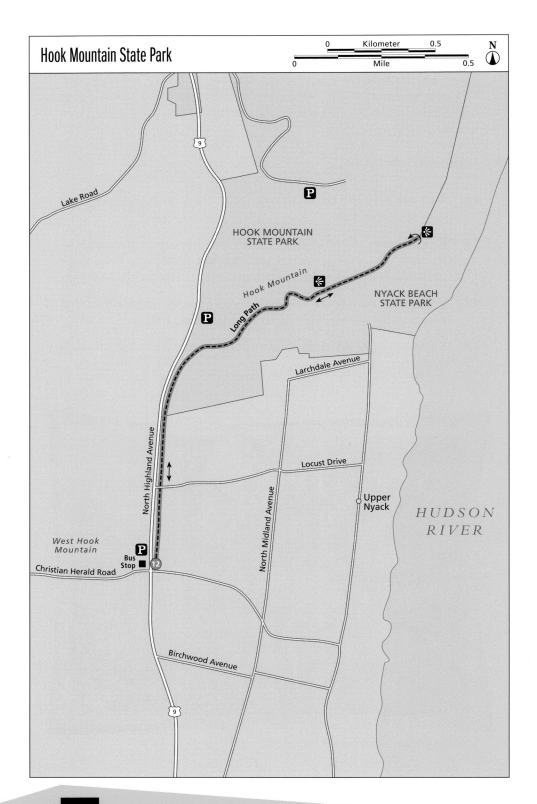

Hook Mountain State Park

1.0 Take a sharp right (east) turn and close the remaining distance to the ridge. The yellow-blazed trail entering from the north connects with a parking area.

1.1 Arrive at the crown, a rounded mass of stone where crickets chirp in the cactus and tall grass. To the north the Tors are visible on the horizon, while south of the park, the Tappan Zee Bridge dominates the view. Soak up the scenery, take a few pictures if you brought a camera, and then continue north on the Long Path.

1.4 Another yellow trail enters from the left (west), at the bottom of the first ridge. Press on for another 0.1 mile.

1.5 Arrive at the second overlook and the end of the hike. Enjoy the panorama southeast over the river and spot Sleepy Hollow and Tarrytown opposite Hook Mountain. The Long Path leads farther into the park, but this is the turnaround point.

3.0 Arrive back at the trailhead, on the west side of US 9W at the corner of Christian Herald Road.

Option: For a full-day, 12-mile hike, follow the Long Path almost to the northern border of the park and then take the white Treason Trail down to the water. Turn right (south) at the bottom of the slope and head back on the paved bike path, which connects with the Upper Nyack Trail in Nyack Beach State Park.

HIKE INFORMATION

Local information: Rockland County Tourism, 18 New Hempstead Rd., New City, NY 10956; (845) 708-7300; http://rockland.org

Local events/attractions: Edward Hopper House Art Center, 82 North Broadway, Nyack, NY 10960-2628; (845) 358-0774; www.hopperhouse.org. Visit the house that iconic American painter Edward Hopper grew up in.

Rockland Center for the Arts, 27 South Greenbush Rd., West Nyack, NY 10994; (845) 358-0877; www.rocklandartcenter.org

Good eats: Turiello's, 76 Main St., Nyack, NY 10960; (845) 358-5440. Italian pizzeria and restaurant open seven days a week.

The Runcible Spoon Bakery, 37 North Broadway, Nyack, NY 10960; (845) 358-9398; www.runciblespoonbakery.com. A gourmet bakery, coffee shop, and lunching spot with cheerful decor from local artists.

🌿 Green Tip:
Consider citronella as an effective natural mosquito repellent.

Local outdoor stores: Eastern Mountain Sports, 66 Rockland Plaza, Nanuet, NY 10954; (845) 623-5282; www.ems.com

Organizations: Palisades Parks Conservancy, Administration Building, Bear Mountain, NY 10911; (845) 786-2701; www.palisadesparksconservancy.org

Friends of Rockland Lake and Hook Mountain, Inc., 17 Collyer Lane, Rockland Lake, NY 10989; (845) 268-7881; www.rocklandlakeandhookmt.org

Rockland Audubon Society, P.O. Box 404, New City, NY 10956; (845) 639-9216; www.rocklandaudubon.org

The Long Path

Not to be confused with Vermont's Long Trail, the Long Path reaches from Fort Lee Historic Park on the western end of the George Washington Bridge to Thatcher State Park near Albany. Taking its name from a line in Walt Whitman's "Song of the Open Road," the path was conceived by Vincent Schaefer of Schenectady, New York, in 1931. His original goal was to create an unmarked trail, but the interruption of the war years in the 1940s stalled efforts to formalize a route until the New York-New Jersey Trail Conference took up the idea several decades later. Since the 1960s the Long Path has grown in fits and spurts, but at present there are no gaps in this aqua-blazed trail, which wanders through eight counties in all. Although it presently approaches 350 miles in length, the various trail groups that maintain it plan to eventually extend this north–south course to the Adirondack Mountains.

Hudson Highlands State Park

Leave the antiques stores and family-run restaurants of Cold Spring behind for a day hike through an easily accessible part of Hudson Highlands State Park. Gaze across at Storm King, watch the boat traffic plying the currents on the Hudson River below, and enjoy spectacular views all the way to the Catskills on clear days.

Start: Between the stone gates at the bottom of the park's paved drive off Route 9D
Nearest town: Cold Spring, NY
Distance: 4.6-mile loop
Approximate hiking time: 3.5 to 4 hours
Difficulty: Moderate to difficult
Trail surface: Woodland dirt footpath; somewhat steep, uneven terrain
Seasons: Mar through Oct
Other trail users: Hunters (seasonally)
Wheelchair accessibility: None
Canine compatibility: Dogs permitted on leashes 10 feet or less
Land status: State park
Fees and permits: None
Schedule: Sunrise to sunset daily

Facilities: The closest public restroom is near the train station at the bottom of Main Street in Cold Spring.
Maps: USGS West Point. North and South Trail maps can be downloaded from the New York State Office of Parks, Recreation & Historic Preservation website. Less detailed black-and-white maps are available at the Washburn trailhead, opposite the Little Stony Point Citizens Association building.
Trail contacts: New York State Office of Parks, Recreation & Historic Preservation, Regional Office Contact Information, P.O. Box 308/9 Old Post Rd., Staatsburgh, NY 12580; (845) 889-4100; www.nysparks.state.ny.us

Finding the trailhead: By car traveling north on US 9, turn left onto Route 301/Cold Spring-Carmel Road. Turn right on Route 9D/Bear Mountain-Beacon Highway and drive 0.7 mile. Park on the shoulder or use the small gravel lot opposite the Little Stony Point Citizens Association building. **By public transportation:** Metro North offers frequent train service to Cold Spring from Grand Central Station in Manhattan. The entrance to the blue-blazed Cornish Trail is on Route 9D/Bear Mountain-Beacon Highway, just over 1 mile northwest of the Cold Spring train station. Walk northwest from the platform to Main Street. Turn right (northeast) and walk uphill 2 blocks to Fair Street. Turn left and proceed 0.7 mile to the foot of Bull Hill (Mount Taurus) and the trailhead. GPS: N41 25.779' / W73 58.065'

THE HIKE

Rich in history and crisscrossed with miles and miles of challenging hiking trails, Hudson Highlands State Park's nearly 6,000 acres of undeveloped land perennially lure outdoor enthusiasts from New York, New Jersey, and Connecticut. Beginning on the Cornish Trail, this hike follows Breakneck Brook to the old Cornish family dairy farm, heads east on the Notch Trail, and then climbs up and over Bull Hill via the Washburn Trail.

A long paved road leads into the park, rising slowly above the road and the train tracks that hug the east bank of the Hudson. To the right, massive boulders and rock outcroppings tower above, while on either side of this initially rather easy path, trees lean under the weight of vines clinging to their branches. As it ascends, the blue-blazed Cornish Trail curves northward, leading past a large abandoned estate, now just a shell of its former self without doors, windows, or a roof to keep the elements at bay. The shell of a greenhouse also stands to the left of the trail just beyond the main house. Here, at mile 0.7, the surface turns to gravel and the way becomes slightly steeper.

Briefly emerging from the mixed woods to cross the Catskill Aqueduct, a gravity-fed water tunnel that carries the resource from the Ashokan Reservoir near Woodstock to New York City, the Cornish Trail merges with the red Brook Trail (approaching from the west) shortly before mile 1.2. As the sound of rushing water from Breakneck Brook grows louder, you may notice monarch butterflies dancing in shafts of sunlight or a pair of gray squirrels chasing each other through the leaf litter. To the left (northwest), a small wooden bridge carries the yellow Undercliff Trail across the waterway and leads to the summit of Breakneck Ridge.

About two-tenths of a mile farther, the remains of the farm come into view and a hard right (east) turn will deliver you to the Notch Trail. Venture a few hundred feet north to explore the crumbling cement cow stalls, barn, and silo owned by the Cornish family until the mid-1940s. Following a dry streambed, the route weaves over the trunks of fallen trees and the remains of old stone walls as it slowly gains elevation. At mile 2.2 the blue blazes lead to the right (south), and a short distance later this trail gives way to the Washburn Trail.

The ascent up the north side of Bull Hill can be strenuous at times, and the trail narrows considerably as it approaches a clearing at the top—some 1,420 feet above sea level. The views north and west of the overlook are impressive, offering a clear line of sight to the Newburgh-Beacon Bridge, the Catskills, and Storm King Mountain on the other side of the Hudson. Depending on the position of the sun, the river can take on many appearances from this height: a milky piece of glass, or a shimmering blue serpent stretching to the horizon.

After a brief rest and another swig of water, continue southwest through the ferns and grasses growing along the trail and begin the somewhat precipitous descent down Bull Hill's south shoulder. Wandering this route late in the day, you may startle a pair of mourning doves or notice birds of prey wheeling in slow circles above the summit. Lowbush blueberry grows here, too, and its colorful fruit can often be spotted ripening in the early summer months.

The last difficult stretch of trail angles sharply downhill and requires sure footing in places. Once you reach the abandoned quarry however, the final section eases its way back to the parking area and the Washburn/Cornish trailhead.

MILES AND DIRECTIONS

0.0   Start from the shoulder of Route 9D, where the blue-blazed Cornish Trail rises gradually northward. The loop is described in a clockwise direction.

0.6   A fork leads to the Brook Trail. Remain on the Cornish Trail by staying to the right.

0.7   The trail, which has switched to a gravel surface, becomes steeper as it climbs the lower slopes of Bull Hill.

View of Cold Spring, Constitution Island, and in the background, the U.S. Military Academy at West Point

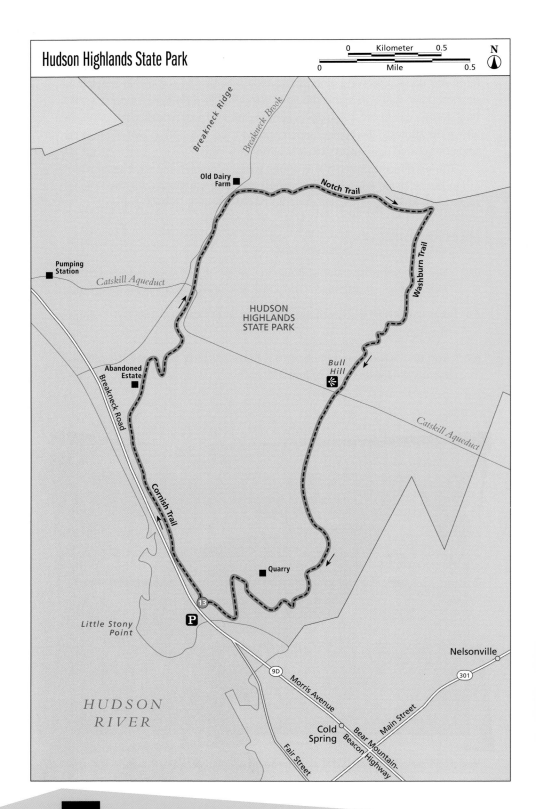

Hudson Highlands State Park

0 Kilometer 0.5
0 Mile 0.5

N

Breakneck Ridge

Breakneck Brook

Old Dairy Farm

Notch Trail

Pumping Station

Catskill Aqueduct

Washburn Trail

HUDSON HIGHLANDS STATE PARK

Bull Hill

Abandoned Estate

Breakneck Road

Cornish Trail

Catskill Aqueduct

Quarry

13

P

Little Stony Point

Nelsonville

301

9D

Morris Avenue

Main Street

HUDSON RIVER

Cold Spring

Bear Mountain-Beacon Highway

Fair Street

1.1 Cross the Catskill Aqueduct and merge with the Brook Trail, entering from the left (west).

1.2 Continue northwest as you pass a short bridge and the yellow-blazed Undercliff Trail, which leads to Breakneck Ridge.

1.4 The trail crosses Breakneck Brook. **(NOTE:** A small log bridge was out at the time this trail was researched.)

1.5 A derelict silo and several abandoned farm buildings come into view. Spend a few minutes investigating these old structures and then turn right (east) on the blue Notch Trail.

2.2 Turn right (south) and zigzag over the remains of low stone walls on your way up the north side of Bull Hill.

2.5 From the three-way intersection, continue south/southwest on the white Washburn Trail as you approach the summit.

2.9 Stop at the top of Bull Hill and admire the views up the Hudson to the northwest. You'll be able to identify Breakneck Ridge and Scofield Ridge, the Newburgh-Beacon Bridge farther north, and Storm King Mountain on the other side of the river.

Although not ancient in origin, trailside rock art can occasionally be found here.

3.2 A second clearing, somewhat lower on the mountain, offers clear sight lines to West Point.

3.4 The Washburn Trail makes a steep, sudden drop downhill. Use caution descending this section of the stony trail or risk losing your footing.

3.5 Continue south, crossing the yellow-blazed Undercliff Trail for the second time.

4.0 A cliff to the left of the trail allows you to peer down on the church steeples, ball fields, and rooftops of Cold Spring and neighboring Nelsonville.

4.3 Enter the old rock quarry at the bottom of Bull Hill and remain on the Washburn Trail as it curves east and then south again, slowly flattening as it nears the road.

4.6 Arrive back at the trailhead and parking area on Route 9D.

HIKE INFORMATION

Local information: Putnam County Visitors Bureau, 110 Old Rte. 6, Bldg. 3, Carmel, NY 10512; (800) 470-4854; www.visitputnam.org

Local events/attractions: The Russel Wright Design Center, P.O. Box 249, Garrison, NY 10524; (845) 424-3812; www.russelwrightcenter.org
Cold Spring River Festival, 97 Main St., Cold Spring, NY 10516; (845) 265-4414; www.coldspringriverfestival.com

Good eats: Whistling Willie's American Grill, 184 Main St., Cold Spring, NY, 10516; (845) 265-2012; www.whistlingwillies.com
Foundry Cafe, 55 Main St., Cold Spring, NY 10516; (845) 265-4504

Local outdoor stores: Hudson Valley Outfitters, 63 Main St., Cold Spring, NY 10516; (845) 265-0221; www.hudsonvalleyoutfitters.com

Organizations: Friends of Fahnestock and Hudson Highlands State Parks, P.O. Box 194, Cold Spring, NY 10516; www.fofhh.org. Founded in 2007 to preserve, protect, and improve these historic and natural resources.
Hudson River Valley Greenway, Capitol Building, Room 254, Albany, NY 12224; (518) 473-3835; www.hudsongreenway.state.ny.us

Inwood Hill Park

Travel back in time on the northernmost corner of Manhattan, where the last rem-
nants of native salt marsh and natural forest survive in spite of witnessing centuries
of human habitation. Wander along pathways laid over terrain that once provided
for Lenape hunters, protected American troops (at Fort Cox), and brought joy to the
Strauss family, who owned Macy's and built an estate in the area.

Start: Payson Avenue park entrance
Nearest town: New York, NY
Distance: 1.8-mile point to point
Approximate hiking time: 1 to 2 hours
Difficulty: Easy
Trail surface: Multiuse paths
Seasons: Year-round
Other trail users: Cyclists, in-line skaters
Wheelchair accessibility: Some of the pathways have a steep incline and others are in need of repair, but many routes are suitable for wheelchairs or motorized scooters.
Canine compatibility: Leashed dogs permitted

Land status: City park
Fees and permits: None
Schedule: Daily from dawn until dusk
Facilities: Restrooms, water fountains, picnic areas
Maps: USGS Yonkers and Central Park, NY. A PDF map of Inwood Hill Park can also be downloaded from the New York City parks department (see below).
Trail contacts: New York City Department of Parks & Recreation, The Arsenal, Central Park, 830 5th Ave., New York, NY 10065; (212) NEW-YORK; www.nycgovparks.org

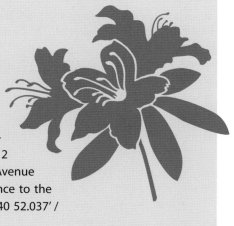

Finding the trailhead: There is no easy parking for this hike, and it is recommended that you take public transportation. Exit the A express train at Dyckman Street and Broadway. Walk northwest on Dyckman for 2 blocks. Turn right (north) on Payson Avenue and immediately look for the entrance to the park, where the trail begins. GPS: N40 52.037' / W73 55.683'

S ituated at the top of Manhattan, nearly 6 miles north of Central Park, Inwood Hill Park doesn't receive even a fraction of the attention that its larger cousin to the south gets when talk turns to green space on the island. And yet with a commanding view of the Hudson, the last salt marsh and natural forest in the borough, and an alleged connection to Peter Minuit, the Dutch governor general of New Netherlands who purchased Manhattan from the Lenape in 1626, it deserves greater recognition. Sculpted by glacial activity some 50,000 years ago, this patch of oak, hickory, and tulip forest takes some of the city out of an urban hike in Inwood.

Pottery, shell middens, and the carbonized remains of food discovered in caves by archaeologists confirm the presence of a Native American settlement before the arrival of the Dutch. After selling the island, Lenape people continued to live in the vicinity of Inwood Hill, which they referred to as Shorakapok, meaning either "the wading place" or "the edge of the river," until about 1715. Six decades later, the Revolutionary War had begun and the largely untested and underprepared Continental Army occupied three forts in the heights of Manhattan, hoping to prevent the British from gaining control of the Hudson. A battalion of Hessians overwhelmed Fort Cockhill, the northernmost of these defenses, in November 1776, all but completing the capture of New York. At the end of the war, when British forces finally evacuated, General Washington rode past Inwood Hill and Fort Cox to reclaim the city.

No diplomacy or military maneuvers are required to reach the top of the park today however, and the wide, multiuse path leading up from Payson Avenue carries walkers to a wooded refuge for animals such as the red-backed salamander, the scarlet tanager, and the eastern mole. In the quiet light of the late afternoon, the view from the overlook at about the 0.5-mile mark can momentarily transport you back in time. Snap back to reality by circling back toward the southern entrance to the park, and then after traveling a little more than 1 mile, follow a path in need of repair down into a shallow valley.

Witch hazel, spicebush, and ivy cover the slopes on either side of the trail, and in the canopy above, wood thrushes, eastern wood peewees, and the occasional red-tailed hawk sound their calls. The slope eventually levels off and the path forks, one branch continuing north while the other curves east, meeting a rock with a plaque explaining that a splendid tulip tree, once one of the oldest and largest trees in Manhattan, stood where the rock is at present. The same historical marker also contends that Peter Minuit conducted his real estate transaction nearby, although this is controversial and more difficult to document.

Let the curved path guide you around the lawn that spreads out from the tree line, and approach the stretch of water between Manhattan and the Bronx still known by its Dutch name, Spuyten Duyvil. Here saltwater cordgrass, salt marsh bulrush, and water hemp shelter fiddler crabs and ribbed mussels, and provide a place for egrets, herons, and kingfishers to feed. This is the salt marsh that once surrounded the island. To find your way back to public transportation, turn right on the waterfront path, walk around the edge of the little cove, and cross two small bridges on a circuitous route to the park entrance on Indian Road.

MILES AND DIRECTIONS

0.0 Start at the park entrance just north of the fenced-in playground on Payson Avenue. A gargantuan sycamore towers overhead. Turn left on the cracked surface of the multiuse path after climbing about 450 feet uphill.

0.1 Continue north past a spur trail on the right. The sound of traffic drifts up to your ears from the western base of the hill.

0.2 Veer right at the fork in the trail instead of heading down toward the Hudson. Walk by two more crossover paths in the next 0.2 mile.

0.4 Turn left on a path that rises gradually to the northwest.

The Henry Hudson Bridge spans Spuyten Duyvil Creek between Manhattan and the Bronx.

Inwood Hill Park

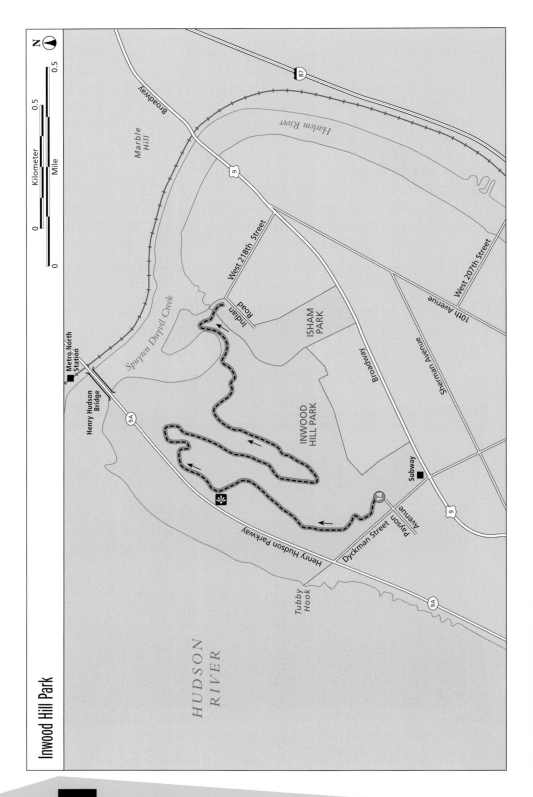

0.5 Behind a rusty iron fence, to the left of the path, lays the river, glittering in the sun against the backdrop of the Palisades. This might be the most enchanting view of the river in Manhattan. Take a left at the fork after the overlook.

0.6 After paralleling the river for a short distance, make a sharp left (north) and then bear to the left (northwest) again.

0.8 Near the toll plaza over the Harlem River, the path starts to curve back to the south. As the high-rise apartment buildings of upper Manhattan come into view through the leaf cover, turn right (south) at the T intersection.

1.1 The path heads east and slopes downhill. Routes leading in several directions intersect here. Once you've almost fully rounded the bend, take the left (northeast) turn and follow this worn trail north again, past broken and neglected lampposts that once lit the way for New Yorkers.

1.4 At the bottom of the slope, follow the path to the right as it curves to meet an open field. A plaque on a rock by the edge of the field explains that an enormous tulip tree stood in this location for close to three centuries.

1.5 Keep left on the semicircular path, proceeding toward the water. Stand by the railing for a while and look across Spuyten Duyvil to Marble Hill and the Bronx, no more than 500 or 600 feet away.

1.7 Cross a small bridge onto the spit of land where the Inwood Hill Park Urban Ecology Center has been since 1995. Turn right (east) and walk over a second bridge. With the ecology center behind, the Harlem River will be on the left.

1.8 Arrive at the park entrance on Indian Road and West 218th Street.

Options: Inwood Hill is crisscrossed with trails. To lengthen or shorten your visit, explore some of the other paths that fan out from the entrances on the eastern side of the park.

🦆 **Green Tip:**
Pack out your dog's waste or dispose of it in a trash can or a hole dug into the ground.

HIKE INFORMATION

Local information: NYC & Company, 810 7th Ave., Third Floor, New York, NY 10019; (212) 484-1200; www.nycgo.com

Local events/attractions: Dyckman Farmhouse Museum, 4881 Broadway, New York, NY 10034-3101; (212) 304-9422; http://dyckmanfarmhouse.org. A small Dutch Colonial–style home dating to 1784.

The Cloisters Museum & Gardens, Fort Tryon Park, 99 Margaret Corbin Dr., New York, NY 10040; (212) 923-3700; www.metmuseum.org/cloisters

Drums Along the Hudson, c/o Lotus Music & Dance, 109 West 27th St., Eighth Floor, New York, NY 10001; (212) 627-1076, ext. 18; www.drumsalongthehudson .org. Manhattan's only open-air powwow is held in Inwood Hill Park every May.

Good eats: Indian Road Cafe & Market, 600 West 218th St., New York, NY 10034-1000; (212) 942-7451; www.indianroadcafe.com

Grandpa's Brick Oven Pizza, 4973 Broadway, New York, NY 10034-1651; (212) 304-1185

Local outdoor stores: Paragon Sports, 867 Broadway, New York, NY 10003; (212) 255-8036; www.paragonsports.com

Tent & Trails, 21 Park Place, New York, NY 10007-2591; (212) 227-1760; www.tenttrails.com

Organizations: The New York City Audubon Society, 71 West 23rd St., Suite 1523, New York, NY 10010; (212) 691-7483; www.nycaudubon.org

East Coast Greenway Alliance, 27B North Road, Wakefield, RI 02879; (401) 789-4625; www.greenway.org. A nonprofit group working to connect local trails into a continuous, traffic-free, multiuser route from Maine to Florida.

> ☘ **Green Tip:**
> *Printing out hike directions or a map at home uses less carbon than it takes to ship a map or drive yourself to a store.*

Jamaica Bay Wildlife Refuge

Take in panoramic views of thousands of acres of salt marsh and mudflat against an urban backdrop in the easternmost section of Gateway National Recreation Area—a sanctuary that also happens to be the city's single best location for spotting dozens of species of migrating birds from all over North America.

Start: Just behind the visitor center off of Cross Bay Boulevard

Nearest town: Broad Channel, NY

Distance: 1.5-mile loop

Approximate hiking time: 1 to 1.5 hours

Difficulty: Easy

Trail surface: Gravel and sand

Seasons: Year-round

Other trail users: Birders

Wheelchair accessibility: Disabled parking is available and the visitor center is wheelchair accessible.

Canine compatibility: Dogs not permitted

Land status: National park

Fees and permits: Free permit required

Schedule: The trails are open daily from dawn to dusk. The visitor center is open from 8:30 a.m. to 5 p.m.

Facilities: A water fountain and public restrooms in the visitor center

Maps: USGS Far Rockaway, NY. Black-and-white maps are stocked at the visitor center and can also be downloaded from the Brooklyn Bird Club's website (see Hike Information).

Special considerations: Beware of ticks and poison ivy. Both are common throughout the refuge and can be an unpleasant souvenir for an otherwise rewarding hike.

Trail contacts: Gateway National Recreation Area, Public Affairs Office, 210 New York Ave., Staten Island, NY 10305; (718) 318-4340; www.nps.gov/gate.
National Parks of New York Harbor Conservancy, Federal Hall National Memorial, 26 Wall St., New York, NY 10005; (212) 825-6880; www.nyharborparks.org/visit/jaba.html

Finding the trailhead: From New York City and Long Island, take the Belt Parkway to exit 17, Cross Bay Boulevard. Continue south on Cross Bay Boulevard across the Joseph Addabbo-North Channel Bridge. The visitor center is approximately 1.5 miles past the bridge, on the right. Enter the parking lot at the stoplight. **By public transportation:** The park is about a 0.5-mile walk from the Broad Channel subway station on the A train. Alternatively, both the Q21 and the Q53 buses make stops at the refuge entrance. GPS: N40 37.008' / W73 49.508'

THE HIKE

This short loop around 45-acre West Pond is an ideal short hike for bird lovers. Located within the Atlantic Flyway, Jamaica Bay attracts hundreds of migrating birds, which stop here to feed or rest during their long journeys. The walk itself is unlikely to tire most visitors, but even experienced hikers will want to take their time along this level footpath for a chance to see birdlife such as tree swallows, green-backed herons, cormorants, hooded mergansers, American oystercatchers, glossy ibises, and many more. Patient, attentive hikers may also be rewarded with a glimpse of painted turtles, diamondback terrapins, the crepuscular muskrat, or horseshoe crabs, an ancient species that spawns in late May and June.

A free permit is an entry requirement, so a stop at the renovated visitor center is necessary before venturing into the refuge. The exhibits and programs at this staffed facility also afford guests an opportunity to learn more about the area's rich natural history. Originally created as part of New York City's park system, Jamaica Bay was transferred to the National Park Service in 1972 when Congress created the larger Gateway National Recreation Area. Then, in 1980, native reptiles and amphibians were reintroduced, the South Field Butterfly and Wildflower Management Zone was defined, and numerous nest boxes were placed around the property to attract kestrels, owls, and bats. Even though the ecosystems here are federally protected, Jamaica Bay continues to lose nearly fifty acres of wetland every year due to rising sea levels and human-environmental interaction.

Leave the visitor center via the rear exit and head due west on the crushed stone path. Within steps of the building you'll marvel at the sheer variety of plant life (salt hay, bayberry, seaside goldenrod, marsh elder, sea lavender). The echo of jet engines from JFK International Airport reaches you from the other side of Cross Bay Boulevard. Airliners won't be the only things filling the skies with sound, however: Keep your ears open for the honk of Canada geese, the whiny cry of gulls, and the high-pitched whistle of the red-winged blackbird.

The cool breeze blowing in from the nearby Atlantic will help you forget the heat on a hot summer day, and more than a dozen benches are scattered along the trail, which arcs northeast after about 0.5 mile. Multiflora rose, prickly pear cactus, and yucca plants can be seen in the sandy soil at your feet, while off in the distance, the spire of the Empire State Building is visible on the horizon. You may encounter more geese once Willow Grove is behind you, but resist the temptation to follow one of them too closely for a snapshot; they may become aggressive and hiss defensively if it's nesting season.

Bear right (south) for the final 0.3 mile beneath the tree cover bordering Phragmites Marsh and pause at the small birding blind just before returning to the visitor center for one last chance to spot one of Jamaica Bay's year-round residents.

MILES AND DIRECTIONS

0.0 Start just behind the visitor center on the West Pond loop. Setting out west from the building, you'll soon pass a spur on the right that leads to the South Garden. The trail is described in a clockwise direction.

0.2 Arrive at the first of thirteen benches scattered along the path. Stop here to watch for birds, or simply to look out over South Marsh toward the town of Broad Channel.

0.5 The spur from the Terrapin Nesting Area enters from the southwest. This short segment can be followed to an overlook.

1.0 Enjoy an expansive vista over West Marsh and Pumpkin Patch Channel. Notice the skyscrapers of Manhattan peeking over the horizon to the northwest.

A goose family, out for a springtime stroll

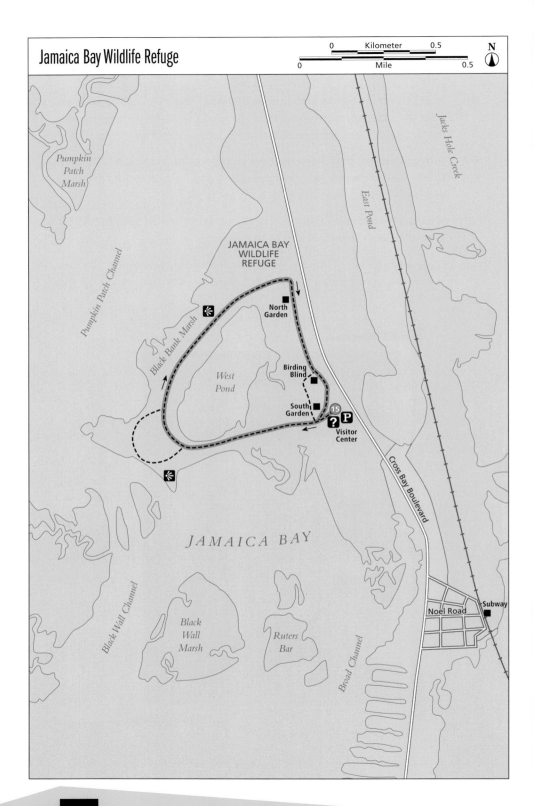

Kilometer

Mile

N

Pumpkin
Patch
Marsh

Jacks Hole Creek

Pumpkin Patch Channel

East Pond

JAMAICA BAY
WILDLIFE
REFUGE

North
Garden

Black Bank Marsh

West
Pond

Birding
Blind

South
Garden

15

Visitor
Center

P

Cross Bay Boulevard

JAMAICA BAY

Black Wall Channel

Black
Wall
Marsh

Ruters
Bar

Broad Channel

Noel Road

Subway

1.2 Turn right (south) at the T intersection and remain on the crushed stone path. Cross Bay Boulevard will be audible on the left as you stroll past the North Garden. Look up at the trees to see nest boxes built for tree swallows, house wrens, barn owls, and bats.

1.4 Encounter a birding blind to the right (west), just beyond another trail intersection. This is an excellent spot for viewing and photographing wildlife in Phragmites Marsh.

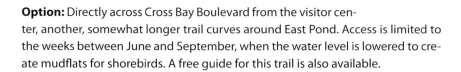

1.5 Arrive back at the trailhead behind the visitor center.

Option: Directly across Cross Bay Boulevard from the visitor center, another, somewhat longer trail curves around East Pond. Access is limited to the weeks between June and September, when the water level is lowered to create mudflats for shorebirds. A free guide for this trail is also available.

HIKE INFORMATION

Local information: Queens Tourism Council, Queens Borough Hall, 120-55 Queens Blvd., Room 309, Kew Gardens, NY 11424; (718) 263-0546; www.discover queens.info

Good eats: Rock-N-Roll Bagels, 20-10 Cross Bay Blvd., Broad Channel, NY 11693; (718) 945-2233; www.rocknrollbagel.com

Rockaway Taco, 95-19 Rockaway Beach Blvd., Queens, NY 11693; (347) 213-7466; http://rockawaytaco.com

Organizations: Brooklyn Bird Club, c/o Alan Baratz, 135 Prospect Park S.W. #E15, Brooklyn, NY 11218; www.brooklynbirdclub.org

American Littoral Society, Northeast Chapter, 28 West 9th Rd., Broad Channel, NY 11693; (718) 318-9344; www.alsnyc.org. A nonprofit environmental organization that seeks to encourage a better scientific and public understanding of the marine environment.

> *Horseshoe crabs, a species that has not changed in the last 400 million years, are more closely related to spiders and scorpions than crabs.*

Long Island Pine Barrens

Discover the other Long Island by navigating across an eco-region that would have covered much of this coastal plain when the European colonists arrived here and displaced the native population. Walk through some of the island's last remaining wilderness on the Paumanok Path, a 125-mile route to Montauk.

Start: Behind the Pine Barrens Trail Information Center
Nearest town: Manorville, NY
Distance: 6.8 miles out and back
Approximate hiking time: 2 to 3 hours
Difficulty: Easy
Trail surface: Grass and dirt footpaths
Seasons: Year-round
Other users: None
Wheelchair accessibility: El's Trail, a 0.6-mile accessible loop, begins at the information center and is marked with blue blazes.
Canine compatibility: Leashed dogs permitted
Land status: County park
Fees and permits: None
Schedule: Daily from sunrise to sunset. The information center is open from May to Oct. Call (631) 852-3449 for hours.
Facilities: Picnic tables, restrooms at the information center

Maps: USGS Wading River, Riverhead, Moriches, and Eastport, NY. The Pine Barrens Trail East map is available for a fee from the Long Island Greenbelt Trail Conference (see below); a simple black-and-white map of El's Wampmissick Trail can be downloaded from http://i231.photobucket.com/albums/ee104/october12007/trail%20guides/ElsWampmissick Trailandmore.jpg.
Trail contacts: Suffolk County Department of Parks, Recreation & Conservation, P.O. Box 144/Montauk Hwy., West Sayville, NY 11796; (631) 854-4949; http://www.co.suffolk.ny.us/depart ments/parks.aspx
Long Island Greenbelt Trail Conference, Inc., P.O. Box 5636, Hauppauge, NY 11788; (631) 360-0753; http://ligreenbelt.org

Finding the trailhead: Take the Long Island Expressway (I-495) east from New York. At exit 70, turn north on Route 111/Eastport Manor Road. Drive 0.2 mile. The trail information center and the parking area are on the right. GPS: N40 52.395' / W72 48.344'

THE HIKE

One of only three pine barrens on the Atlantic coastal plain of the United States—the others being a relatively short distance away in Cape Cod and southern New Jersey—Long Island's temperate coniferous forest is often overshadowed by the parks and beaches on its coast. These natural attractions are also worth visiting, of course, but the pine barrens are a unique feature of the state, an eco-region characterized by sandy soils and the presence of scrubby oak trees alongside medium-size pitch pines, with their egg-shaped cones and tufts of stiff needles on their trunks. Begin near the Peconic River at the trail information center in Manorville to pick up some information about the environment and the wildlife before setting out on this easy trek.

Three stacked trails lead from the information center. The first (blazed blue) is handicapped accessible, the Orange Trail is a 1.2-mile loop, and the short, yellow-blazed segment creates a circuit out of a bend in the much longer Paumanok Path. Walking by several benches spaced somewhat evenly along its length, you'll turn left at the first fork in the blue-blazed El's Trail and then left (north) again onto the Orange Trail. There is virtually no elevation change on this flat out-and-back route, which travels over fallen pine needles, tree roots, and the margins of white cedar swamps. Quietness will pervade the forest as you hike farther into county parkland; at times crickets might be all you hear besides your own footsteps.

When you cross Mill Road to join the Paumanok Path (the Algonquin word for Long Island), you'll be following a westward course toward Rocky Point and

Don't forget to look for signs of life on the forest floor.

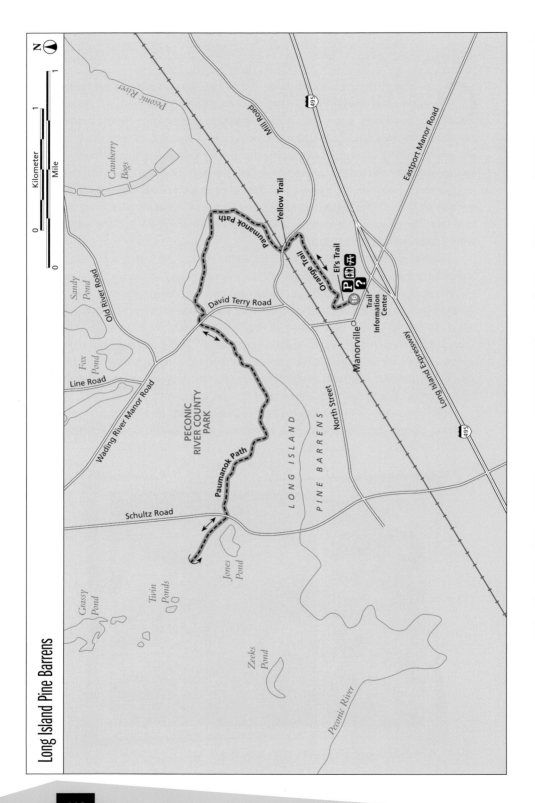

Long Island Pine Barrens

Long Island Sound. As you walk, notice the variety of understory plants that share space with the pitch pine: the white, slightly translucent Indian pipe, bayberry, low-bush blueberry, and blue huckleberry; sassafras and swamp azalea. The pines and blackjack oaks in these stunted forests have the ability to recover quickly after a wildfire, and blackened trunks and a thinning of the tree species around mile 3 are a reminder of an enormous blaze that consumed thousands of acres of land in late August and early September 1995. Known as the Sunrise Fire, it reportedly generated walls of flame 2,000 feet high in places. In some cases, it can take the forest up to thirty years to fully recover from a large blaze.

Lacking any major landmarks, the end point for this hike can be somewhat arbitrary, although staff at the trail information center will tell you that many people turn around at Jones Pond, on the western side of Shultz Road. One way to Jones Pond is just over 3 miles. If you're feeling adventurous, bushwhack to the edge of the water, where you could get lucky and see a large (and secretive) tiger salamander, a yellow-freckled spotted turtle, or birds like prairie and pine warblers. Finding your way back from the small, lily-covered pool shouldn't be difficult with only one trail to worry about.

For variety's sake, on the return trip stick with the Paumanok Path east until it merges with the Orange Trail (heading south), or take the other half of the Orange loop back to the parking area and trailhead, when it meets the Yellow Trail on the south side of Mill Road.

MILES AND DIRECTIONS

0.0 Start behind the Pine Barrens Trail Information Center and walk north on El's Trail.

0.1 Turn right with the trail, then bear left (east) at the fork, and immediately turn left (north) onto the Orange Trail.

0.6 Make a left onto the Yellow Trail; pass under a power line.

0.7 Cross Mill Road and look for white blazes to the left (north), near the railroad tracks.

1.1 Turn left (west) sharply where an unmarked trail enters.

1.6 Cross another unmarked spur.

1.8 Walk across David Terry Road and over a small bridge on the other side of the road. You're now in Peconic River County Park.

2.8 Enter an area where the forest thins and the trees that still stand appear to be dead or bare of leaves—most likely the result of a wildfire in the recent past.

3.0 Cross a third unmarked trail as you continue west. Emerge from the woods a few steps later and traverse Shultz Road.

3.4 Unless you're planning to reach Rocky Point and the westernmost terminus of the Paumanok Path, turn back just beyond Jones Pond to complete the hike.

6.8 Arrive back at the trailhead at the trail information center on Eastport Manor Road.

HIKE INFORMATION

Local information: Long Island Convention & Visitors Bureau and Sports Commission, 330 Motor Parkway, Suite 203, Hauppauge, NY 11788; (877) FUN-ON-LI; www.discoverlongisland.com

Local events/attractions: The Ward Melville Heritage Organization, P.O. Box 572, Stonybrook, NY 11790; (631) 751-2244; www.wmho.org. Take a tour of a gristmill listed on the National Register of Historic Places.

Vail-Leavitt Music Hall, 18 Peconic Ave., Riverhead, NY 11901; (631) 727-5782; www.vail-leavitt.org. Check out the performance schedule at this historic venue for some post-hike entertainment.

Good eats: Anton's Pizzeria, 611 Montauk Hwy, Center Moriches, NY 11934; (631) 878-2528; www.lavolperestaurant.net. Brick oven pizza with toppings like prosciutto and arugula, or mozzarella and fresh basil.

J & R's Steak House, 4362 Middle Country Rd., Calverton, NY 11933; (631) 727-7218; www.jandrssteakhouse.com. Hungry hikers can earn a place in this restaurant's hall of fame by taking the seventy-six-ounce steak challenge.

Lobster Roll, 3225 Sound Ave., Riverhead, NY 11901; (631) 369-3039; www.lobsterroll.com

Hike tours: The Long Island Trail Lovers Coalition and the Long Island Greenbelt Trail Conference regularly organize hikes and events. See www.litlc.org and www.ligreenbelt.org for details.

Organizations: Long Island Pine Barrens Society, 547 East Main St., Riverhead, NY 11901; (631) 369-3300; www.pinebarrens.org

Central Pine Barrens Joint Planning and Policy Commission, P.O. Box 587/3525 Sunrise Hwy., Second Floor, Great River, NY 11739; (631) 224-2604; http://pb.state.ny.us

Long Island Trail Lovers Coalition, c/o Ken Kindler, Open Space & Trails Advocate, P.O. Box 1466, Sayville NY 11782; (631) 563-4354; www.litlc.org

East Hampton Trails Preservation Society, P.O. Box 2144, Amagansett, NY 11930; www.easthamptontrails.org. A nonprofit dedicated to the protection and preservation of over 280 miles of trails on Long Island's East End.

Nassau–Suffolk Trail

Cut across Long Island from south to north, beginning in the Massapequa watershed and finishing with a short section of trail in Bethpage State Park. Admire wildflowers, observe migrating birds, and see the landscape through new eyes on this easily accessible trek suitable for hikers of all ages and levels of experience.

Start: At the signed trailhead at the corner of Ocean Avenue and Merrick Road
Nearest town: Massapequa, NY
Distance: 7.0 miles point to point
Approximate hiking time: 3.5 to 4.5 hours
Difficulty: Easy
Trail surface: Woodland dirt footpath, gravel, and paved multiuse path
Seasons: Year-round
Other trail users: Joggers, cyclists, and in-line skaters
Wheelchair accessibility: The Bethpage Bikeway, a paved multiuse path, runs parallel to this piece of the greenbelt trail, enabling disabled individuals to cover roughly the same distance in stages or in a single outing.
Canine compatibility: Dogs not permitted
Land status: County park

Fees and permits: None
Schedule: Daily from dawn to dusk
Facilities: Public restrooms can be found at the Bethpage Public Library on Powell Avenue.
Maps: USGS Huntington and Amityville, NY. A detailed map is also available by mail from the Long Island Greenbelt Trail Conference (see below).
Trail contacts: Nassau County Department of Parks, Recreation, and Museums, Administrative Building, Eisenhower Park, East Meadow, NY 11554; (516) 572-0200; www.nassaucountyny.gov/agencies/parks
Long Island Greenbelt Trail Conference, Inc., P.O. Box 5636, Hauppauge, NY; (631) 360-0753; www.ligreenbelt.org

Finding the trailhead: From the city, take the Southern State Parkway east and then go south on Route 107/Hicksville Road via exit 29. Cross Sunrise Highway and then turn left on Lakeview Avenue. This road meets Ocean Avenue after 4 short blocks. Turn right (south) and look for parking near Massapequa Lake. **By public transportation:** Walk south from the Massapequa Long Island Railroad station, crossing Sunrise Highway/Route 27 onto Ocean

Avenue at the stoplight. Continue south on the sidewalk, merging onto the paved multiuse path on your left where Prospect Place meets Ocean Avenue. Find the kiosk indicating the trailhead at the intersection of Ocean Avenue and East Merrick Road. Enter here and follow the white blazes north. GPS: N40 40.022' / W73 28.230'

THE HIKE

With Long Island as densely populated as it is, outdoor activities may seem to be few and far between. But, in fact, numerous hiking opportunities are no more than a short drive or train ride from downtown Manhattan. The Nassau–Suffolk Trail is the longest route across the largest island in the lower forty-eight states, a 20-mile trek that connects the town of Massapequa in the south with Cold Spring Harbor in the north. By starting out from the southern coast, it's possible to tackle an easier section in a day hike from one train station to another.

Begin your walk just off East Merrick Road, near the site of a Victorian resort that entertained guests with its bathing pavilion and boathouse between 1888 and 1916. From here the narrow track keeps close to the shores of Massapequa Lake, a relatively small body of water where large blue and green dragonflies dart about, swans glide over the lake's surface, and terns wheel and dive in the air above. Tread quietly and a glimpse of a great blue heron may be another reward. Brambles reach out for bare legs and T-shirts during the first mile or so, but the path widens somewhat as the landscape gradually transitions from marsh to mixed woodland.

Moving through small clearings, you may notice that the Massapequa Preserve is a bit too well loved in places—the occasional fire pit or collection of empty beer cans mar this otherwise pristine piece of property surrounding Massapequa Creek. But on a late spring afternoon you're far more likely to hear the squeaky call of a gray catbird or the far-off clatter of the Long Island Railroad than you are the sound of teenage revelers. Peaceful may be the single best description for this long, leisurely hike.

After crossing busy Sunrise Highway, the trail skirts around the first of several ponds where, depending on the season, it's possible to see nesting ospreys, cygnets swimming alongside their long-necked parents, or mallard ducklings waddling in line behind their watchful mother. The Nassau–Suffolk briefly overlaps with the paved bikeway here, but soon you'll be stepping back onto the soft natural trail surface and roaming amongst shoulder-high ferns, sassafras trees, and here and there, a small, spiky-leafed American holly. Watch for the spotted woodpecker called the northern flicker in the canopy above, and listen for the rubber-band twang of native frog species as you circle the other ponds.

Just before the halfway mark, the path leads across Linden Street and then over the Southern State Parkway via a pair of bridges. Until it enters Bethpage State Park around mile 6.4, the next stretch of trail is somewhat less scenic, sandwiched between the community of South Farmingdale and the noisy Bethpage State Park-way. Once it enters the park, the Nassau–Suffolk becomes quieter again and small hills emerge, but the elevation change is minimal and won't pose a challenge for most hikers. A dirt bike course, complete with ramps and obstacles, cuts through the trail in the final mile, and to the right several of the famed Bethpage golf fair-ways are visible beyond the tree line.

Exit the park by turning left on Manchester Drive. Next, make an immedi-ate right onto Plainview Road (which becomes Powell Avenue after it crosses the expressway), jog left on Broadway and then immediately right onto Benkert Street. Follow the sidewalk west 1.5 blocks to the Bethpage train station.

A painted turtle sunbathes on a submerged log.

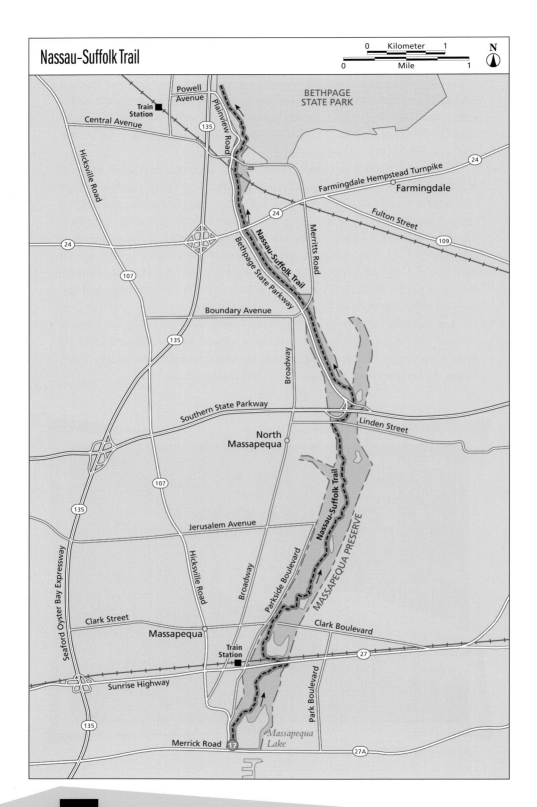

Nassau-Suffolk Trail

Powell Avenue

Train Station

Central Avenue

Hicksville Road

Plainview Road

135

BETHPAGE STATE PARK

Farmingdale Hempstead Turnpike

Farmingdale

24

Fulton Street

24

107

24

Nassau-Suffolk Trail

Bethpage State Parkway

Merritts Road

109

Boundary Avenue

Broadway

135

Southern State Parkway

Linden Street

North Massapequa

Nassau-Suffolk Trail

MASSAPEQUA PRESERVE

Jerusalem Avenue

Seaford Oyster Bay Expressway

107

135

Hicksville Road

Broadway

Parkside Boulevard

Clark Street

Clark Boulevard

Massapequa

Train Station

27

Park Boulevard

Sunrise Highway

135

Merrick Road

17

Massapequa Lake

27A

0   Kilometer   1

0   Mile   1

N

0.0 Start at the kiosk at the corner of Ocean Avenue and East Merrick Road. Pay attention to the white trail blazes as you move north into the Massapequa Preserve. The initial part of the route overlaps with the paved multiuse path on your left in several places.

0.3 Make a sharp right (east) turn, followed by a left (north) turn at a small clearing. Don't be tempted to take one of the unmarked trails that occasionally intersect with the Nassau–Suffolk route.

0.7 Walk across the paved multiuse trail.

0.8 Turn right onto the sidewalk alongside Sunrise Highway and cross over the road at the stoplight on Lakeshore Boulevard.

1.2 Staying on the bikeway, circle the southern shore of a large pond and then look for white blazes to the left after a few hundred feet.

1.5 Cross Clark Street/Boulevard and reenter the preserve, continuing northeast.

1.8 Make a left onto a gravel road to get around a second pond and cross a tiny bridge about one-tenth of a mile later.

2.0 Take a left (west) turn into the woods and then a second left onto another gravel road bordering a third small pond.

2.4 Cross a bridge and stick to the western shore of the pond, veering left, farther away from the water, after about one-tenth of a mile.

2.9 Turn right (east) after traversing another small bridge spanning an intermittent stream.

3.5 Turn right (east) on Linden Street, stay on the sidewalk for a few hundred feet, and then get back onto the trail on the other side of Linden, just east of the Southern State Parkway entrance ramp. Use the bikeway to get over this road, as well as the Bethpage State Parkway, and follow the multiuse path approximately 0.5 mile to rejoin the Nassau–Suffolk Trail.

4.0 Leave the bikeway and reenter the woods on the Nassau–Suffolk Trail.

4.7 Back on the paved route, you'll parallel the highway and walk below an overpass for Merritts Road. The Nassau–Suffolk Trail returns to the woods on the other side.

5.5   Pass underneath the Hempstead Turnpike.

6.4   Just beyond the railroad trestle, veer right off the bikeway and follow the white blazes over a low hill and into Bethpage State Park.

6.9   After traveling 0.5 mile in a wooded area adjacent to a golf course, the Nassau–Suffolk Trail intersects with Manchester Drive. Turn left (south) here and follow it to Plainview Road.

7.0   Arrive at the Bethpage State Park entrance on Plainview Road.

Note: To reach the Bethpage train station, walk south toward the park exit on Manchester Drive and turn right (west). Cross over the Seaford-Oyster Expressway and continue west on Powell Avenue for about 0.3 mile. At Broadway, turn left (south) and then make an immediate right on Benkert Street. Walk west another 0.2 mile to reach the train station on Railroad Avenue.

HIKE INFORMATION

Local information: Long Island Convention & Visitors Bureau and Sports Commission, 330 Motor Parkway, Suite 203, Hauppauge, NY 11788; (877) FUN-ON-LI; www.discoverlongisland.com

Local events/attractions: American Airpower Museum, 1230 New Hwy., Farmingdale, NY 11735; (631) 293-6398; www.americanairpowermuseum.com

Old Bethpage Village Restoration, 1303 Round Swamp Rd., Old Bethpage, NY 11804; (516) 572-8400; www.nassaucountyny.gov/agencies/Parks/wheretogo/museums/central_nass_museum/old_bethpage_rest.html. A nineteenth-century living history museum including farms, businesses, and homes.

Good eats: Massapequa Diner, 4420 Sunrise Hwy., Massapequa, NY 11758; (516) 799-5234

Village Coffee Shop, 357 Broadway, Bethpage, NY 11714-3008; (516) 822-8739. Lunch specials.

Organizations: Long Island Trail Lovers Coalition, P.O. Box 1466, Sayville NY; (631) 563-4354; www.litlc.org

Friends of Massapequa Preserve, 90 Pennsylvania Ave., Second Floor, Massapequa, NY 11758; (516) 541-2461; www.fdale.com/FMP/FMP.htm. A nonprofit organization designed to restore and preserve the largest passive-use park in Nassau County.

> 🐾 **Green Tip:**
> *If you see someone else littering,*
> *muster up the courage to ask them not to.*

Old Croton Aqueduct

Trace a section of the route clean drinking water took to reach New York City from 1842 to 1965. Bring your camera, pack a picnic lunch, and get some light exercise by visiting this green corridor—a National Historic Landmark.

Start: The intersection of Main Street and Church Street in Ossining
Nearest town: Ossining, NY
Distance: 10.1 miles out and back
Approximate hiking time: 4 to 5 hours
Difficulty: Easy
Trail surface: Grass, hard-packed dirt, gravel
Seasons: Mar through Oct
Other trail users: Joggers, dog walkers, cyclists
Wheelchair accessibility: The section of the trail up to the weir at 0.2 mile is a multiuse path.
Canine compatibility: Dogs permitted on leashes 10 feet or less
Land status: State historic park
Fees and permits: None
Schedule: Daily from sunrise to sunset

Facilities: Croton Gorge Park has restrooms, drinking fountains, and a picnic area. Restrooms can also be found at the Ossining Urban Park Visitor Center.
Maps: USGS Ossining, NY. Maps are available at the visitor center in Ossining and via download from the New York State parks website (see below). The Friends of the Old Croton Aqueduct also sell a glossy map at various area locations.
Trail contacts: New York State Office of Parks, Recreation & Historic Preservation, Regional Office Contact Information, 15 Walnut St., Dobbs Ferry, NY 10522; (914) 693-5259; www.nysparks .com/parks/96/details.aspx

Finding the trailhead: To drive from the city, take I-87 north toward Albany to exit 12. Follow the Saw Mill River Parkway north for 16 miles, then merge onto the Taconic State Parkway. Go about 1 mile to Saw Mill River Road/Route 100/9A north. Follow Saw Mill River Road/Route 9A; after 3.2 miles, turn left on Route 133 west/Croton Avenue and follow this road into Ossining. **By public transportation:** Although it's an uphill march, the walk from the Ossining train station is only about 0.5 mile from the trailhead. Cross over the railroad tracks and turn right onto Secor Road. Proceed through the intersection with South Water Street and continue northeast when Secor Road merges into Main Street. Look for a trail sign and historical marker near the center of town, where Main and Church Streets form a fork. GPS: N41 09.686' / W73 51.754'

THE HIKE

When engineer Major David B. Douglass set out to build the Croton Aqueduct in 1837, he didn't have recreation in mind. The challenge of providing clean drinking water to New York City was a very real one; a problem that required a solution as large as the urban population 26.2 miles south of the then new Croton Reservoir. So he designed a gravity-fed water supply system, an 8.5-foot by 7.5-foot brick tunnel that was intended to continue delivering this essential resource to the city for a full century. But as great as the achievement was, the architects of the aqueduct (John B. Jervis managed the construction) underestimated the demand exerted by the biggest city in the United States; work on a new tube consequently began in 1885.

To walk atop even a 5-mile section of the Old Croton Aqueduct is to understand both the enormity of this engineering feat and its significance to the quickly growing metropolis that was busy transforming itself into a world capital. Starting from the town center of Ossining, hikers first cross the distinctive double arch that once carried 100 million gallons of water over Sing Sing Gorge every day. On the northern side of this stone structure, a large weir built in 1882 once controlled water flow into the aqueduct. When its massive iron gate was lowered into the chamber, the entire lower aqueduct could be drained in approximately two hours, permitting maintenance and repairs downstream.

Before this section of the trail reaches the Croton Gorge Unique Area, and then Croton Gorge Park, it runs through several communities, crossing local streets and in some cases edging along property lines. For anyone hiking on an empty stomach, the smell of backyard barbecue may be more than a little distracting. That and the countless thickets of wild raspberry that droop under the weight of ripening fruit in June and July. The 1843 Kane mansion near the first mile mark—an old stone home that shows signs of a more recent addition—helps take hungry minds off snacking, as does the first tall ventilating tower on the route.

Spaced about a mile apart, these vents were meant to keep the water fresh as it was transported to New York in the long, dark, brick tunnel. Look for three more of these landmarks along the 3.5 miles of trail that remain. Bypass busy Route 9A and detour around the GE Management Institute by using Ogden Road and Old Albany Post Road, and then prepare for the day's only small incline as you close in on the midpoint. Half a mile after leaving the second ventilating tower behind, a sign for the Croton Gorge Unique Area will appear. In many ways these final 2 miles before the reservoir are the nicest part of this out-and-back trek.

Lawn mowers and road noise are exchanged for the sound of children happily playing in the Croton River to the west, and the soft crunch of acorns and pinecones underfoot. Twenty or thirty feet above the greenway, limber trees lean toward each other and begin to resemble the central aisle of a temple or a cathedral. If it's near dusk, joggers and dog walkers on their evening circuits are likely to smile and nod "hello."

At mile 4 the trail slices through an enormous stony obstacle, and before long the final vent comes into view. Inside the boundaries of Croton Gorge Park, the massive dam emerges from behind the foliage. Cutting across an access road, the path jogs right and left in quick succession before reaching the wall of stone that holds back the reservoir. Retrace your steps to return to Ossining and the trailhead.

MILES AND DIRECTIONS

0.0 Start at the historical marker just off Main Street in Ossining.

0.1 Stand atop the arch that carried water over Sing Sing Gorge and consider this feat of engineering.

0.2 Walk by the stout weir chamber built in 1882. Crossing North Malcolm Road, the trail shifts from pavement to grass.

Roadside sculpture on the Old Albany Post Road

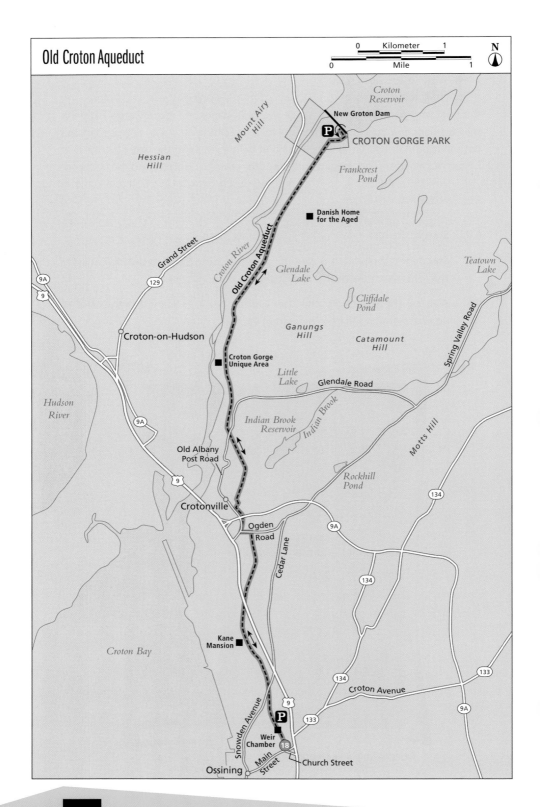

Croton
Reservoir

New Groton Dam

P

CROTON GORGE PARK

Mount Airy Hill

Hessian Hill

Frankcrest Pond

Danish Home for the Aged

Grand Street

Croton River

Old Croton Aqueduct

Glendale Lake

Teatown Lake

129

Cliffdale Pond

9A

9

Croton-on-Hudson

Ganungs Hill

Catamount Hill

Spring Valley Road

Croton Gorge Unique Area

Little Lake

Glendale Road

Hudson River

9A

Indian Brook Reservoir

Indian Brook

Motts Hill

Old Albany Post Road

Rockhill Pond

134

9

Crotonville

Ogden Road

9A

Cedar Lane

134

134

Kane Mansion

Croton Bay

133

Croton Avenue

9A

134

Snowden Avenue

9

P

133

18

Weir Chamber

Main Street

Church Street

Ossining

0.5 Walk past the Northside Fire House on Snowden Avenue; so far, your route has paralleled US 9.

0.9 Now behind the Engelhard Corporation, enter a wide lawn. A large stone home, the Kane mansion, is on the left. Several hundred feet later, the trail veers to the right (east) and then crosses North Highland Avenue/US 9.

1.5 On the opposite side of Piping Rock Drive, descend a somewhat steep, eroded slope and catch sight of the first cylindrical vent at the bottom of this drop.

1.8 Make a sharp left onto Ogden Road instead of letting the aqueduct's right of way guide you into Route 9A. Head downhill, turn right (north) on Old Albany Post Road, continue under Route 9A, and then immediately look for the trail again on the right near the entrance to the GE property.

2.2 Ascend a small hill and then stroll across Indian Brook Service Road at the bottom of Hillcrest Avenue.

2.6 Encounter the second stone ventilation tower.

3.1 Enter the Croton Gorge Unique Area. The river will be at the bottom of the gorge to your left (west).

3.4 Cross Quaker Bridge Road for the second time and continue into Old Croton Trailway State Park.

3.6 Stop briefly to inspect the third vent.

4.0 Thread a somewhat narrow channel of rock that had been blasted away to make way for the water tunnel, and then move underneath large towers carrying power lines over the river.

4.6 Walk past the fourth and final vent. Keep to the left (onto the grass instead of the gravel surface) for a good look at the dam. After 0.2 mile, climb up to the trail bed and proceed to Croton Dam Road, where you'll turn left.

5.0 Step out onto the dam and soak up the view. The Taconic State Parkway is visible at the northern end of the reservoir, and the sound of rushing water fills your ears. Then turn around and walk the trail in the other direction.

10.1 Arrive back at the trailhead on Main Street in Ossining.

18

Local information: Westchester County Tourism & Film, 222 Mamaroneck Ave., White Plains, NY 10605; (914) 995-8500; www.westchestertourism.com

Local events/attractions: Ossining Urban Park Visitor Center, 95 Broadway, Ossining, NY 10562; (914) 941-3189; http://townofossining.com/depts/parksrec.htm

Ossining Historical Society Museum, 196 Croton Ave., Ossining, NY 10562; (914) 941-0001; www.ossininghistorical.org

Jug Tavern of Sparta, P.O. Box 8977, Scarborough, NY 10510; www.jugtavern.org. Built in 1760 and listed in the National Register of Historic Places.

Local outdoor stores: Kelloggs & Lawrence, 26 Parkway, Katonah, NY 10536; (914) 232-3351; www.kelloggsandlawrence.com

Hike tours: The Friends of the Old Croton Aqueduct (see below) lead guided walks on the trail and give tours of the aqueduct tunnel in Ossining.

Organizations: The Friends of the Old Croton Aqueduct, 15 Walnut St., Dobbs Ferry, NY 10522-2109; www.aqueduct.org

Croton Friends of History, P.O. Box 193, Croton-on-Hudson, NY 10520; www.crotonfriendsofhistory.org. A small nonprofit organization dedicated to preserving and promoting the history of Croton-on-Hudson and the Hudson Valley.

Other resources: Historic Hudson River Towns, 180 Rte. 100, Katonah, NY 10536; (914) 232-6583; www.hudsonriver.com

A Boat to Save the River

Troubled by the dangerous levels of pollution and contamination present in the Hudson River and its watershed, Pete Seeger, already a folk music legend in 1966, decided to educate the public about the importance of conservation by building a sailboat with the help of fellow activists. Modeled after the Dutch cargo vessels that were a common sight on the Hudson in the eighteenth and nineteenth centuries, the single-masted sloop could carry a maximum of fifty passengers. Launched three years later, the 106-foot-long boat was called *Clearwater,* and became one of the first ship-based environmental classrooms in the country. For more than four decades now, the Clearwater organization has worked with schools, community leaders, and other non-profit groups to protect the Hudson River valley's ecosystems and promote environmental education. Its accomplishments are varied and numerous, but above all, the advocacy of this pioneering group has reintroduced thousands of people to one of the nation's most historic waterways.

Pawling Nature Preserve

Spend an afternoon on land deemed "a living museum for Man's use" when it was gifted to The Nature Conservancy in 1958. Hunt for salamanders in ridgetop wetlands, wander through a hemlock forest, and discover a colorful variety of rare plant species such as lavender devil's bit, yellow wild flax, and scarlet Indian paintbrush.

Start: At the Appalachian Trail map kiosk on Route 22

Nearest town: Pawling, NY

Distance: 6.5-mile lollipop

Approximate hiking time: 3 to 4 hours

Difficulty: Moderate

Trail surface: Grassy open fields and dirt footpaths

Seasons: Year-round

Other trail users: None

Wheelchair accessibility: None

Canine compatibility: Dogs not permitted

Land status: Private preserve

Fees and permits: None

Schedule: Daily from dawn until dusk

Facilities: None

Maps: USGS Pawling and Dover Plains, NY. Maps are occasionally found at trailheads, and a PDF can be downloaded from the Oblong Land Conservancy's website (see Hike Information).

Trail contacts: New York State Office, The Nature Conservancy, 195 New Karner Rd., Suite 200, Albany, NY 12205; (518) 690-7850; www.nature.org/wherewework/ northamerica/states/newyork/

Finding the trailhead: By car from the New York City metro area, take the Hutchinson River Parkway north, continuing through the southwestern corner of Connecticut on I-684 north. After 29 miles, take Route 22 north. Stay on Route 22 for 16 miles and look for parking on the right just past the Appalachian Trail train station and the garden center on the other side of the road. **By public transportation:** Metro North's Harlem Line stops at the Appalachian Trail just north of Pawling. Service is infrequent, however, so check the schedule before leaving. From the station platform, walk to Route 22, turn left (north), proceed a few hundred feet, and then look for the map kiosk on the other side of the road. There is a small parking area just north of the trailhead on Route 22. GPS: N41 35.632' / W 73 35.207'

Composed primarily of mica schist, Hammersly Ridge is perhaps best known today to Appalachian Trail (AT) thru-hikers, who must surmount this final hurdle before reaching the Connecticut state border and the next leg of their journey. Long before it became one of the many pieces of the 2,179-mile national scenic trail however, generations of local farmers used this landform for grazing sheep and cattle. Here and there, stone walls dating as far back as the mid-eighteenth century can still be seen, marking boundaries that no longer hold any meaning. Fittingly, the approach to Pawling Nature Preserve from the west includes a mile walk through pastures on either side of historic Hurd's Corners Road.

Rising slowly from the floor of the Harlem Valley, the AT hugs the tree line between neighboring properties as it covers its last few miles in New York State. Thistle, goldenrod, and black-eyed Susan are just a few of the flowers that thrive on the edges of the grassy route toward the preserve. Between the trailhead and the preserve boundary, a pair of stiles, or sets of steps, help hikers over electric fences—otherwise the way is obstacle free. Old fence posts painted with white blazes serve as guides. At mile 1, consult the map at the Pawling kiosk, add your name to the notebook kept there, and then move on northeast.

The next 0.75 mile involves some strenuous exercise as the trail labors up the side of Hammersly Ridge, leveling off at about 1,020 feet. Eastern gray squirrels romp amidst the dark cylindrical shapes of fallen trees as tiny winter wrens trill from the underbrush and black-throated green warblers utter their persistent, buzzing vocalization from the branches of hemlocks that grow throughout this park. Turn onto the Red Trail heading north, briefly rejoin the AT where several sections of boardwalk transport hikers over particularly muddy areas, and then make a left (northwest) on the Green Trail in the direction of the Wingdale trailhead.

Dipping down to the occasionally dry channel of a creek that isn't labeled on the map, the Green Trail soon intersects the short Orange Loop Trail, which traces the intermittent stream's opposite bank. Before it reaches the Wingdale trailhead on Sprague Road, look for blazes to your left that lead uphill. You might also notice walking fern or the flowering, shade-loving hobblebush as you navigate the northwestern corner of Pawling. Dead trees that are riddled with holes drilled by hungry woodpeckers might get your attention, too. Quickly gain close to 300 feet in elevation on the way to an overlook. Time your trip with peaking fall foliage, and enjoy a kaleidoscope of reds and yellows on the surrounding hillsides.

Rather than follow the Orange Trail all the way back to the creekbed where you first encountered it, bear right (south) on the Green Trail again and cut across the ridge's northeastern side. Watch closely for the green plastic trail markers on this segment of the hike; they can be hard to spot from a distance, especially with a significant amount of leaves obscuring the footpath itself. Less than 200 feet after passing mile 4, the Green Trail runs straight into the Red Trail once more. Turn right, ramble south across the top of the ridge, and then head back down to the train station on the Appalachian Trail.

MILES AND DIRECTIONS

0.0   Start at the Appalachian Trail map kiosk on Route 22, directly across from Native Landscapes Garden Center. Notes left by thru-hikers accompany warnings, guidelines, and a large map of the AT from the Hudson to Connecticut.

0.2   Cross Hurd's Corners Road and continue over the stile through the field to the northeast.

0.3   Walk across a small plank bridge spanning a trickle of a creek. Look for posts marked with the white Appalachian Trail blazes.

1.0   Arrive at the Pawling Nature Preserve map kiosk and the preserve boundary. Turn right (east) and continue on the AT.

1.9   Make a left turn (north) on the Red Trail, climbing the flank of Hammersly Ridge to about 1,020 feet.

Farming continues to be a way of life for some in the Harlem Valley.

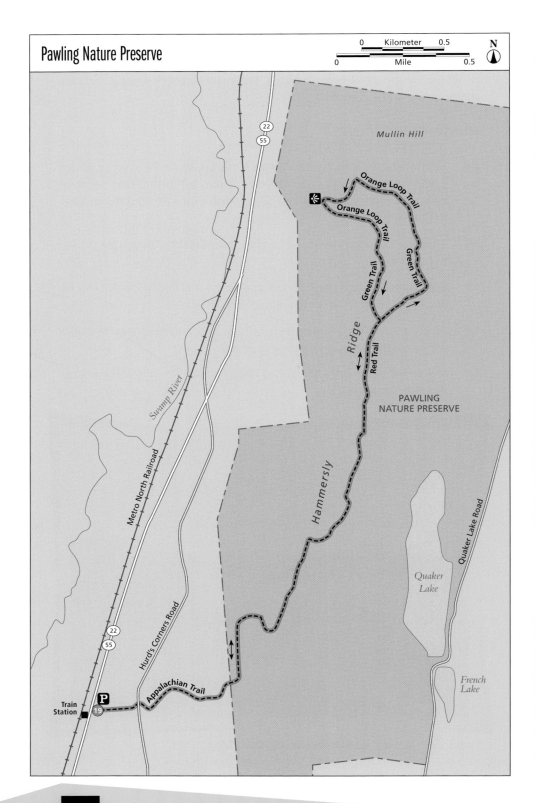

Mullin Hill

Orange Loop Trail

Orange Loop Trail

Green Trail

Green Trail

Green Trail

Ridge

Red Trail

PAWLING
NATURE PRESERVE

Hammersly

Quaker Lake Road

Quaker
Lake

French
Lake

Swamp River

Metro North Railroad

Hurd's Corners Road

Appalachian Trail

22
55

22
55

P

Train
Station   19

0   Kilometer   0.5

0   Mile   0.5

N

2.5 Cover a short distance on a few sections of boardwalk that traverse a patch of wet ground.

2.6 Turn left onto the AT again at a U intersection.

2.7 Make a sharp left (northwest) onto the Green Trail (a small sign affixed to a tree reads Wingdale), traveling in a counterclockwise direction.

2.9 Join the Orange Loop Trail on the left (west) and cross a creekbed. Keep to the left (south) bank of the little waterway.

3.3 Turn sharply left—almost backtracking—and start to climb up a somewhat steep slope.

3.5 Reach a scenic viewpoint that looks over Route 22 and the Metro North Railroad in the Harlem Valley. Descend the high point via the Orange Loop Trail.

3.7 Take the Green Trail on the right (south), up and over the ridge.

4.1 Turn right at the T intersection where the Green Trail meets the Red Trail. Use the same route you took inbound to return.

6.5 Arrive back at the AT map kiosk and trailhead on Route 22.

Option: Add a little over 1 mile to your hike by turning left on the Red Trail after descending from the overlook. Upon completing 0.2 mile, proceed northeast on the AT for another 0.1 mile, and then resume hiking on the Red Trail as it circles around to the south again, sloping down into Duell Hollow. When you come to a bridge and see yellow blazes, turn right, climb the ridge until you meet the AT one more time, and then turn left to exit the preserve.

HIKE INFORMATION

Local information: Dutchess County Tourism, Suite Q-17, 3 Neptune Rd., Poughkeepsie, NY 12601; (845) 463-4000; www.dutchesstourism.com

Local events/attractions: The Institute for American Indian Studies, 38 Curtis Rd., Washington, CT 06793; (860) 868-0518; www.birdstone.org. Open Mon to Sat from 10 a.m. to 5 p.m., and Sun from 12 to 5 p.m.

Sloane Stanley Museum, 31 Kent-Cornwall Rd. (Rte. 7), Kent, CT 06757; (860) 927-3849; www.cultureandtourism.org/cct/cwp/view.asp?a=2127&q=302262. Home of the artist, author, and illustrator Eric Sloane.

Good eats: Big W's Roadside Bar-B-Q, 1475 Rte. 22, Wingdale, NY 12594; (845) 832-6200; www.bigwsbbq.com

McKinney & Doyle's Fine Foods Cafe, 10 Charles Colman Blvd., Pawling, NY 12564; (845) 855-3875; www.mckinneyanddoyle.com

Towne Crier Cafe, 130 Rte. 22, Pawling, NY 12564; (845) 855-1300; http://townecrier .com. Live music four nights a week, and American cuisine for dinner and brunch on weekends.

Local outdoor stores: Great Blue Outfitters, 3198 Rte. 22, Patterson, NY 12563; (845) 319-6172; www.greatblueoutfitters.com

Backcountry Outfitters, 5 Bridge St., Kent, CT 06757; (860) 927-3377; www.bc outfitters.com

Organizations: The Oblong Land Conservancy, P.O. Box 601, Pawling, NY 12564; (845) 855-5993; www.oblongland.org. A community-founded land trust established to conserve open space in and around Pawling and Dover.

Dutchess Land Conservancy, P.O. Box 138/4289 Rte. 82, Millbrook, NY 12545; (845) 677-3002; www.dutchessland.org

Oblong Trail Association, 582 North Quaker Hill Rd., Pawling, NY 12564; (845) 855-0693; www.oblongtrails.com

Cary Institute of Ecosystem Studies, Plant Science Building, 2801 Sharon Turnpike (Rte. 44), Millbrook, NY 12545; (845) 677-5343; www.ecostudies.org. Regularly hosts free events for the public.

> 🍃 **Green Tip:**
> *Stay on the trail. Cutting through from one part of a switchback to another can destroy fragile plant life.*

Rockefeller State Park Preserve

Meander about this green oasis just 30 miles from New York and even closer to the setting of Washington Irving's most famous story. Let carriage roads carry you past cattle pastures, ash trees, and rock formations.

Start: Just behind the preserve visitor center

Nearest town: Pleasantville, NY

Distance: 5.9-mile interlocking loops

Approximate hiking time: 3 to 4 hours

Difficulty: Easy to moderate, with one short climb

Trail surface: Gravel and crushed stone pathways

Seasons: Mar through Oct

Other trail users: Joggers, equestrians, birders; cross-country skiers (seasonally) and bow hunters (limited to hunting season)

Wheelchair accessibility: None

Canine compatibility: Dogs permitted on leashes 10 feet or less

Land status: State park

Fees and permits: None

Schedule: Daily from sunrise to sunset

Facilities: Bathrooms, vending machines, and an exhibition space at the park entrance

Maps: USGS White Plains, NY. A black-and-white hiking map can be printed out from the Friends of the Rockefeller State Park Preserve website or the New York State parks website (see below).

Trail contacts: New York State Office of Parks, Recreation & Historic Preservation, Regional Office Contact Information, 125 Phelps Way, Pleasantville, NY 10570; (914) 631-1470; www .nysparks.state.ny.us

Finding the trailhead: By car from New York, take the Taconic State Parkway north and exit onto CR 117 to Pleasantville. Turn left at the end of the ramp and proceed through three stoplights. The entrance to the preserve will be on the left after approximately 2 miles. **By public transportation:** Take Metro North to the Tarrytown station and hail one of the taxis waiting outside the station. The 4-mile ride to the preserve shouldn't take more than ten minutes. GPS: N41 06.682' / W73 50.180'

I n his haunting story about Sleepy Hollow, Washington Irving wrote that "the place still continues under the sway of some witching power, that holds a spell over the minds of the good people." He was, of course, referring to the fictional Headless Horseman, and yet the 1,418-acre area of the Pocantico Hills that has been set aside for all to enjoy does in fact possess an enchanting quality for modern visitors. Instead of gloomy lanes and eerie, ominous woods however, Rockefeller State Park Preserve is characterized by rolling fields, gurgling streams, and a sizeable man-made lake. Created by a gift from the Rockefeller family in 1983, the park and visitor center (designed by Lo Yi Chan and opened in 1994) do have one thing in common with Ichabod Crane, Irving's main character, though: They serve an educational purpose for the community.

One particular subject of study is birdlife. An impressive 182 species of birds have been recorded in the hemlock stands, hayfields, and wooded shrub swamps on either side of Route 117. This count includes commonly seen birds such as hairy woodpeckers, northern cardinals, and white-throated sparrows, as well as the much less-frequently spotted prairie warbler, gray-cheeked thrush, and black-billed cuckoo. Pick up a checklist at the visitor center if you wish to record some of the species you see during your time in the park.

The first geographic feature to appear once you've left the visitor center behind is Swan Lake, a long, lily-strewn body of water that attracts waterfowl, artists, and amateur photographers. Find peace by lingering here awhile, but don't forget that Rockefeller Preserve has 20 miles of carriage roads waiting to be explored. Alongside these well-maintained arteries you might notice some of the plants that inhabit the landscape: common milkweed, wild raspberry, and in shady, damp areas, the striped jack-in-the-pulpit. Deer are also abundant in the park, contentedly munching their way through a wide range of grasses, shrubs, vines, and woody plants.

Once you've crossed the Pocantico River, take the Gory Brook Road Trail under the highway into the park's quiet middle section, named the Eagle Hill Area after its highest point. Only the buzz of cicadas will accompany you deeper into the mixed hardwood forest. This meandering route eventually leads over thirteen small bridges spanning Gory Brook; pause on any one of them to observe damselflies folding their wings at their sides when they alight on a surface, or dozens of water striders skating on the glassy liquid surface below. To complete this irregular-shaped loop hike, follow the Pocantico River Trail south to the Old Sleepy Hollow Road Trail and let it guide you back toward the park entrance and trailhead in the northeast. Before leaving, be sure to visit the gallery with its rotating exhibits by local artists.

MILES AND DIRECTIONS

0.0   Start behind the visitor center off Route 117. Take Brother's Path south toward Swan Lake.

0.4   Turn right at the fork onto Farm Meadow Trail and then take the next right on Ash Tree Loop, which curves up a modest grade.

0.8   Veer to the northwest (left) on the Overlook Trail, which enters from the southeast. Keep right where Ash Tree Loop circles back to the south and then make another left (west) on the Old Sleepy Hollow Road Trail 0.1 mile later.

1.1   Cross Old Sleepy Hollow Road and continue down the broad path over the Pocantico River. Turn left (south) on the other side of the bridge and then take a right, gradually climbing up Eagle Hill.

A confused hiker asks the locals for directions.

Rockefeller State Park Preserve

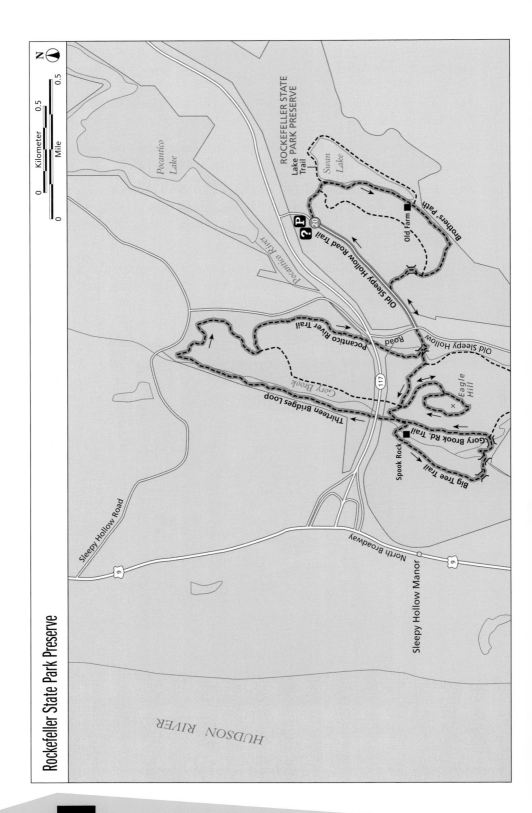

1.4 Make a sharp left on the carriage road leading to an overlook.

1.7 Arrive at the top of Eagle Hill for a partially obstructed view of the Hudson River, Kykuit, and the Tappan Zee Bridge.

2.2 Follow a single switchback to the left across Gory Brook Trail and then make a right onto Witch's Spring Trail over a small bridge. Pass Spook Rock to the left of the gravel path and merge onto the Big Tree Trail.

2.7 Cross a wide stone bridge, turn left (east) on the other side of Gory Brook and then left again (north) on the trail of the same name. Walk by boulders that have tumbled down Eagle Hill to the right of the trail.

3.3 Pass under Route 117 and continue walking north on the Thirteen Bridges Loop. This trail weaves back and forth up a low hill, turning back toward the visitor center.

4.5 Turn left (east) on the Pocantico River Trail and walk past a short spur that leads to Sleepy Hollow Road.

5.0 Stroll beneath the highway overpass, turn left (east) to rejoin the Old Sleepy Hollow Road Trail, and cover the last few hundred feet to the end of the loop portion of your route.

Ducks, such as these mallards, are drawn to the bodies of water in this preserve.

5.9 Arrive back at the trailhead at the edge of the large parking lot southwest of the visitor center.

HIKE INFORMATION

Local information: Westchester County Tourism & Film, 222 Mamaroneck Ave., White Plains, NY 10605; (914) 995-8500; www.westchestertourism.com

Local events/attractions: Lyndhurst, 635 South Broadway, Tarrytown, NY 10591; (914) 631-4481; http://lyndhurst.wordpress.com. Tour the magnificent Gothic mansion occupied by New York City mayor William Paulding and railroad tycoon Jay Gould.

Kykuit, the Rockefeller Estate, 381 North Broadway (Rte. 9), Sleepy Hollow, NY 10591; (914) 631-3992; www.hudsonvalley.org/content/view/12/42/. Open daily except Tues from May 8 through Nov 7.

Washington Irving's Sunnyside, 89 West Sunnyside Lane, Tarrytown, NY 10591; (914) 591-8763; www.hudsonvalley.org/content/view/13/43/

Good eats: Captain Lawrence Brewing Company, 99 Castleton St. #1, Pleasantville, NY 10570-3461; (914) 741-2337; www.captainlawrencebrewing.com. Tastings held on Fri from 4 p.m. to 7 p.m., and Sat from 12 to 6 p.m.

Blue Hill Cafe at Stone Barns, 630 Bedford Rd., Pocantico Hills, NY 10591; (914) 366-9600; www.stonebarnscenter.org/visit/dining

Lefteris Gyro, 1 North Broadway, Tarrytown, NY 10591; (914) 524-9687; www.lefterisgyro.com. Gyro, souvlaki, and other authentic Greek dishes at reasonable prices.

Local outdoor stores: American Terrain Outdoors, 175 East Post Rd., White Plains, NY 10601; (914) 682-3971; www.americanterrain.com

Eastern Mountain Sports, 693 White Plains Post Rd., Eastchester Shopping Center, Scarsdale, NY 10583; (914) 725-0024; www.ems.com

Hike tours: Friends of the Rockefeller State Park Preserve periodically lead guided hikes and discovery walks around the preserve.

Organizations: Friends of the Rockefeller State Park Preserve, Inc., P.O. Box 8444, Sleepy Hollow, NY 10591; (914) 762-0209; www.friendsrock.org

New York City Audubon, 71 West 23rd St., Suite 1523, New York, NY 10010; (212) 691-7483; http://nycaudubon.org

Schunemunk Mountain State Park

Begin under the Moodna Viaduct, the highest and longest railroad trestle east of the Mississippi, and then climb the tallest mountain in Orange County. Survey the landscape for miles from two parallel ridges, trace part of a Moodna Creek tributary, and check out a group of megaliths.

Start: Trailhead on Otterkill Road, underneath the viaduct

Nearest town: Salisbury Mills, NY

Distance: 7.1-mile lollipop

Approximate hiking time: 5 to 6 hours

Difficulty: Difficult, with several steep climbs and one section of scrambling over exposed rock

Trail surface: Rocky trails, bare rock, and dirt footpaths

Seasons: May through Oct

Other trail users: Hikers only

Wheelchair accessibility: None

Canine compatibility: Leashed dogs permitted

Land status: State park

Fees and permits: None

Schedule: Daily from dawn until dusk

Facilities: None

Maps: USGS Cornwall-on-Hudson, NY; New York–New Jersey Trail Conference West Hudson Trails Map 114. A topo map of Schunemunk can be downloaded from the Hil-Mar Lodge website: www .hil-marlodge.com/schunemunk .htm.

Special considerations: Watch out for timber rattlesnakes, an animal that is rarely seen but is a poisonous species and can be dangerous.

Trail contacts: Palisades Interstate Park Commission, Administration Building, Bear Mountain, NY 10911; (845) 786-2701; www.nysparks.com

Finding the trailhead: From the New York State Thruway/I-87 north, take exit 16 onto US 6 heading west. Travel 5 miles and then follow signs for Route 208 north. After about 3 more miles, make a slight right onto Clove Road/CR 27. After 4.4 miles, turn right onto Otterkill Road. Look for the parking area and trailhead on the left. **By public transportation:** It's possible to reach Schunemunk by train via the Port-Jervis line (exit at Salisbury Mills) on Metro North, or by a Coach USA bus to Mountainville. The walk from the train station is lengthy, although much of it is along country roads. Exit the station onto Route 94 and walk to the left (east) 0.6 mile. Turn right (south) on Jackson Avenue and continue on this road for 1 mile. When it intersects Otterkill Road, turn right (west) and walk 0.6 mile to the trailhead, which will be on the left. GPS: N41 25.572' / W74 05.888'

THE HIKE

S erving as a scenic backdrop for the sculpture placed around the property of the Storm King Art Center, Schunnemunk Mountain cuts a striking figure in the Hudson Highlands, rising as it does to an imposing height of almost 1,700 feet. Schunnemunk is, in fact, tall enough to be seen from most places in Orange County. Relatively new as parks go—New York State only officially acquired the property in 2003—this long land formation is characterized by its double crest. The two ridges on either side of Baby Brook are actually a geological downfold, rather than a dramatic feature like a gorge or a canyon.

Making Schunnemunk even more interesting is the puddingstone conglomerate visible in the higher elevations. A reddish-purple in color, this caprock is speckled with white quartz and pink sandstone millions of years old. To study the geology up close and to appreciate the grandeur of this mountain, spend a long afternoon among the ancient megaliths, twisted pines, and the swampy lowland between the two ridges. Discoveries await within the boundaries of the park, none more welcome perhaps, than a bit of solitude.

Seen from afar, this mountain thrusts its wide shoulders out in a challenge to day hikers, daring them to try to reach the top. Climbing the northern slope, half a mile into the Trestle Trail, unprepared visitors may be having second thoughts. Fortunately, the packed soil path levels off (temporarily) and a single bench presents the weary with a chance for a rest and a view. Thick grass chokes the trail in places from this spot on, as the white blazes guide you to a second overlook where the sun-baked shelf of rock is splotched with gray-green lichen.

The red-blazed Barton Swamp Trail picks up where the Trestle Trail leaves off, carrying you up and over a weather-worn hump of rock in a counterclockwise direction and intersecting with the Long Path. This long-distance trail can be traced south all the way to Fort Lee, New Jersey, but only about 1.5 miles of it overlap with this particular route. Undulating over the exposed stone on top of the narrow western ridge, the Long Path provides several views and then, just before mile 3, it meets a crossover trail.

Choosing your steps carefully, descend into the valley and then climb a series of switchbacks up the other, steeper side. Although short, this might be the most arduous part of the hike. The clatter of dry stones cascading behind will chase you up the cliff. Now on the eastern ridge, you'll stay with the Jessup Trail for approximately 2 miles, to where it dives down into Taylor Hollow and runs into the Barton Swamp Trail. Until then the yellow blazes (painted on the stone at boot level in many places) keep you in the open. And at the highest point on this ramble across Schunnemunk, the former site of a fire tower, your elevation will be 610 feet above the observation deck of the Empire State Building.

Duck under the branches of the jack pines that cloak the eastern ridge in a thick green mantle, and pick your way over the varied topography that makes the Highlands such an ideal destination for city dwellers in search of some fresh air and exercise. The yellow blazes curve east at Taylor Hollow, mirroring the course of Baby Brook. To return to the Trestle Trail and close the loop, ford the brook and make a final scramble up the red-blazed trail. Then retrace your steps to the trailhead.

MILES AND DIRECTIONS

0.0 Start just west of the viaduct, where white blazes leading from the parking lot on Otterkill Road lead south and uphill. Turn right to stay on the white-blazed Trestle Trail after climbing about 450 feet.

Opened in January 1909, the Moodna Viaduct is 3,200 feet long and 193 feet tall at its highest point.

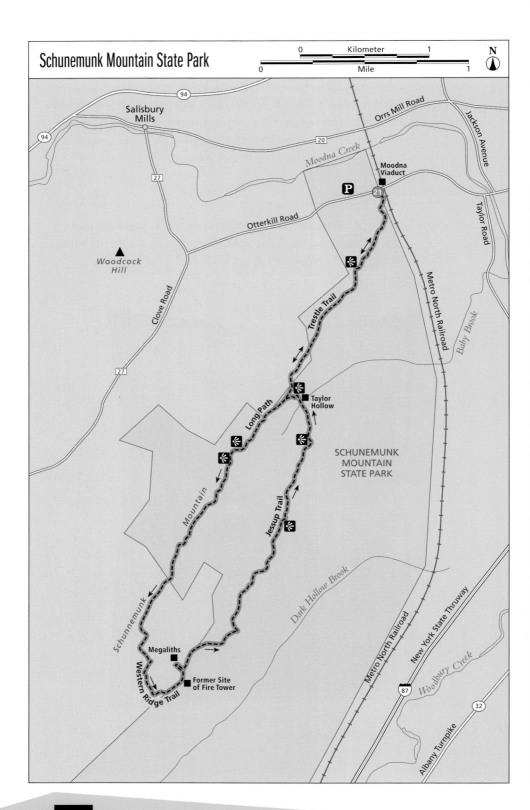

Schunemunk Mountain State Park

0 — Kilometer — 1
0 — Mile — 1

N

Salisbury
Mills

94

20

27

Orrs Mill Road

Jackson Avenue

Moodna Creek

Moodna
Viaduct

P

21

Taylor Road

Otterkill Road

*Woodcock
Hill*

Clove Road

Metro North Railroad

Baby Brook

Trestle Trail

27

Long Path

Taylor
Hollow

SCHUNEMUNK
MOUNTAIN
STATE PARK

Mountain

Jessup Trail

Dark Hollow Brook

Schunemunk

Megaliths

Former Site
of Fire Tower

Western Ridge Trail

Metro North Railroad

New York State Thruway

Woodbury Creek

87

32

Albany Turnpike

0.5 After a fairly relentless 0.5 mile, steadily gaining roughly 500 feet in elevation, you'll reach a tiny spur leading to an overlook with a wooden bench. Look down on the viaduct and Salisbury Mills with the knowledge that you'll be twice as high above these landmarks later in the day.

1.2 Reach a second clearing with views to the east toward Storm King and the Hudson.

1.4 The Trestle Trail ends where it meets the Barton Swamp Trail. Follow the red blazes right (west) over a hump of bare rock and then turn left (south) on the Long Path.

1.7 From a third viewpoint, gaze down on Woodcock Hill and Clove Road. On a clear, sunny afternoon it's possible to make out the Shawangunk Mountains to the northwest, their deeper blue outline barely discernible against the sky.

2.2 At 1,440 feet, you now have a near 360-degree view of Orange County, an impressive vantage point that encourages lingering. Continue south on the ridgeline in the direction of the aqua blazes.

2.9 Turn left (southeast) on the blue-blazed Western Ridge Trail and proceed slowly down the bumpy, uneven puddingstone. You'll briefly join the red Barton Swamp Trail in the valley, but then return to blue blazes up a nearly vertical section where you'll need your hands free to pull yourself over the wall of rock.

3.3 Make a left (north) turn on the yellow Jessup Trail, which is also blazed with the Highland Trail's teal diamond. Much of the next mile will be above the trees.

3.5 Stop on the spot where an old fire tower once stood, 1,670 feet above sea level. On a sunny afternoon there's no better place for a lunch break, but if the day is cool or overcast, you may want to seek shelter from the wind. To see the megaliths, turn left (west) at the white blazes painted on the stone and walk for slightly less than 0.2 mile.

4.0 Drop below 1,600 feet and keep left at the junction to remain on the Jessup Trail. Just past this intersection is another outstanding view to the east.

4.6 Meet the Sweet Clover Trail, which runs across the park to Taylor Road in the east. Keep following the yellow blazes north.

5.2 Yet another view will delay hikers who aren't relying on public transportation for the return trip to New York.

5.5 Proceed straight on the Jessup Trail (northwest) through the four-way trail intersection, cross Baby Brook, and climb back up the western ridge on the red Barton Swamp Trail.

5.7 Veer to the right to reconnect with the Trestle Trail. Let the white blazes guide you back downhill to the viaduct.

7.1 Arrive back at the trailhead on Otterkill Road.

Options: Add another mile or more to this hike by remaining on the Long Path until it crosses the Jessup Trail (rather than using the blue connector trail), or follow the Dark Hollow Trail (black blazes) to the Otterkill Trail (red blazes) on the return trip.

HIKE INFORMATION

Local information: Orange County Tourism, 124 Main St., Goshen, NY 10924; (845) 615-3860; www.orangetourism.org

Local events/attractions: Museum Village, 1010 Rte. 17M, Monroe, NY 10950; (845) 782-8248; www.museumvillage.org. A nineteenth-century living history museum with frequent events.

Harness Racing Museum and Hall of Fame, 240 Main St., Goshen, NY 10924; (845) 294-6330; www.harnessmuseum.com

Bethlehem Art Gallery, 58 Orrs Mills Rd., Salisbury Mills, NY 12577; (845) 496-4785

Local outdoor stores: The North Face (at Woodbury Commons), 498 Red Apple Court, Suite 461, Central Valley, NY 10917; (845) 928-4900; www.thenorthface.com

Hike tours: Outdoor Bound, Inc., 154 Grand St., Suite 610, New York, NY 10013; (212) 579-4568; www.outdoorbound.com

Organizations: New York-New Jersey Trail Conference, 156 Ramapo Valley Rd. (Rte. 202), Mahwah, NJ 07430-1199; (201) 512-9348; www.nynjtc.org

The Nature Conservancy, 195 New Karner Rd., Suite 200, Albany, NY 12205; (518) 690-7850; www.nature.org

Open Space Institute, 1350 Broadway, New York, NY 10018-0983; (212) 290-8200; www.osiny.org

🌿 **Green Tip:**
Carpool or take public transportation to the trailhead.

Staten Island Greenbelt

Seven different trails crisscross this expansive swath of green space near the center of Staten Island, offering visitors numerous opportunities to try to spot a variety of bird species that aren't often found in the other boroughs. This mid-length circuit leads into the swampy Bloodroot Valley, past old hospital buildings, and finally up to the summit of Moses' Mountain, a small hill created with construction debris from the Staten Island Expressway.

Start: At the nature center on Rockland Avenue

Nearest town: Willowbrook, NY

Distance: 4.3-mile lollipop

Approximate hiking time: 2 hours

Difficulty: Easy

Trail surface: Woodland dirt footpath, gravel, and stony, uneven terrain

Seasons: Year-round

Other trail users: Joggers, dog walkers, mountain bikers

Wheelchair accessibility: The 1-mile Nature Center Trail is suitable for disabled visitors.

Canine compatibility: Leashed dogs permitted, although sections of trail can be narrow and somewhat overgrown.

Land status: City park

Fees and permits: None

Schedule: Daily from sunrise to sunset

Facilities: Restrooms are located in the Greenbelt Nature Center, the Greenbelt Recreation Center, and the Greenbelt Environmental Education Building in High Rock Park. Picnic tables can be found in High Rock Park and Willowbrook Park, which also has ball fields, an archery range, and a carousel.

Maps: USGS Arthur Kill and The Narrows, NY. Main trails are well marked, but pick up a free map at the nature center or download it from the Greenbelt Conservancy's website (see below).

Trail contacts: New York City Department of Parks & Recreation, The Arsenal, Central Park, 830 Fifth Avenue, New York, NY 10065; (212) NEW-YORK; www.nyc.gov/parks Greenbelt Conservancy, 200 Nevada Ave., Staten Island, NY 10306; (718) 667-2165; www.si greenbelt.org

22

Finding the trailhead: From the Verrazano Narrows Bridge, exit off Route 278 west onto Bradley Avenue. Continue to the intersection of Bradley and Brielle Avenues. Follow Brielle Avenue south for 0.75 mile to its end at the Greenbelt Nature Center and trailhead. **By public transportation:** To reach the greenbelt from the ferry terminal at St. George, take the S62 bus to the corner of Bradley Avenue and Victory Boulevard. Transfer to the S57, which stops at Brielle and Rockland Avenues, across the street from the Greenbelt Nature Center and trailhead. GPS: N40 35.311′ / W74 08.328′

THE HIKE

Staten Island might not seem like an obvious place to commune with nature, but the greenbelt offers some of the best hiking trails within the five boroughs. Consisting of 2,800 acres of woodlands, wetlands, lakes, ponds, and meadows, the greenbelt is also the largest of the five flagship parks in New York City. The highest natural elevation on the eastern seaboard south of Maine is also on the eastern edge of the greenbelt. Todt Hill, named after the Dutch word for "dead," rises above the Moravian Cemetery, which was once a burial ground for early colonists.

Wandering off under a canopy of oak, beech, tulip, and sweet gum trees, you'll soon be strolling through one of the last undisturbed forests in New York City. Fern, cat briar, and thickets of the devil's walking stick—a prickly shrub—line the occasionally muddy stretches of trail that lead through the Bloodroot Valley toward Sea View Hospital where, through the links of barbed-wire fence, you'll catch glimpses of derelict buildings built between 1905 and 1938 to house tuberculosis patients.

Returning along an unblazed path that descends to Manor Road, the smell of fragrant wisteria blossoms will overtake you before you arrive at the short, stony loop that spirals up to the top of Moses' Mountain. Keep an eye out for the occasional wild blackberry or blueberry bush as you hike. On a clear day, New Jersey is just visible to the west, across Arthur Kill.

Back at the bottom of this artificial feature, which was created with construction rubble from the expressway, enter High Rock Park and follow the Green and Yellow Trails as they weave back and forth over a stream that twists and turns past bright purple violets, skunk cabbage, invasive garlic mustard, and, unfortunately, poison ivy. Pick up the Blue Trail and let it guide you by the greenbelt headquarters.

Although the final section of this hike never veers far from the somewhat noisy traffic that passes through the park, it eventually climbs the flank of Heyerdahl Hill and merges with the short trail that circles the nature center. Alert walkers may be lucky enough to spot a northern oriole, a brown snake warming itself in the sun, or a bright blue robin's egg that has fallen from its nest into the leaf litter on the forest floor. Combine this short hike with a visit to Historic Richmond Town nearby and it's possible to imagine Staten Island as it would have appeared to the first Dutch settlers who arrived here in the mid-seventeenth century.

MILES AND DIRECTIONS

0.0 Start at the Greenbelt Nature Center on Rockland Avenue. The Nature Center Trail begins at a footbridge to the left of the building. Turn left (east) at the first T intersection. Join the Blue Trail and descend into Buck's Hollow.

0.4 Remain on the Blue Trail by turning left at the four-way crossing. Walk east over a trickle of water on a worn plank bridge and climb three steps to the shoulder of the road.

0.7 Arrive at another four-way intersection. Turn left (uphill) and listen to crickets chirping from their hiding places in the tall grass. A rusty chain-link fence marking the property line of the Sea View Hospital is covered in a tangle of brown vines.

0.9 At the bottom of Bloodroot Valley, turn right before stepping onto a small bridge. The blue blazes continue north around the hospital but don't link

An uncommon sight: the tiny turquoise egg of a robin

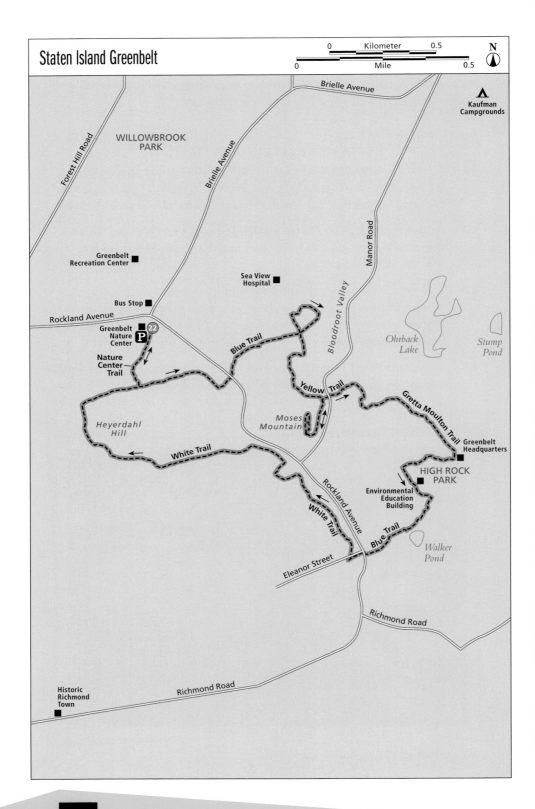

Staten Island Greenbelt

0   Kilometer   0.5

0   Mile   0.5

N

Brielle Avenue

Kaufman
Campgrounds

WILLOWBROOK
PARK

Forest Hill Road

Brielle Avenue

Manor Road

Greenbelt
Recreation Center

Sea View
Hospital

Bloodroot Valley

Ohrback
Lake

Stump
Pond

Bus Stop

Rockland Avenue

Greenbelt
Nature
Center

22

P

Blue Trail

Yellow Trail

Gretta Moulton Trail

Nature
Center
Trail

Heyerdahl
Hill

Moses
Mountain

Greenbelt
Headquarters

White Trail

HIGH ROCK
PARK

White Trail

Rockland Avenue

Environmental
Education
Building

Blue Trail

Walker
Pond

Eleanor Street

Richmond Road

Richmond Road

Historic
Richmond
Town

with any other trails at the terminus. Walk up a gentle slope into new-growth forest.

1.0 Return to the four-way intersection and veer left (south), downhill.

1.1 Cross a well-built bridge that spans a cheerful little creek. On the other side of the water, take the left fork to the east.

1.3 Make a sharp right (south) turn and follow the trail marked by white blazes with a yellow bull's-eye.

1.5 After circling around the rather modest topographical feature, arrive at the top of Moses' Mountain (224 feet). Retrace your steps to the bottom of the hill.

1.7 Cross Manor Road, veer left (northeast) onto the Gretta Moulton Trail, and then follow the green blazes at the next two forks.

2.0 Keep to the right as you come down a small slope. The green blazes will briefly overlap with the yellow as they angle southward. Watch for picnic tables and an informational kiosk up ahead.

2.1 Pick up the Blue Trail again at the edge of the fences of the Moravian Cemetery, and let it guide you partway around the park road loop. It will lead you past a studio building after another 0.2 mile.

2.5 Make three right turns in quick succession to end up pointed west. Walker Pond, an overgrown and sadly polluted body of water, will be on your left.

2.8 Cross Rockland Avenue again and look for Eleanor Street up ahead on the right. Turn right (north) a few hundred feet down this dead-end street.

2.9 Cross a stream at the bottom of Egbertville Ravine and advance north up the slope on the other side.

3.2 Walk through the Meisner Avenue intersection, steering left. The White Trail resumes on the right, just off London Road.

3.4 Keep right (northwest) where the red and yellow blazes break away from the trail they've been sharing. Stay on the White Trail.

3.8 Walk by another intersection with the Red Trail. You may not have noticed the subtle elevation gain, but you're now at 300 feet.

4.0 Turn right (east) on the Nature Center Trail and make a left (north) after 0.1 mile. This should look familiar.

4.3 Arrive back at Mitchell Crossing, the footbridge next to the nature center, and the trailhead.

HIKE INFORMATION

Local information: Visit Staten Island, 1110 South Ave., Suite 57, Staten Island, NY 10314; (347) 273-1257; www.visitstatenisland.com

Local events/attractions: The Jacques Marchais Museum of Tibetan Art, 338 Lighthouse Ave., Staten Island, NY 10306; (718) 987-3500; www.tibetanmuseum.org. Houses objects of cultural, historical, and spiritual signifi- cance to the living traditions of Tibetan Buddhism.
Historic Richmond Town, 441 Clarke Ave., Staten Island, NY 10306; (718) 351-1611; www.historicrichmondtown.org. New York City's living history village and museum complex includes an eleven-acre organic farm and one of the oldest homes in the country.

Good eats: Victory Boulevard, leading uphill from the ferry terminal, is littered with ethnic restaurants: Mexican, Sri Lankan, Trinidadian, and more. Try Taco Azteca, 75 Victory Blvd. (718-273-6404); or Island Roti Shop, 65 Victory Blvd. (718-815-7001).
Schaffer's Tavern, 2055 Victory Blvd., Staten Island, NY 10314; (718) 494-9696. German food and imported beers.

Hike tours: Guided hikes focusing on local ecology and history are frequently offered by the Greenbelt Conservancy. See their calendar for details.

Organizations: Council on the Arts & Humanities for Staten Island, Snug Harbor Cultural Center, 1000 Richmond Terrace, Staten Island, NY 10301; (718) 447-3329; www.statenislandarts.org

The tiger-striped eastern swallowtail, one of several species of butterfly that call the Staten Island Greenbelt home, lives for just two short weeks.

Storm King State Park

Scale the shoulders of a giant named by the nineteenth-century editor, journalist, and poet Nathaniel Parker Willis. From a majestic perch at the summit of Storm King Mountain, you can watch peregrine falcons soar on the air currents above while barges glide by on the waters of the Hudson River far below.

Start: Parking lot on Mountain Road

Nearest town: Cornwall, NY

Distance: 4.5-mile lollipop

Approximate hiking time: 3 to 4 hours

Difficulty: Moderate to difficult

Trail surface: Rocky trails, woods roads, and exposed rock

Seasons: May through Oct

Other trail users: Deer hunters (seasonally)

Wheelchair accessibility: None

Canine compatibility: Leashed and muzzled dogs permitted

Land status: State park

Fees and permits: None

Schedule: Daily from dawn until dusk

Facilities: None

Maps: USGS Cornwall-on-Hudson and West Point, NY; New York-New Jersey Trail Conference West Hudson Trails Map 113

Trail contacts: Palisades Interstate Park Commission, Bear Mountain, NY 10911; (845) 786-2701; www.nysparks.com

Finding the trailhead: Take exit 17 off the New York State Thruway and then the next right onto Route 300/Union Avenue. Drive south to Vails Gate, where Route 300 intersects with Route 32. Follow Route 32 for about 1.7 miles and then turn left onto Quaker Avenue toward Cornwall. Make your next right on US 9W and head south 2.7 miles until you see a sign for Mountain Road. Turn left, drive past the Storm King School, and look for a small parking lot and the trailhead on the right after roughly 1.3 miles. GPS: N41 25.938' / W74 00.720'

23

With a poetic name and a picturesque location on the west bank of the Hudson, Storm King practically begs to be climbed. By following the Stillman Trail to its open summit—as well as the top of adjacent Butter Hill—hikers will find themselves looking out over a landscape painted in vivid blues, browns, greens, and purples. The park itself came into being with an 800-acre donation from Dr. Ernest Stillman, and has slowly grown in size to encompass nearly 2,000 acres of the Hudson Highlands.

Today, six main trails snake through the park, each rapidly ascending from one of the roads along its borders to heights topping out at over 1,200 feet. And, more so on Storm King's tall gray cliffs than perhaps any other spot in the lower Hudson Valley, it's possible to gaze for miles both up and down the river. To pause on the crown of this imposing mountain on the eastern edge of the Appalachians is to feel like a king indeed.

Taking off from the Mountain Road entrance, the yellow-blazed Stillman Trail (which is also blazed with the teal diamond of the Highlands Trail for most of the way) eases hikers into what will ultimately be a reasonably challenging climb. For the first 0.5 mile however, the going is easy. The initial view of the glittering Hudson materializes after just twenty minutes on the trail, offering a glimpse of Cornwall-on-Hudson and the Newburgh bridge farther upriver. Soon yellow blazes point up the slope you've been following, and water bars placed periodically along the route are evidence of an attempt to minimize erosion on this steeper section.

When the Stillman Trail meets the blue- and red-blazed Bluebird Trail, the going gets tougher and you may find yourself pausing to catch your breath against the sturdy trunk of one of the many oak trees that populate the park. The dry, clattering sound of rocks cascading downhill may flush out mourning doves as you move in the direction of the summit. Nearing the top, a short detour leads to Butter Hill, where you can admire the surrounding mountains from its balding pate: Black Rock and Schunnemunk to the west, and Storm King and Breakneck Ridge to the east.

Descend back to the cairn that marked the terminus of the Bluebird Trail. Climb east in the direction of the yellow blazes first, and then look for the solid blue blazes of the Howell Trail. This passage of the hike involves a fair amount of up and down, and for much of the way you'll be traversing rugged terrain in a counterclockwise direction. Where the blue blazes meet the Bypass Trail just after mile 2, turn left (east), following the white blazes that hug the southern slope of Storm King. Ten minutes of walking will deliver you to a weather-worn shelf of rock that looks down on the town of Cold Spring across the river, and directly below, the CSX railroad.

The payoff is around a final bend, 0.1 mile north of the overlook at the end of the Bypass Trail. An open summit that plunges almost straight down also provides a majestic view for miles and miles. The river widens considerably at this spot, creating the illusion that Storm King rises uncontested from the waterway like a mighty island. The ruins of a Scottish-style castle on (Pollepel) Bannerman's Island—destroyed by an explosion in 1920 and then further damaged by fire—can be seen clearly from this high point, as can Dennings Point and the Newburgh-Beacon Bridge.

To return to your car, follow the yellow blazes/teal diamonds around the nose of the mountain and proceed carefully downhill. Loose stone on a narrow track makes for treacherous footing in places. At mile 3.5, the small cairn will look familiar—to the left is the Bluebird Trail you took on the outbound trip. Stay to the right on the Stillman Trail and arrive back at the gate and trailhead in another mile.

MILES AND DIRECTIONS

0.0 Start from the parking area, stepping over the large chain intended to prevent vehicles from accessing the yellow-blazed Stillman Trail. This route begins by following a woods road up a gentle incline.

0.4 Cross an old stone bridge and then look for yellow trail blazes to the left (north) after another few hundred feet. Leave the woods road behind at this point.

The view north from Storm King encompasses Bannerman's Island, Breakneck Ridge, and the Newburgh-Beacon Bridge.

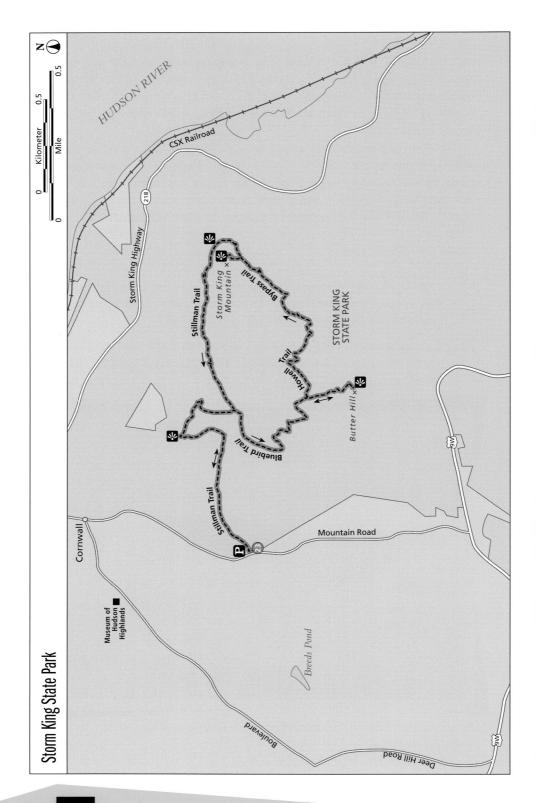

Storm King State Park

0.6 Reach a clearing and a scenic view to the northeast about 500 feet above the river.

0.9 The trail forks. Follow the Bluebird Trail's red/blue blazes to the right (west) up a fairly short but challenging ascent.

1.1 At the cairn, turn left onto a grassy path and continue along the well-defined path. (Ignore the erroneous turn blazes at 1.3 miles.) Proceed up a steep staircase of stone.

1.5 A second, larger cairn signals the end of the blue- and red-blazed Bluebird Trail. Back on the yellow Stillman Trail, continue southwest (straight ahead) through blueberries and scrub.

1.7 Arrive at the summit of Butter Hill. You will have views in all directions and a patch of warm rock to stretch out on for a few minutes before tackling the next climb.

1.9 Back at the intersection with the Bluebird Trail, turn right to remain on the Stillman Trail and head toward the summit of Storm King, gaining elevation as you go. Stay to the right at the fork to pick up the blue Howell Trail, which plunges back down the southern face for several hundred feet.

2.2 Turn left (east) off of the Howell Trail onto the white-blazed Bypass Trail.

2.4 Turn around on the ledge for a view back to Butter Hill and US 9W.

2.6 The Bypass Trail ends. The Stillman Trail leads in two directions from here: up to the main overlook (left), and back down the north face of the mountain (straight ahead). Dash up for the view and then start downhill from the end of the Bypass Trail.

3.4 After following the trail downhill along the rather sheer slope of Storm King, descend a short flight of wooden stairs built into the cliff.

3.5 Return to the original junction with the Bluebird Trail and keep to the right.

4.5 Arrive back at the trailhead and the Mountain Road parking area.

🐾 **Green Tip:**
For rest stops, go off-trail so others won't have to get around you. Head for resilient surfaces without vegetation.

Local information: Orange County Tourism, 124 Main St., Goshen, NY 10924; (845) 615-3860; www.orangetourism.org

Local events/attractions: Storm King Art Center, Old Pleasant Hill Road, Mountainville, NY 10953; (845) 534-3115; www.stormking.org. Open Wed through Sun from Apr 1 to Nov 14.

Hudson Highlands Nature Museum, 25 Boulevard, Cornwall-on-Hudson, NY 12520; (845) 534-7781; www.hhnaturemuseum.org

Good eats: Woody's, 30 Quaker Dr., Cornwall, NY 12520; (845) 534-1111; www.woodysallnatural.com. Arguably the best burger in the Hudson Valley. (The milkshakes aren't bad, either.)

Hudson Street Cafe, 237 Hudson St., Cornwall-on-Hudson, NY 12520; (845) 534-2450; www.hudsonstreetcafe.com

Hike Tours: Storm King Adventure Tours, 178 Hudson St., Cornwall-on-Hudson, NY 12520; (845) 534-7800; www.stormkingadventuretours.com

Organizations: Scenic Hudson, One Civic Center Plaza, Suite 200, Poughkeepsie, NY 12601; (845) 473-4440; www.scenichudson.org. A pioneering environmental group dedicated to protecting and restoring the Hudson River.

New York-New Jersey Trail Conference, 156 Ramapo Valley Rd., Mahwah, NJ 07430-1199; (201) 512-9348; www.nynjtc.org

The Castle in the Hudson

Stand atop Storm King or Sugarloaf Mountain and you can't miss it: a rocky island near the eastern shore of the Hudson crowned by what looks to be, for all intents and purposes, the ruins of a majestic castle. Your eyes do not deceive you. Needing a larger place to store the military equipment he had amassed as a professional munitions dealer, New Yorker Francis Bannerman began to build a castle on the tiny landmass just north of Breakneck Point in 1901. Styled after the fortified residences of his native Scotland, it would serve as a warehouse and a summer retreat for the family for many years after Bannerman himself passed away in 1918. Harsh winters, vandalism, and a powder house explosion have damaged the structure considerably, but several tour companies lead seasonal trips out to the island (also known as Pollepel) by kayak and passenger boat. While officially part of Hudson Highlands State Park, the island is maintained by The Bannerman Castle Trust, Inc.

Sugarloaf Hill

This hike in the east Hudson Highlands promises views of West Point, Anthony's Nose, the Bear Mountain Bridge, and a curious mansion called Castle Rock. Cover the distance out and back in a matter of hours or use a full day to explore the Osborn Preserve section of Hudson Highlands State Park, which includes a short segment of the Appalachian Trail.

Start: Arden Point trailhead in the Metro North parking area

Nearest town: Garrison, NY

Distance: 4.9 miles out and back

Approximate hiking time: 2.5 hours

Difficulty: Easy to moderate, with one short but serious climb

Trail surface: Open meadow, level dirt footpath, and a few sections of steeper, forest paths

Seasons: Mar through Oct

Other trail users: Hunters (seasonally)

Wheelchair accessibility: None

Canine compatibility: Dogs permitted on leashes 10 feet or less

Land status: State park

Fees and permits: None

Schedule: Daily from sunrise to sunset

Facilities: None

Maps: USGS Peekskill, NY. A map of Castle Rock Unique Area can be downloaded from the New York State Department of Environmental Conservation website (see below).

Trail contacts: New York State Office of Parks, Recreation & Historic Preservation, Regional Office Contact Information, P.O. Box 308/9 Old Post Rd., Staatsburgh, NY 12580; (845) 889-4100; www.nysparks.state.ny.us

New York State Department of Environmental Conservation, Region 3 Headquarters, 21 South Putt Corners, New Paltz, NY 12561; (845) 256-3000; www.dec.ny.gov/lands/34747.html

Finding the trailhead: By car from US 9 north, turn left on Route 403/Cat Rock Road. Continue northwest across Route 9D; at this point the name changes to Lower Station Road. Look for parking and the trailhead on the left after 0.6 mile. Alternatively, there is a limited amount of parking at the Castle Rock Unique Area off Route 9D. **By public transportation:** The hamlet of Garrison is just over an hour's ride from Grand Central Station by train. From the northbound platform, enter the gravel parking lot and walk toward Lower Station Road. A sign for the Arden Point Trail is near the tree line at the southeastern corner of the lot. GPS: N41 22.795' / W73 56.829'

Starting out in the wooded area bordering the train tracks, this trip to the top of Sugarloaf Hill (so named for the conical shape that refined sugar was sold in until the nineteenth century) is hardly a strenuous hike, and yet it offers a pleasant vantage point from which to view the Bear Mountain Bridge and the US Military Academy at West Point. Bothersome mosquitoes whining at ear level may slow your pace somewhat, but strong hikers can reach the summit in less than two hours. Walking almost due south over flat terrain, you'll pass a brick structure that's been all but reclaimed by native vegetation, and a small wooden bridge will carry you across Arden Brook. Reaching a fork after nearly 0.5 mile, bear slightly to the left (southeast) instead of taking the bridge over the railroad, and watch for white trail markers reading Marcia's Mile.

The trail soon jogs left (east), up a small incline and around a diminutive pond. Emerging from the woods after 0.2 mile, you'll pick up the route to Sugarloaf on the other side of Route 9D. Having carefully crossed the road, step over a low stone wall and traverse an overgrown field blanketed with bright white daisies and yellow buttercups, roughly aiming for the red barn on the hill up ahead. Peering down from its perch above the river valley, Castle Rock, with its medieval appearance and red slate roof, gives its name to the surrounding acres. Built as a retirement home for the nineteenth-century railroad baron William Henry Osborn, the residence remains private property, although the Osborn family gifted much of the former estate to New York.

Following the gravel drive for a short distance, the trail now turns left (east) again, cutting through a second meadow on its way to a gazebo that is sometimes obscured by low-hanging tree branches. Turn around here, before proceeding into Hudson Highlands State Park, for your first good look at West Point.

Beyond this point the Sugarloaf trail zigzags south, guiding you around old stone walls, rocky creekbeds, and the occasional rotting log as you gradually gain 200 feet in elevation. An unmarked trail enters from the left as you circle back toward the Hudson. Stick to the red blazes and don't be confused by this spur, which leads into private property. The throaty sound of frogs calling out to each will tell you that a pond is nearby; once you've passed this small body of water, the junction with the blue-blazed Osborn Loop trail will be about 0.2 mile farther along.

Make a sharp right (west) turn here and begin a short but steep ascent to a thin ridge that runs southwest to a rocky overlook. From this height above the river it's possible to see Bear Mountain Bridge, West Point, and the shapes of watercraft 600 feet below your perch. On a sunny summer day, you're likely to share this overlook with other hikers, in addition to the hawks and vultures winging by overhead.

From the summit, retrace your steps to return to the Arden Point trailhead and the Garrison train station.

MILES AND DIRECTIONS

0.0   Start at the signed Arden Point trailhead located at the southeastern limit of the Metro North parking lot. Follow this flat trail south past a crumbling brick building facade on the right.

0.2   Cross the wooden bridge over Arden Brook.

0.5   The red Arden Point Trail heads across the railroad tracks to the right. Stay on the blue-blazed trail for a short distance and then veer to the left (southeast), in the direction of the plastic Marcia's Mile tags tacked to tree trunks.

0.8   Head left (east) over a tiny ridge and through a clearing. Sugarloaf awaits beyond this patch of parkland along the river. Cross Route 9D and continue east into Castle Rock Unique Area. Red blazes now lead through a meadow and uphill toward the tree line.

1.5   Turn right (south) onto a woods road where the field ends. A small wooden gazebo stands at this intersection, providing a view west.

1.6   After initially using a woods road, the Sugarloaf trail makes another right turn (east), climbs uphill alongside a stream, and eventually veers right once more where the slope levels off. Many trees in this area appear to have been badly damaged by a forest fire.

Some of the creatures native to the region have more than four legs.

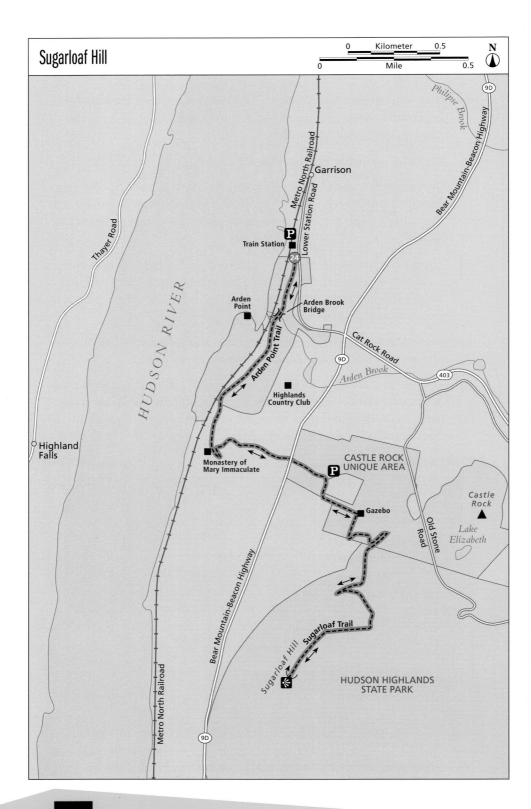

Sugarloaf Hill

Kilometer 0 — 0.5
Mile 0 — 0.5

N

Philipse Brook

9D

Metro North Railroad

Garrison

Lower Station Road

Bear Mountain-Beacon Highway

P
Train Station

24

Arden Point

Arden Brook Bridge

Arden Point Trail

HUDSON RIVER

Cat Rock Road

9D

Arden Brook

403

Highlands Country Club

Highland Falls

Monastery of Mary Immaculate

P

CASTLE ROCK UNIQUE AREA

Gazebo

Thayer Road

Castle Rock

Lake Elizabeth

Old Stone Road

Bear Mountain-Beacon Highway

Sugarloaf Hill

Sugarloaf Trail

HUDSON HIGHLANDS STATE PARK

Metro North Railroad

9D

2.3   Beyond a small pond, the blue Osborn Loop trail enters from the left (east) while the Sugarloaf Trail turns right (west). Begin to ascend the hill on the Sugarloaf Trail, quickly gaining close to 200 feet in elevation. Follow the narrow ridge southwest.

2.4   Rest at the scenic overlook, have a snack, listen for the long horn of an Amtrak engine on the train tracks below, and watch as birds of prey wheel and glide on the air currents. Once you've regained your energy, retrace your route back.

4.9   Arrive back at the Arden Point trailhead.

Option: Another 4.5 miles can be added to this hike by continuing straight (south) through the junction with the Osborn Loop, sticking to the blue-blazed trail. Turn left (east) before reaching Canada Hill, and then return north along the ridgeline on a section of the Appalachian Trail.

HIKE INFORMATION

Local information: Putnam County Visitors Bureau, 110 Old Rte. 6, Bldg. 3, Carmel, NY 10512; (800) 470-4854; www.visitputnam.org

Local events/attractions: Garrison Art Center, 23 Garrison's Landing/P.O. Box 4, Garrison, NY 10524; (845) 424-3960; www.garrisonartcenter.org

Boscobel House and Gardens, 1601 Rte. 9D, Garrison, NY 10524; (845) 265-3638; www.boscobel.org. A large neoclassical-style mansion built in 1808 for the Dyckman family. Decorated with Federal period art and surrounded by gardens and orchards, this property also hosts the Hudson Valley Shakespeare Festival.

Local outdoor stores: Hudson Valley Outfitters, 63 Main St., Cold Spring, NY 10516; (845) 265-0221; www.hudsonvalleyoutfitters.com

Hike tours: Wild Earth Adventures, P.O. Box 88, Suffern, NY 10901; (845) 357-3380; www.wildearthadventures.com

Organizations: Friends of Fahnestock and Hudson Highlands State Parks, P.O. Box 194, Cold Spring, NY 10516; www.fofhh.org. Founded in 2007 to preserve, protect, and improve these historic and natural resources.

Hudson River Valley Greenway, Capitol Building, Room 254, Albany, NY 12224; (518) 473-3835; www.hudsongreenway.state.ny.us

Other resources: The Open Space Institute, a research and conservation organization, offers a free "Train to the Trail" brochure in the publications section of their website, www.osiny.org.

Study native and endangered wildflower species, learn about the natural history of the Hudson Highlands, and stretch your legs on 15 miles of hiking trails that radiate out from the nature center around Teatown Lake, Shadow Lake, and, farther west, Cliffdale Farm.

Start: Behind the nature center; south of Teatown Lake
Nearest town: Croton-on-Hudson, NY
Distance: 3.5-mile interlocking loops
Approximate hiking time: 2 hours
Difficulty: Easy to moderate
Trail surface: Primarily dirt footpaths, with some sections of grass and gravel
Seasons: Year-round
Other trail users: Joggers; cross-country skiers and snowshoers (seasonally)
Wheelchair accessibility: None
Canine compatibility: Leashed dogs permitted
Land status: Nonprofit membership organization
Fees and permits: No fees, but donations strongly encouraged
Schedule: Daily from sunrise to sunset
Facilities: Bathrooms, water fountain, gift shop, nature center, bee and butterfly garden, working maple sugar house
Maps: USGS Ossining, NY. A color map of the hiking trails can be printed from the Teatown Lake Reservation website (see below) or purchased for a small fee at the nature center (closed Mon).
Trail contacts: Teatown Lake Reservation, 1600 Spring Valley Rd., Ossining, NY 10562; (914) 762-2912; www.teatown.org

Finding the trailhead: Take the Saw Mill River Parkway north from New York and exit onto the Taconic State Parkway. Follow the Taconic State Parkway north and exit at Route 134/Ossining. Turn left at the bottom of the exit ramp onto Route 134/Kitchawan Road, passing under the Taconic parkway. Drive for 0.25 mile and turn right on Spring Valley Road. Drive 1 mile, bearing left at the fork on Spring Valley Road, to reach the nature center. The main parking lot will be on the right immediately after the nature center. The trailhead is behind the center. GPS: N41 12.695' / W73 49.617'

THE HIKE

N ew York doesn't lack for hikes that appeal to birders, history lovers, and those who like nothing more than a good view. Fans of wildflowers however, need look no further than Teatown Lake Reservation, a parcel of land originally gifted to the Brooklyn Botanic Garden by the Swopes family in 1963. Beginning as a humble outreach center that offered a few nature classes and activities, the reservation has evolved into a larger center of environmental education for Westchester County, a nonprofit organization with a robust range of public offerings including a unique island refuge for over 230 species of wildflowers.

Created by Director of Education Warren Balgooyen, with assistance from Marjorie Swope, in 1982, Wildflower Island is the centerpiece of Teatown, containing several diverse habitats (dry woodland, low moist woodland, marsh, and bog) within its two-acre shape. Although it can only be visited on specific days for half of the year, a trip over the wooden bridge is not to be missed. Arrive in April to see blue, white, and cream-colored violets in bloom. Turn up in May and observe

The painted lady butterfly is also known as the thistle butterfly, due to its fondness for the nectar of this particular plant.

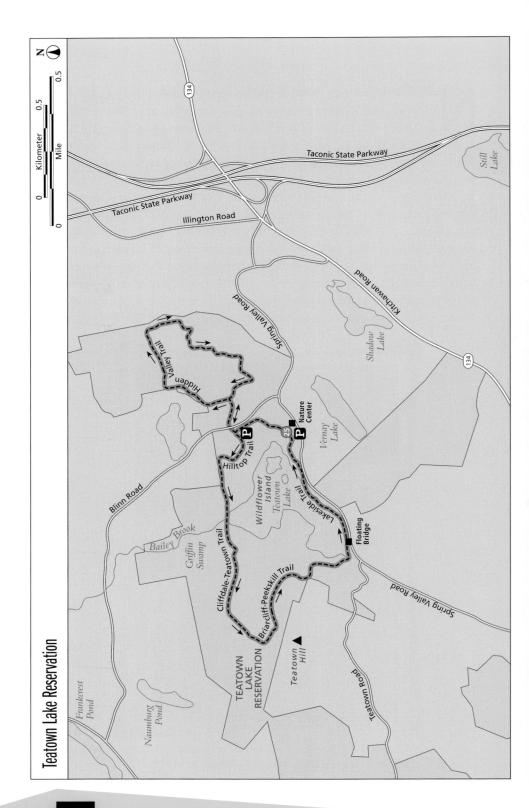

Teatown Lake Reservation

Still Lake

Taconic State Parkway

Taconic State Parkway

Illington Road

134

Kitchawan Road

Spring Valley Road

Shadow Lake

134

Valley Trail

Hidden

Nature Center

25

Vernay Lake

Hilltop Trail

Wildflower Island

Teatown Lake

Lakeside Trail

Floating Bridge

Blinn Road

Bailey Brook

Griffin Swamp

Cliffdale-Teatown Trail

Briarcliff-Peekskill Trail

Spring Valley Road

Frankcrest Pond

TEATOWN LAKE RESERVATION

Teatown Hill

Teatown Road

Naumburg Pond

N

Kilometer

0   0.5

0   0.5

Mile

the bell-shaped Jacob's ladder flower or the five pink petals of the ragged robin. The bright orange butterfly weed blooms in June, attracting its namesake insects. July brings the black-eyed Susan to life, along with the yellow flag iris, the heraldic symbol for French royalty.

But before getting lost in the flowering plants that thrive on the island, spend some time exploring the vernal pools, rocky outcroppings, and shrublands scattered around the rest of Teatown. A very short distance down the Hidden Valley Trail, pause to gawk at the caged animals such as the solitary porcupine, one of the largest rodents on the planet, or the omnivorous opossum, which boasts fifty teeth—more than any other North American mammal. In the northeastern section of the reservation, expect to encounter a narrow trail that winds through a pine grove, a damp marsh, and an abundance of mountain laurel. After completing this first loop in a clockwise direction, backtrack to the Hilltop Trail and walk west to the lake.

This 0.5-mile length of the path maneuvers around several stone walls and then dead-ends near the water, where you'll briefly join the Lakeside Trail to begin the second loop. Head back under tree cover on the Cliffdale/Teatown Trail as it snakes west past a shortcut trail and Griffin Swamp to the north. Turn left and follow the yellow and green blazes up the flank of Teatown Hill on the Briarcliff/Peekskill Trail, which crosses the white blazes of the Cliffdale/Teatown Trail at the northeastern edge of this landform. This is the toughest section of the hike, but fortunately it's only 1 mile back to the nature center from the top of the hill. Take a water break at the summit and then continue south in a counterclockwise direction, following the yellow and green blazes, until they meet the shore trail at the southwestern corner of the lake. Use the floating bridge that parallels Teatown Road to get across the water, and stick to the Lakeside Trail for the remaining 0.5 mile back to the trailhead.

MILES AND DIRECTIONS

0.0 Start behind the nature center, south of the lake. The large map board should help with orientation.

0.1 Head northeast on the Hidden Valley Trail past the Lakeside parking lot.

0.2 Walk by the orange Hilltop Trail and cross Blinn Road to begin the first of the two loops on this hike.

0.3 Step through a gap in an old stone wall and enter a meadow on the side of a small hill. Make a sharp left (north) at the four-way intersection to remain on the red-blazed Hidden Valley Trail.

0.6 Having traced the edge of the property line, turn right (east) and continue past the Overlook trailhead, which rises sharply up the cliff to your left.

0.8 Turn right (south) and use a short stretch of boardwalk to get over a patch of marshy terrain. Proceed up the steep slope ahead.

1.3 Take another sharp right onto a woods road and then keep left where the trail forks at the meadow. Retrace your steps westward back to the orange-blazed Hilltop Trail. The second loop starts here.

1.7 Arrive at the top of another hill, where a bench offers a resting place for the weary. The elevation here is approximately 400 feet.

1.9 The Hilltop Trail ends on the north shore of Teatown Lake. A dam at the end of Bailey Brook led to the freshwater lake you see here. Stick to the Lakeside Trail for 100 feet or so and then walk west on the white-blazed Cliffdale/Teatown Trail.

2.3 Turn left (southwest) on the Briarcliff/Peekskill Trail and begin to work your way around Teatown Hill. The trail steepens after about 0.1 mile and rapidly climbs 200 feet up a stony slope.

2.5 Arrive at the top of Teatown Hill. Follow the yellow and green blazes east down the other side and underneath the electric towers.

2.9 Rejoin the Lakeside Trail and continue south through the forest.

3.0 Turn left (east) and cross the southern part of the lake on a floating bridge also called the Bergman Boardwalk.

3.4 Pass the wrought iron gates leading to Wildflower Island, to the left of the Lakeside Trail. Admission to the island is by guided tour only (a small fee for members; a larger fee for nonmembers).

3.5 Arrive back at the trailhead and the main parking area on the west side of the nature center.

> **🌿 Green Tip:**
> *Never let your dog chase wildlife.*

HIKE INFORMATION

Local information: Westchester County Tourism & Film, 222 Mamaroneck Ave., White Plains, NY 10605; (914) 995-8500; www.westchestertourism.com

Village of Croton-on-Hudson, 1 Van Wyck St., Croton-on-Hudson, NY 10520; (914) 271-4781; http://village.croton-on-hudson.ny.us

Local events/attractions: Van Cortlandt Manor, 525 South Riverside Ave., Croton-on-Hudson, NY 10520; (914) 271-8981; www.hudsonvalley.org/content/view/15/45/

Brinton Brook Sanctuary, Saw Mill River Audubon, 275 Millwood Rd., Chappaqua, New York 10514; (914) 666-6503; www.sawmillriveraudubon.org/Brinton.html. Three miles of hiking trails on 156 acres north of Croton.

John Jay Homestead State Historic Site, 400 Jay St./P.O. Box 832, Katonah, NY 10536; (914) 232-5651; www.nysparks.com/historic-sites/4/details.aspx. Home of the president of the Continental Congress, the first chief justice of the US Supreme Court, and the second governor of New York State.

Good eats: Grouchy Gabe's Grill, 8 Old Post Rd. South, Croton-on-Hudson, NY 10520; (914) 271-9690; www.grouchygabe.com. Soups, salads, paninis, and wraps in a deli/art gallery.

The Black Cow Coffee Company Inc., 64 Maple St., Croton-on-Hudson, NY 10520; (914) 271-7544; www.blackcow.com

Blue Pig Ice Cream Factory, 121 Maple St., Croton-on-Hudson, NY 10520; (914) 271-3850. Up to three scoops of gourmet, all-natural ice cream at reasonable prices.

Local outdoor stores: American Terrain Outdoors, 175 East Post Rd., White Plains, NY 10601; (914) 682-3971; www.americanterrain.com

Kelloggs & Lawrence, 26 Parkway, Katonah, NY 10536; (914) 232-3351; www.kelloggsandlawrence.com

Hike tours: Teatown regularly schedules bird walks, guided tours of Wildflower Island, and seasonal festivals for all ages. Check the online calendar for details.

Organizations: Hudson River Valley Greenway, Capitol Building, Capitol Station, Room 254, Albany, NY 12224; (518) 473-3835; www.hudsongreenway.state.ny.us

Friends of John Jay Homestead, P.O. Box 148, Katonah, NY 10536; (914) 232-8119; www.johnjayhomestead.org

Van Cortlandt Park

An oasis of green at the top of the Bronx, Van Cortlandt Park has watched the area evolve from rich farmland into a corridor for trains and drinking water, and exists today as fourth largest park in New York City, encompassing 1,146 acres.

Start: The Van Cortlandt House Museum

Nearest town: Riverdale, NY

Distance: 6.5 miles out and back

Approximate hiking time: 2 to 3 hours

Difficulty: Easy

Trail surface: Worn pavement, crushed stone, packed earth

Seasons: Year-round

Other trail users: Joggers, dog walkers, cyclists, equestrians

Wheelchair accessibility: Disabled parking is available and portions of the trail are wheelchair accessible.

Canine compatibility: Leashed dogs permitted

Land status: City park

Fees and permits: None

Schedule: Daily from dawn to dusk

Facilities: Restrooms can be found at four different points along this hike and a picnic area is located southwest of the museum, just behind the pool.

Maps: USGS Flushing, NY. A glossy, full-color map of the park is available at the nature center.

Trail contacts: New York City Department of Parks & Recreation, The Arsenal, Central Park, 830 5th Ave., New York, NY 10065; (212) NEW-YORK; www.nycgovparks.org

Finding the trailhead: Take the Number 1 Train to 242nd Street/Van Cortlandt Park. Leave the subway platform and cross over to the park side of Broadway. Keeping the park on your right, walk away from the subway up Broadway to the driveway into Van Cortlandt Park, flanked by planter boxes. The park can also be reached via MTA Bus BX9, which travels along the western edge of the park and stops at 262nd and 244th Streets; the BXM3 express bus that stops at 244th Street; and Westchester Bee-Line buses 1, 2, and 3. Many of these bus stops are located adjacent to the park driveway leading to Van Cortlandt House Museum. GPS: N40 53.482' / W73 53.698'

I n 1694, Jacobus Van Cortlandt, the son of a wealthy Dutch merchant, began purchasing land for a wheat plantation in what is now the Bronx. His only son, Frederick, eventually inherited the property and built a stately home in the Georgian
style here in 1748. The plantation and the mills thrived, and during the Revolutionary War, both George Washington and British General Sir William Howe used the
house as a temporary headquarters. The family sold the entire estate to the City of
New York in 1886, and ten years later, it was restored as a historic house museum,
the first such landmark in the city.

Beginning alongside the wrought iron fence that surrounds the old home,
follow the paved path east, past the nature center and the tennis courts. At the T
intersection, bear right (southwest) to join the John Kieran Nature Trail. Shadows
will stretch over this short section of the hike as you move away from open fields
and meadows into the shelter of woodland. Turn left (southeast) at the southern
end of Van Cortlandt Lake and listen for American robins whistling and starlings
buzzing and chirping in the underbrush. Crossing a small bridge, you'll have a better view of the lake, initially created when Jacobus Van Cortlandt dammed Tibbetts
Brook to power a gristmill and a sawmill.

At different times, both George Washington and British General Sir William Howe used Van Cortlandt
House as their headquarters during the American Revolution.

At this point the route merges with the Putnam Trail, a former rail bed for the New York Central Railroad. Here and there, decaying railroad ties are still visible. As the flat and occasionally muddy track heads north, you'll pass by a curious collection of thirteen pillars just to the left. The Grand Central Stones, as they're called, were actually placed there by the railroad to determine the most durable building material for the facade of Manhattan's Grand Central Terminal. The two columns of Indiana limestone on the far right (which happened to be the cheapest to transport) ended up as the stone of choice.

Shortly before the 1-mile mark, turn left (west), skirt the fenced-off golf course, and duck under overhanging branches on the way to the edge of the parade ground. Emerging from this narrow, rather overgrown section of trail at a towering sycamore tree, you'll make a sharp right (north) turn and continue for about 0.1 mile on the wide, paved path before reentering the woods. Near the summit of Vault Hill is the burial plot of the Van Cortlandt family, a stone-walled structure perched atop the Fordham gneiss that protrudes from this part of the park. Just above the cemetery, a rocky outcropping more than 165 feet above sea level offers views of the Manhattan skyline on clear afternoons.

From here the hike heads downhill on a well-maintained cross-country running course and then, once across the Henry Hudson Parkway, turns right (northeast) to meet the Cass Gallagher Nature Trail in the Northwest Forest. Ascending a steep staircase, this leaf-covered trail leads through thickets of fragrant multiflora rose, past patches of bright green fern, and beneath a canopy of tulip, white oak, hickory, and black cherry trees. Keep walking north over the small dips and rises in the cracked pavement until the trail guides you west and then south once again. Faint gold blazes on tree trunks will be helpful at forks and intersections. Away from the more heavily trafficked areas of the park, it's possible to see an eastern cottontail or the occasional pheasant.

The Cass Gallagher Nature Trail meets the John Muir Nature Trail just west of Rockwood Circle. Turn right (northwest) and follow this route a short distance to the turnaround point. Peer into the riding stable here and then return to the Van Cortlandt House the way you came.

Over half of Van Cortlandt Park is a protected nature preserve, which means scenic trails abound in this expanse of public land bordering Westchester County.

MILES AND DIRECTIONS

0.0 Start next to the Van Cortlandt House Museum on the paved multiuse path. Walk by the nature center and the tennis courts.

0.4 Turn right (southwest) on the John Kieran Nature Trail. Follow it around the southern end of Van Cortlandt Lake and make a left at the bridge onto the Putnam Trail.

0.8 Veer right (east) off the Putnam Trail after passing the Grand Central Stones and take the path that hugs the lake shoreline, weaving between birches and willows.

0.9 Rejoin the Putnam Trail and proceed north over a bridge on the western side of the lake where Tibbetts Brook flows into it from the north.

1.1 Make a sharp left (west) back onto the John Kieran Nature Trail, passing between the golf course (behind a chain-link fence on the right) and a marshy area to the left.

1.3 Turn right (north) at a huge sycamore tree on the edge of the parade ground. Stay on the paved multiuse path briefly, then take the next right (northeast) turn and immediately look for a trail heading into the woods on the left.

1.5 Make a left off the crushed stone cross-country route you joined on your way up the hill and stop at the Van Cortlandt family burial vault.

1.6 Climb up and over the bare stone above the vault to reach an overlook above the parade ground, with views south toward Manhattan. Turn around and find the cross-country trail that leads down the back of Vault Hill to an overpass across the Henry Hudson Parkway.

1.8 Turn right before you reach Rockwood Circle. Parallel the parkway for a short stretch as it curves east. Then jog left off the crushed gravel trail onto the Cass Gallagher Nature Trail.

1.9 Take the staircase to the right (east) and watch for Cass Gallagher's fading gold blazes as the trail wriggles deeper into the Northwest Forest on its way to the Westchester County line.

2.4 Cross the cross-country route again, but continue straight through the intersection as the Cass Gallagher Trail gains some elevation and circles back south. Rather than choose other side trails, keep to the left.

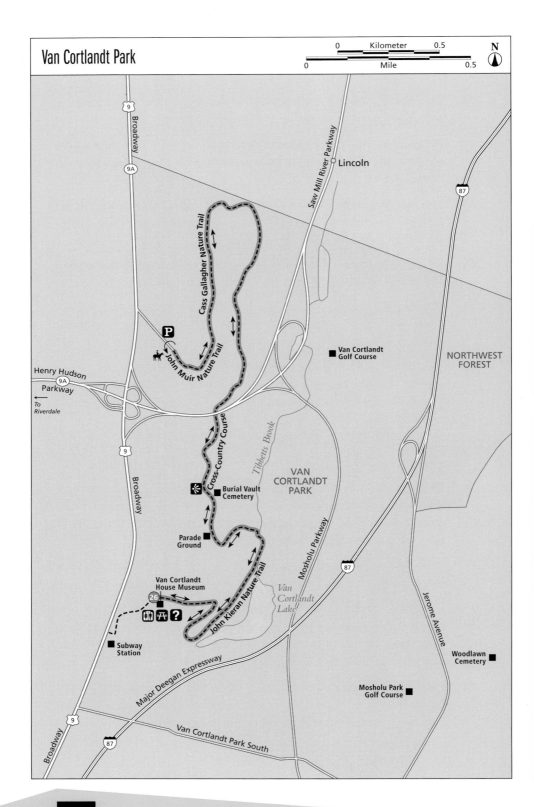

Van Cortlandt Park

0 — Kilometer — 0.5

0 — Mile — 0.5

N

Broadway

9

9A

Cass Gallagher Nature Trail

Lincoln

Saw Mill River Parkway

87

P

John Muir Nature Trail

Van Cortlandt Golf Course

NORTHWEST FOREST

Henry Hudson

9A

Parkway

To Riverdale

9

Broadway

Cross-Country Course

Tibbetts Brook

VAN CORTLANDT PARK

Burial Vault Cemetery

Parade Ground

Mosholu Parkway

87

Van Cortlandt Lake

Van Cortlandt House Museum

26

John Kieran Nature Trail

Jerome Avenue

Subway Station

Woodlawn Cemetery

Major Deegan Expressway

Mosholu Park Golf Course

9

Broadway

87

Van Cortlandt Park South

2.9   Proceed south through another intersection with the cross-country course. Veer right (west) at two consecutive forks as the terrain flattens and make a sharp right (northwest) onto the John Muir Nature Trail.

3.2   Pass the riding stable on the left and arrive at a sign indicating the start of the John Muir Trail. Learn a bit about the naturalist and author who inspired the route and then retrace your footsteps back to the beginning of the hike.

6.5   Arrive back at the trailhead next to the Van Cortlandt House Museum.

HIKE INFORMATION

Local information: The Bronx Tourism Council, The Bronx County Building, 851 Grand Concourse, Suite 123, Bronx, NY 10451; (718) 590-3518; www.ilovethe bronx.com

Local events/attractions: Van Cortlandt House Museum, Broadway at West 246th Street, Bronx, NY 10471; (718) 543-3344; www.vancortlandthouse.org. This eighteenth-century Georgian mansion is the oldest building in the Bronx. Closed Mon and major holidays.
Wave Hill, West 249th Street and Independence Avenue (front gate)/675 West 252nd St. (mailing), Bronx, NY 10471; (718) 549-3200; www.wavehill .org. A twenty-eight-acre public garden and cultural center overlooking the Palisades.

Local outdoor stores: Paragon Sports, 867 Broad-way, New York, NY 10003; (212) 255-8036; www .paragonsports.com
Tent & Trails, 21 Park Place, New York, NY 10007-2591; (212) 227-1760; www.tenttrails.com

Organizations: Friends of Van Cortlandt Park, 124 Gale Place, Apt. GrA, Bronx, NY 10463; (718) 601-1553; www.vancortlandt.org
New York City Audubon, 71 West 23rd St., Suite 1523, New York, NY 10010; (212) 691-7483; www.nycaudubon.org. A grassroots community organization that works for the protection of wild birds and habitat in the five boroughs.

Walkway Over the Hudson

Feel like you're walking on water with a visit to New York's newest park and arguably, one of the most breathtaking views in the Empire State. Instead of a simple out-and-back hike on the longest pedestrian walkway in the world, follow the loop trail and cross back over the river via the Franklin D. Roosevelt Mid-Hudson Bridge.

Start: Parking lot on Haviland Road
Nearest town: Highland, NY
Distance: 3.7-mile loop
Approximate hiking time: 2 hours
Difficulty: Easy
Trail surface: Pavement, multiuse cement slabs
Seasons: Year-round
Other trail users: Joggers, cyclists, in-line skaters
Wheelchair accessibility: Disabled parking is located at both ends of the bridge; motorized scooters are allowed in addition to wheelchairs.
Canine compatibility: Dogs permitted on leashes 6 feet long or less
Land status: State historic park
Fees and permits: None
Schedule: Daily from 7 a.m. until sunset

Facilities: Restrooms at both ends of the bridge
Maps: USGS Poughkeepsie, NY. A map of the walkway loop trail is available at the trailhead and can be downloaded from the New York State parks department website or the Walkway Over the Hudson organization's website (see below).
Special considerations: The loop trail is not for people with a fear of heights.
Trail contacts: Walkway Over the Hudson State Historic Park, 87 Haviland Rd. (west entrance/park office), Highland, NY 12528; (845) 834-2867; www.nysparks.com Walkway Over the Hudson, P.O. Box 889, Poughkeepsie, NY 12602; (845) 454-9649; www.walkway.org

Finding the trailhead: Driving north on US 9W, make a right-hand exit onto Haviland Road. Continue down Haviland for approximately 0.5 mile until you see a sign for the park entrance. Walkway Over the Hudson can also be accessed from the Metro North Poughkeepsie station on the other side of the river. GPS: N41 42.641' / W73 57.269'

THE HIKE

or all of its recreational, economic, and historic importance, the Muhheakantuck (to use the Mohican name), or the North River (as the Dutch first referred to it), is certainly pleasing to the eye. Many of the hikes near New York City culminate in peaks or ledges that elevate the Hudson, the state's largest waterway, to a thing of beauty. But nowhere can it be better appreciated than from New York's newest park: Walkway Over the Hudson.

Extending from Poughkeepsie on the east bank to Highland on the west, this trail became the world's longest elevated walkway when it opened to the public in October 2009. And the structure it sits atop was no less exceptional in its day either. When the Highland railroad bridge started carrying trains in 1889, it was the only all-rail route over the Hudson south of Albany. Much of the early freight that rode those rails was coal bound for New York City. But it also had another claim to fame at the time it was built: It was the longest cantilevered truss bridge in the world.

Stepping out onto the deck of the walkway, you'll be 212 feet above the riverbed, which was created by an ice field some 16,000 years ago. Today birds such as

From Highland, New York, the Walkway Over the Hudson stretches 6,767 feet to Poughkeepsie, making it the world's longest pedestrian bridge.

ring-billed gulls, double-breasted cormorants, and common mergansers feed on the aquatic life supported by the waterway, although spotting them without binoculars may be somewhat difficult. Nonetheless, the unique perspective afforded by this historic park encourages visitors to proceed along the multiuse path at a leisurely pace.

Nearing Poughkeepsie on the east side of the Hudson, you'll learn about the history of this city's once busy docks, where ferries carried goods and passengers over the half-mile distance before the bridge was completed. Now a center of education, with four colleges including Vassar and the Culinary Institute of America in the area, in the nineteenth century Poughkeepsie's prosperity was due to the lumber yards, paper mills, whale rendering businesses, and breweries that sprung up here. The walkway passes over the Mount Carmel district as it enters the seat of Dutchess County, just north of the historic downtown.

To continue back across the Hudson via the well-marked Walkway Loop Trail, take the staircase on the left (north) just as it the park links with the Dutchess Rail Trail. At the bottom of the steps, turn left on Washington Street and then right on Verrazano Boulevard, which follows Fallkill Creek. The 1-mile walk to the Mid-Hudson Bridge leads through Wheaton Park and past the Poughkeepsie train station; a connecting trail from Main Street grants access to Waryas Park and the Mid-Hudson Children's Museum on the waterfront.

The appeal of taking the Mid-Hudson Bridge back to Highland in the west— besides the chance to see one of the peregrine falcons that nest here—is the ability to admire the Walkway Over the Hudson at a distance. From the multiuse path over the Mid-Hudson, walkers can survey the full length of the old railroad bridge while watercraft dart under its steel beams. Back in Ulster County, take one last look at the bridges from Johnson-Iorio Memorial Park, and then let Haviland Road guide you uphill to the walkway's western trailhead.

When racing toward their prey in a vertical dive called a stoop, peregrine falcons can reach speeds of 200 miles per hour or more.

MILES AND DIRECTIONS

0.0 Start by the informational kiosk at the Scenic Hudson Gate, a very short walk from the walkway's parking area.

0.5 Stand approximately mid-bridge and let your eyes wander over the topography of the river valley. Look for the campuses of the Culinary Institute of America and Marist College upriver, while 0.5 mile south, the gray silhouette of the Mid-Hudson Bridge blends into the sky.

1.4 At the end of the bridge, take the staircase on the left down to Washington Street and turn left (south). Pass under the walkway, look for a Loop Trail sign, and make a right turn (west) on Verrazano Boulevard.

1.8 Turn left (south) on Mill Street, cross to the sidewalk on the west side of the street, and enter Wheaton Park.

1.9 Take a left (south) on Davies Place and walk in the direction of the Poughkeepsie train station. Pass beneath the overpass and then turn right (west) on Main Street.

2.2 Turn left (south) on Rinaldi Boulevard and then right (west) on Gerald Drive. You should see a sign for Riverview Condos.

2.5 Arrive at the entrance to the Mid-Hudson Bridge and follow the ramp up to the deck.

Catch a view of the Franklin D. Roosevelt Mid-Hudson Bridge from Johnson-Iorio Memorial Park.

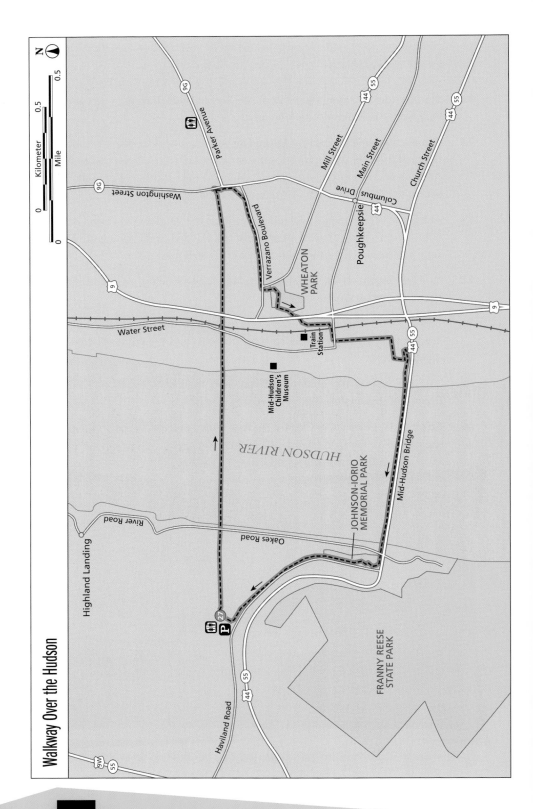

Walkway Over the Hudson

N

Kilometer
0   0.5   0.5
Mile
0   0.5

Parker Avenue

9G

Washington Street

9G

Verrazano Boulevard

WHEATON PARK

Water Street

9

Mill Street

Main Street

Columbus Drive

Poughkeepsie

44

Church Street

44 55

44 55

Train Station

Mid-Hudson Children's Museum

HUDSON RIVER

Mid-Hudson Bridge

JOHNSON-IORIO MEMORIAL PARK

River Road

Highland Landing

Oakes Road

FRANNY REESE STATE PARK

Haviland Road

44 55

9W 55

44 55

2.7 Reach the first Bridge Music listening station. Joseph Bertolozzi, a local composer and percussionist, recorded the sounds the bridge made when struck by a variety of objects, including a sledgehammer and a small log. He then mixed and edited them into a musical suite.

3.0 Arrive at the second Bridge Music listening station.

3.2 Enter Johnson-Iorio Memorial Park and take a minute to look back at the Mid-Hudson Bridge. There are benches in this small park if you want to rest longer.

3.7 Arrive back at the trailhead and parking lot on Haviland Road.

Option: Just south of the Mid-Hudson Bridge, a short connecting trail links the Walkway Loop to an easy 2.5-mile nature trail in Franny Reese State Park.

HIKE INFORMATION

Local information: Ulster County Tourism, 10 Westbrook Lane, Kingston, NY 12401; (845) 340-3566; www.ulstercountyalive.com

Local events/attractions: Historic Huguenot Street, 18 Broadhead Ave., New Paltz, NY 12561; (845) 255-1889; www.huguenotstreet.org. Learn about the founders of New Paltz by touring this National Historic Landmark district.

New Paltz Third Saturday, 350 Libertyville Rd., New Paltz, NY 12561; (845) 430-8470; www.newpaltzarts.org. A monthly art walk with stops at fourteen different galleries, museums, and cultural venues.

Mid-Hudson Children's Museum, 75 North Water St., Poughkeepsie, NY 12601-1720; (845) 452-4873; www.mhcm.org

Good eats: Gilded Otter Brewing Company, 3 Main St., New Paltz, NY 12561-1742; (845) 256-1700; www.gildedotter.com

Mariner's on the Hudson, 46 River Rd., Highland, NY 12528; (845) 691-4711; www.marinersonhudson.com

Local outdoor stores: Eastern Mountain Sports, 2521 South Rd., Spackenkill Plaza, Suite B, Poughkeepsie, NY 12601; (845) 463-3207; www.ems.com

Rock & Snow, 44 Main St., New Paltz, NY 12561-1799; (845) 255-1311; www.rockandsnow.com

Organizations: Scenic Hudson, One Civic Center Plaza, Suite 200, Poughkeepsie, NY 12601; (845) 473-4440; www.scenichudson.org. A pioneering environmental group dedicated to protecting and restoring the Hudson River.

Hudson Valley Rail Trail Association, Inc., 12 Church St., Highland, NY 12528; (845) 691-2066; www.hudsonvalleyrailtrail.net

Visit the largest park in Westchester County for some big rewards: namely a dramatic overlook, a bit of exercise along well-groomed woods roads, and a small cave named after a nineteenth-century vagrant. If there's still daylight left after this mid-length circuit, stop at the popular Trailside Nature Museum to learn about the area's natural history.

Start: At the map kiosk by the Michigan Road parking area

Nearest town: Katonah, NY

Distance: 5.4-mile loop

Approximate hiking time: 2 to 3 hours

Difficulty: Easy to moderate

Trail surface: Dirt and gravel woods roads with several steeper, rockier spur trails

Seasons: Year-round

Other trail users: Mountain bikers, dog walkers, equestrians; cross-country skiers (seasonally)

Canine compatibility: Leashed dogs permitted, but not in picnic areas

Wheelchair accessibility: None

Land status: County park

Fees and permits: A small vehicle entry fee for residents; a larger fee for nonresidents

Schedule: Daily from 8 a.m. until dusk. The Trailside Nature Museum is open from 9 a.m. to 4 p.m., Tues through Thurs, and Sat.

Facilities: Restrooms, campground, sleeping shelters, picnic areas, playgrounds, fishing sites, art gallery, and the Trailside Nature Museum

Maps: USGS Peach Lake and Pound Ridge, NY. A map of the park is available at some of the trailheads and a PDF can be downloaded from the Trailside Nature Museum website (see below).

Trail contacts: Westchester County Department of Parks, Recreation and Conservation, 25 Moore Ave., Mount Kisco, NY 10549; (914) 864-PARK; http://parks.westchestergov.com/ The Trailside Nature Museum at Ward Pound Ridge Reservation, Routes 35 & 121 in Cross River, NY 10518; (914) 864-7322; www.trailsidemuseum.org

Finding the trailhead: From I-84 north, take exit 6 east on Route 35 toward the town of Cross River. Drive approximately 4 miles and turn right (south) on Route 121. The entrance to the park is on the left. Proceed east on Reservation Road until you reach the visitor center and main gate. Make the first right (south) after the gate on Michigan Road and follow this for approximately 1 mile until you reach the parking area. GPS: N41 14.848' / W73 35.641'

THE HIKE

Before it was farmed in the eighteenth and nineteenth centuries, or transformed into a recreation area during the early twentieth century, the Lenni-Lenape Indians hunted and fished the territory encompassing Ward Pound Ridge Reservation. They built wigwams in the maple, hickory, and oak forest, and drove tall wooden stakes into the ground to construct a large enclosure for trapping game. In 1938, "Poundridge" acquired the name of a powerful local Republican chairman, William Lukens Ward. Known as the Duke of Westchester, this politician from Greenwich, Connecticut, played a large part in the creation of parklands throughout the county in the late 1920s. Today the reservation that occupies 4,365 acres just east of the Cross River Reservoir endures as one of his greatest public achievements.

Beyond the park entrance and Reservation Road, which cuts across the northern third of Ward Pound, miles upon miles of hiking trails lead to hills and hollows, meadows and marshes. Many of the woods roads that crisscross the park, along with the camping shelters and the Trailside Nature Museum, were built by the Civilian Conservation Corps (CCC), a Depression-era program that put young, unemployed men to work around the country developing forest lands. In New York alone, 102 camps provided jobs, food, shelter, and other services to over 220,000 citizens. One such temporary settlement—Camp Merkel—stood close to where this hike begins at the end of Michigan Road.

A hiker peers into the maw of Leatherman's Cave.

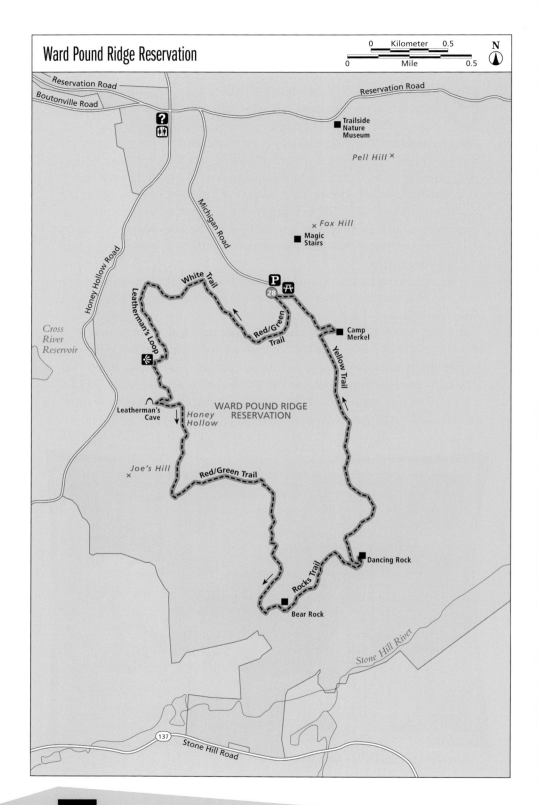

Ward Pound Ridge Reservation

0   Kilometer   0.5

0   Mile   0.5

N

Reservation Road

Boutonville Road

Reservation Road

Trailside Nature Museum

Pell Hill ×

Michigan Road

× Fox Hill

Magic Stairs

Honey Hollow Road

P 28

White Trail

Leatherman's Loop

Red/Green Trail

Camp Merkel

Cross River Reservoir

Yellow Trail

Leatherman's Cave

Honey Hollow

WARD POUND RIDGE RESERVATION

Joe's Hill ×

Red/Green Trail

Rocks Trail

Dancing Rock

Bear Rock

Stone Hill River

137

Stone Hill Road

Walk past the map kiosk on the flat trail surface, which alternates between gravel and sand or very fine soil, and let it gently carry you into the western section of the park. First the Red/Green Trail, and then a white-blazed route, circuitously winds over the rolling terrain to reach two highlights on the short Leatherman's Loop: an overlook where the scenic landscape around the Cross River Reservoir can be admired, and a little cave that probably once sheltered a hermit known simply as the Leatherman. According to folk history and legends from the latter half of the nineteenth century, a man clad in a bizarre assortment of leather clothing would wander back and forth from central Connecticut to Westchester and Putnam Counties, relying on the generosity of strangers and sleeping in caves. Besides Ward Pound, he is also thought to have regularly stayed at Bull's Hill Cave in Bedford Hills and Helicker's Cave in Armonk. Some evidence, and indeed a gravestone in the Sparta Cemetery in Ossining, suggests that he might have been Jules Bourglay of Lyon, France.

Once you've satisfied your curiosity about the cave, continue south on the white-blazed trail, moving around the base of Joe's Hill and then through Honey Hollow. Jog left (east) on the Red/Green Trail again and then, at mile 3, turn right onto the newly marked Rocks Trail (RT) and let the white blazes guide you to the Bear Rock Petroglyph, another point of interest for history buffs. Along with the large bear contour clearly inscribed on the surface of a large granite boulder, a number of other designs can be detected and have been debated by scholars. Press on to the northeast from here, making a short detour to stop at Dancing Rock, partially hidden in the chokeberry, witch hazel, and mountain laurel rooted in the soil atop Stone Hill.

The green, red, and white trails diverge just beyond mile 4: Unless you want to lengthen your hike and/or see the Indian Rock Shelter, make sure to stick with the white blazes and head north/northeast at this junction. Roughly 0.2 mile farther on, the wide gravel path you've trod through the southern section of the park will meet an even broader woods road blazed in yellow. This trail carries you the remaining distance back to Michigan Road. Linger at Camp Merkel before getting back in the car—if overgrown foundations, lonely cement steps, or old, rusted water fountains seem intriguing.

MILES AND DIRECTIONS

0.0   Start at the map kiosk by the Michigan Road parking area. Walk southeast on the Red/Green Trail, keeping to the right at the first fork.

0.2   Stay to the right at the next fork, following the Red/Green Trail up a small rise, and then merge onto a trail marked with white blazes that runs northwest.

0.6   Remain on the White Trail, but turn left at the T intersection.

0.9   At the bottom of a gradual decline, steer to the left where the White Trail heads over a footbridge. (Taking the right fork leads out of the park to Honey Hollow Road.)

1.2   Continue south (in the same counterclockwise direction you've been traveling) on Leatherman's Loop.

1.4   Stand and stare out over an arm of the Cross River Reservoir at an elevation of approximately 750 feet. Munch on some trail mix, rehydrate, and then move on toward Leatherman's Cave, located underneath this overlook.

1.5   After descending about 200 feet, follow Leatherman's Loop to the right, and then up a spur trail to the cave itself. Head back down the talus slope to the loop trail and turn left on a rocky woods road.

1.8   Turn right (south) at the T intersection and enter Honey Hollow.

2.2   Make a sharp left on the Red/Green Trail and stay to the right (east) when this path forks.

3.0   Turn right (southwest) in the direction of the white blazes when the Red/Green Trail begins to loop back to the north. After 0.1 mile, stay to the right and pass under a power line, and then make an immediate left (east) on the other side of the cleared area.

3.3   Arrive at the Bear Rock Petroglyph.

3.6   Turn right (southeast) onto a white-blazed spur trail to access the flat, table-like slab of granite known as Dancing Rock. Let the white blazes guide you back to the Rocks Trail.

4.3   The Red Trail swoops across your path, but continue north with the white blazes.

4.5   Meet the Yellow Trail, which enters from the east, and keep walking north.

4.9   Turn right (east) on a spur trail to pass through the site of a former Civilian Conservation Corps (CCC) camp. Turn left and complete a small loop to resume your route north on the Yellow Trail.

5.4   Arrive back at the trailhead at the Michigan Road map kiosk.

HIKE INFORMATION

Local information: Westchester County Tourism & Film, 222 Mamaroneck Ave., White Plains, NY 10605; (914) 995-8500; www.westchestertourism.com

Local events/attractions: John Jay Homestead State Historic Site, 400 Jay St./ P.O. Box 832, Katonah, NY 10536; (914) 232-5651; www.nysparks.com/historic-sites/4/details.aspx

Caramoor Center for Music and the Arts, 149 Girdle Ridge Rd./P.O. Box 816, Katonah, NY 10536; (914) 232-5035; www.caramoor.org

Wolf Conservation Center, 7 Buck Run, South Salem, NY 10590; (914) 763-2373; www.nywolf.org. Offers regular weekend educational programs for a small fee.

Local outdoor stores: Kelloggs & Lawrence, 26 Parkway, Katonah, NY 10536; (914) 232-3351; www.kelloggsandlawrence.com

Organizations: Friends of Westchester County Parks, 25 Moore Ave., Mount Kisco, NY 10549; (914) 864-7032; www.friendsofwestchesterparks.com

North American Butterfly Association, 4 Delaware Rd., Morristown, NJ 07960; www.naba.org. The New York chapter organizes a butterfly census every year at Ward Pound.

Friends of John Jay Homestead, P.O. Box 148, Katonah, NY, 10536; (914) 232-8119; www.johnjayhomestead.org

A view west over the Cross River Reservoir toward Katonah

New Jersey

Hewitt Brook feeds into the north end of the Monksville Reservoir. See Hike 29.

Thirty species of mammals, one hundred species of birds, and more than four hundred types of plant life have been recorded in Pyramid Mountain Natural Historic Area. See Hike 32.

Long Pond Ironworks

Travel to the New Jersey state line for a historical hike through an eighteenth- and nineteenth-century iron mining community. Roam across the New York border into the massive Sterling Forest parklands and clamber up Big Beech Mountain to survey miles and miles of landscape from the southern end of Sterling Ridge.

Start: Next to the visitor center on the Greenwood Lake Turnpike
Nearest town: Ringwood, NJ
Distance: 7.4-mile lollipop
Approximate hiking time: 4 to 5 hours
Difficulty: Moderate due to distance and elevation change
Trail surface: Rocky forest trails
Seasons: Year-round
Other trail users: Mountain bikers, equestrians; hunters and cross-country skiers (seasonally)
Wheelchair accessibility: None
Canine compatibility: Leashed dogs permitted
Land status: State park
Fees and permits: None

Schedule: Daily from dawn to dusk
Facilities: Restrooms at visitor center
Maps: USGS Greenwood Lake, NJ; New York-New Jersey Trail Conference Sterling Forest Trails Map 100; DeLorme *New Jersey Atlas & Gazetteer,* p. 20. Free black-and-white self-guided tours of the historic district are available at the visitor center.
Trail contacts: Long Pond Ironworks State Park, 1304 Sloatsburg Rd., Ringwood, NJ 07456-1799; (973) 962-7031; www.state.nj.us/dep/parksandforests/parks/longpond.html

Finding the trailhead: From either I-78, I-280, or I-80 west, take I-287 north toward the New York State border. Leave the highway near Oakland at exit 57 and turn left (north) on West Oakland Avenue, which will soon become Skyline Drive. After about 5.2 miles, turn right onto CR 511/Greenwood Lake Turnpike and continue north/northwest, passing through the town of Ringwood. Travel another 5 miles, cross the causeway over Monksville Reservoir, and look for the historic district parking area on the right, in front of the visitor center. GPS: N41 08.469' / W74 18.550'

THE HIKE

Without some knowledge of local history, the appearance of an entire village in the middle of New Jersey's vast Skylands territory might come as a surprise. And yet the facts remain—for well over a century Long Pond and the town of Hewitt were home to hundreds of families engaged first in the iron industry, later in the ice cutting business, and finally in recreation. In 1987 the area was donated to the state division of parks and forestry, and today many of the buildings that were homes, furnaces, and farms survive as a historic district maintained by the Friends of Long Pond Ironworks.

Working north from the Monksville Reservoir, each step on the Sterling Ridge/Highlands Trail is a step further back in time. Once the parking lot is out of sight, the present falls away and nineteenth-century architecture starts to mix with structures from the eighteenth, namely the Stone Double House on Hewitt Brook. Investigate the many ruins on Long House Road and then cross the Wanaque River to see the wilderness as it might have looked before mines and forges altered the landscape.

On the other side of the river, mounds and depressions scattered to the right are evidence of Long Pond Village, a small colonial settlement that preceded the town of Hewitt. Leave these reminders of the past behind and march north up a stony trail. On hot afternoons when school is out, you may hear the splashes and happy shouts of teenagers cooling off in one of the naturally occurring pools sculpted by the creative force of moving water.

After about 1 mile, the large boulders that have been a common sight thus far thin out, and the Sterling Ridge/Highlands Trail jogs to the right at a fork. Grasshoppers leap out of the way as you close the distance between the start of the loop and Big Beech Mountain.

Two inspiring views—one at about 1,000 feet and the other at close to 1,200 feet—come at the price of a tough climb, including a tight switchback up a broad shoulder of stone. Less than 0.5 mile later, you'll cross into New York and then descend the west side of the ridge via a partially washed-out gully of a path that spiders have strung their wispy webs across at regular intervals. Pause on the bridge spanning Jennings Creek to hear frogs squeak to one another as they jump into the waterway for safety. You are now on the Lake-to-Lake Trail, which runs for more than 1.5 miles before meeting a clearing designated for seasonal hunters' parking.

An unmarked but relatively easy-to-find trail heads southeast from the gate at the eastern end of the parking lot. Running down almost 300 feet into Jennings Hollow, it meets a yellow-blazed loop. Turn right (south) and follow the Jennings Hollow Trail past a secluded patch of wetlands, across the shallow creek, and around a squat little hill that sits between Sterling Ridge and the Wanaque River. Expect a muddy passage through the hollow as you close the loop. The Long Pond

Ironworks Visitor Center awaits your return roughly 1 mile south from the intersection with the Sterling Ridge/Highlands Trail.

MILES AND DIRECTIONS

0.0 Start next to the visitor center on the Greenwood Lake Turnpike.

0.2 Cross a small wooden bridge over Hewitt Brook and then go right (east) at the fork up ahead. What remains of an old company store stands on the left.

0.4 Before reaching the Long Pond Iron Furnaces, turn right on the teal-blazed Highlands Trail and walk over the Wanaque River using a narrow footbridge. Pass the site of a former charcoal site on the other side of the water and continue north.

1.1 Keep to the right (northeast) and remain on the Sterling Ridge/Highlands Trail at the fork, beginning a loop walk in a counterclockwise direction. The elevation gain here is gradual but steady.

1.3 The teal blazes jog to the northwest, passing through an intermittent streambed.

The Stone Double House, built in the 1760s, is thought to be the oldest residence in the historic district.

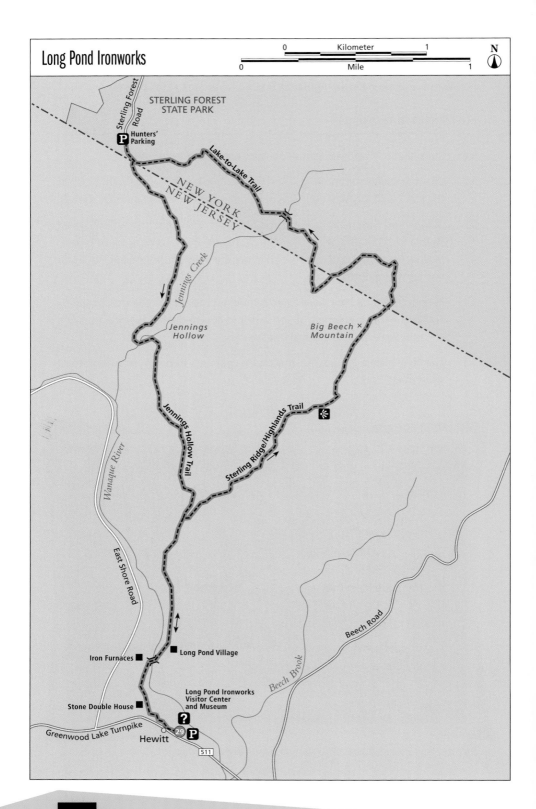

0   Kilometer   1

0   Mile   1

N

STERLING FOREST
STATE PARK

Sterling Forest Road

P Hunters'
Parking

Lake-to-Lake Trail

NEW YORK
NEW JERSEY

Jennings Creek

Jennings
Hollow

Big Beech ×
Mountain

Jennings Hollow Trail

Sterling Ridge/Highlands Trail

Wanaque River

East Shore Road

Beech Road

Iron Furnaces ■   ■ Long Pond Village

Beech Brook

Stone Double House ■

Long Pond Ironworks
Visitor Center
and Museum

?

29

P

Greenwood Lake Turnpike

Hewitt

511

1.9   After a somewhat tough climb, the trees thin out and offer a magnificent view to the southeast. Admire the hills in Tranquility Ridge County Park before moving on.

2.1   Follow a switchback up a steep section of trail and then rest at the top of Big Beech Mountain (1,200 feet).

2.5   Descend the mountain and cross the state line into New York. Continue north 0.2 mile past an unmarked woods road.

2.7   Turn left (west) on the Lake-to-Lake Trail, a route that stretches across Sterling Forest State Park from Little Sterling Lake to Greenwood Lake.

3.2   Reenter New Jersey and stick to the white blazes as the trail wanders northwest again.

3.5   Cross a bridge spanning Jennings Creek and stay left at the fork about 0.2 mile farther down the forest path.

4.4   Arrive at a gate and a grassy seasonal parking area for hunters. Immediately turn left (south) on an unmarked trail and follow it approximately 300 feet down a ridge into Jennings Hollow.

4.9   At the bottom of the slope, turn right (south) onto the yellow-blazed Jennings Hollow Trail.

5.3   Watch carefully for the yellow blazes to veer left (east) around a swamp. Do not follow the woods road that continues southwest to East Shore Road.

5.6   Reach the start of the Jennings Hollow loop and proceed south.

6.2   Walk over a short plank bridge and rejoin the Sterling Ridge/ Highlands Trail. The remaining mile covers the terrain alongside the Wanaque River that you traversed at the outset of this lollipop hike.

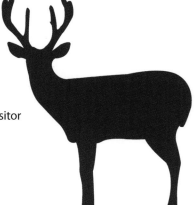

7.4   Arrive back at the trailhead and visitor center on Greenwood Lake Turnpike.

Local information: Borough of Ringwood, 60 Margaret King Ave., Ringwood, NJ 07456; (973) 962-7037; www.ringwoodnj.net

Passaic County, Passaic County Administration Building, Freeholder's Office, 401 Grand St., Paterson, NJ 07505; (973) 881-4402; www.passaiccountynj.org

Local events/attractions: Ringwood Manor, Sloatsburg Road, Ringwood, NJ 07456; (973) 962-2240; www.ringwoodmanor.com

New Jersey Botanical Garden, 2 Morris Road, Ringwood, NJ 07456-0302; (973) 962-7527; www.njbg.org

Good eats: Goldberg's Famous Bagels & Cafe, 55 Skyline Dr., Ringwood, NJ 07456; (973) 962-4800

Pizza One, 1185 Ringwood Ave., Haskell, NJ 07420-1567; (973) 835-1600; www.njpizzaone.com

Local outdoor stores: Ramsey Outdoor, 835 Rte. 17 South, Ramsey, NJ 07446; (201) 327-8141; www.ramseyoutdoor.com

Hike tours: The Friends of Long Pond Ironworks offer tours on the second Saturday of the month from Apr through Nov.

Organizations: The Friends of Long Pond Ironworks, Inc., P.O. Box 809, Hewitt, NJ 07421; (973) 657-1688; www.longpondironworks.org

North Jersey Highlands Historical Society, P.O. Box 248, Ringwood, NJ 07456; www.northjerseyhistory.org

New York-New Jersey Trail Conference, 156 Ramapo Valley Rd., Mahwah, NJ 07430; (201) 512-9348; www.nynjtc.org

Lime Kilns and Pig Iron

Between 1767 and 1882, the upper Wanaque River valley region (now Passaic County) was a major iron-making site. The second ironmaster, Robert Erskine, supplied George Washington's Continental Army with raw material for military equipment, and the blast furnaces at Long Pond and Ringwood continued to spit out bars of cast iron called "pigs" during the Civil War. Work continued until new ore and coalfields farther west forced the closure of the ironworks at Long Pond. By exploring the National Historic District on foot, the remains of the mining and smelting infrastructure that Peter Hansclever first expanded in the eighteenth century can still be seen today. As many as eight furnaces can be viewed in the greater area, along with lime kiln ruins, a sawmill, the two surviving iron industry waterwheels in the Highlands, and numerous residences once occupied by farmers, charcoal burners, and miners.

Monks Mountain

This short loop is ideal for those seeking a more leisurely walk through part of a state park that encompasses close to 3,000 acres. Highlights include a sweeping vista of Monksville Reservoir and several low peaks to the south, along with views down into the pits and shafts of a nineteenth-century iron ore mine.

Start: At the boat launch/parking area just south of the Greenwood Lake Turnpike causeway over Monksville Reservoir

Nearest town: Ringwood, NJ

Distance: 2.3-mile loop

Approximate hiking time: 1 to 1.5 hours

Difficulty: Easy, with one moderately challenging climb

Trail surface: Rocky forest trails

Seasons: Year-round

Other trail users: Birders, mountain bikers, equestrians; hunters and cross-country skiers (seasonally)

Wheelchair accessibility: None

Canine compatibility: Leashed dogs permitted

Land status: State park

Fees and permits: None

Schedule: Daily from sunrise to sunset

Facilities: None

Maps: USGS Greenwood Lake, NJ; DeLorme *New Jersey Atlas & Gazetteer*, p. 20

Trail contacts: Ringwood State Park, 1304 Sloatsburg Rd., Ringwood, NJ 07456-1799; (973) 962-7031; www.state.nj.us/dep/parksandforests/parks/longpond.html

Finding the trailhead: From either I-78, I-280, or I-80 west, take I-287 north toward the New York State border. Leave the highway near Oakland at exit 57 and turn left (north) on West Oakland Avenue, which will soon become Skyline Drive. After about 5.2 miles, turn right onto CR 511/Greenwood Lake Turnpike and continue north/northwest, passing through the town of Ringwood. In another 4.5 miles, before crossing the causeway over Monksville Reservoir, turn left at Beech Road into the boat launch/parking area. GPS: N41 08.172' / W74 18.460'

E very once in a while a long hike doesn't appeal, or for some reason isn't fea-
sible. To get most of the best features of a lengthy trek in just a couple of miles
then, would seem like an ideal scenario. Enter Monks Mountain. Located west
of the town of Ringwood, a mere 2 miles from the New York State border, this short
loop offers the challenge of a decent climb, the payoff of a pleasant view, and a
dash of history for good measure. Experiencing it all though, won't take much
more than an hour for fit walkers. Consequently, it would be easy to combine this
circular trail with a visit to Ringwood Manor or the New Jersey
Botanical Garden, both of which are a short drive away.

From the trailhead, you will immediately plunge into
the woods on the north side of the mountain, edging
southwest around the shoreline of the artificial lake
named for the Monks family and the little village that
is now underwater. Through the trees boaters can be
seen on the reservoir, casually paddling toward one
shore or another. The white blazes that mark the trail
soon lead up the slope, and you'll do well to reorient
accordingly—there are no other paths leading to the
top. Crossing a gravel woods road, the incline begins to
steepen somewhat, but the real work isn't apparent until
you've traveled about 0.6 mile. From here the trail makes itself
difficult, rising abruptly to more than 700 feet.

After leveling off, the narrow path runs east along the summit,
intersecting with a blue-blazed spur trail to the right (south) at the 1-mile
mark. Take this brief side trip to look out over the water to Board Mountain,
Horse Pond Mountain, and Harrison Mountain. Here at the overlook, scrub pines
share real estate with prickly pear cactus, New Jersey's only native cactus plant.
Happy to grow in patches of sandy, rocky soil with lots of sunlight, this succulent
brightens with color from June to August when it flowers.

Back on Monks Trail, the route leads downhill, turning sharply left (north)
where another spur leads to a second boat launch. Avoid the temptation to proceed straight ahead from here, where a woods road will guide you right into some
of the trenches and open pits that bear testament to the Monks (Winston) Mine
that operated on this site for close to thirty years, beginning in the 1860s. The scars
on the landscape caused by this industry are visible from the trail, and it's best to
avoid getting too close to any shafts, for both your own safety and for the sake of
the vegetation, which may be fragile. Instead, let the undulating path steer you
around the lower slopes of the mountain's northeastern face, ultimately—and
quickly—delivering you back to the trailhead at the Beech Road parking lot.

MILES AND DIRECTIONS

0.0 Start at the boat launch/parking area just south of the causeway over Monksville Reservoir.

0.2 Glimpse the water through the trees to your right. Turn left (east) uphill and cross a gravel access road.

0.4 Pass underneath power lines.

0.6 The steepest part of the hike begins here. Climb to an elevation of about 700 feet.

1.0 Turn right (south) on the blue spur trail for a clear view over the reservoir toward Horse Pond Mountain and Harrison Mountain.

1.3 Walk by a spur trail entering from the right (east) that leads to another parking area.

1.4 Stop to peer into the mine holes on the right side of the trail.

1.6 Step over a tiny stream, then turn left (north) and walk uphill past Monks Mine.

White oaks produce longer, pointed acorns while the nut of the red oak is shorter and fatter.

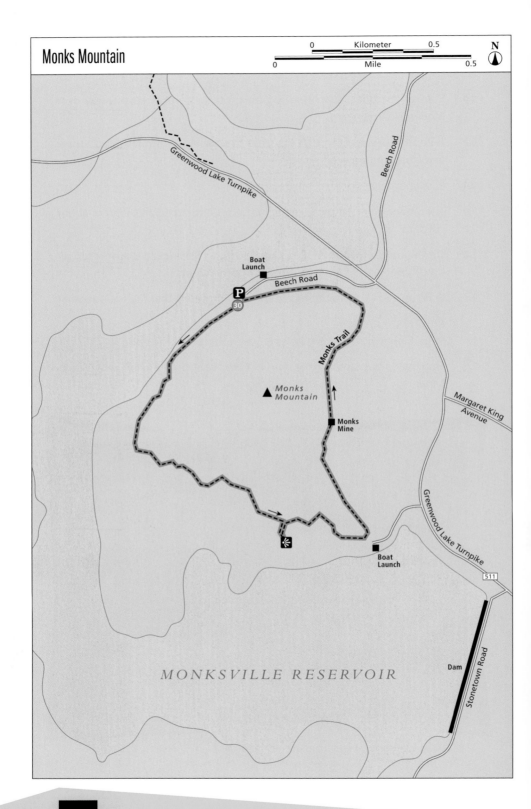

Monks Mountain

Boat Launch

Beech Road

Beech Road

P
30

Monks Trail

Monks
Mountain

Monks
Mine

Margaret King
Avenue

Greenwood Lake Turnpike

Greenwood Lake Turnpike

Boat
Launch

511

MONKSVILLE RESERVOIR

Dam

Stonetown Road

N

0   Kilometer   0.5

0   Mile   0.5

1.9 Keep to the left at the fork in the trail, then detour around a large fallen tree about 0.2 mile later. Traffic on Greenwood Lake Turnpike will be audible.

2.3 Arrive back at the trailhead at the southwestern end of the parking area.

HIKE INFORMATION

Local information: Borough of Ringwood, 60 Margaret King Ave., Ringwood, NJ 07456; (973) 962-7037; www.ringwoodnj.net
Passaic County, Passaic County Administration Building, Freeholder's Office, 401 Grand St., Paterson, NJ 07505; (973) 881-4402; www.passaiccountynj.org
Local events/attractions: Ringwood Manor, Sloatsburg Road, Ringwood, NJ 07456; (973) 962-2240; www.ringwoodmanor.com
Weis Ecology Center, 150 Snake Den Rd., Ringwood, NJ 07456; (973) 835-2160; www.njaudubon .org/SectionCenters/SectionWeis/Introduction.aspx.
Managed by New Jersey Audubon, the complex includes a nature store, bird-feeding station, a butterfly garden, and trail access.
Good eats: Prime 15 Steakhouse and Grill; 15 Greenwood Lake Turnpike, Ringwood, NJ 07456; (973) 831-9494; www.prime15.com
Alpine Deli and Pork Store, 1141 Greenwood Lake Turnpike, Ringwood, NJ 07456; (973) 728-1646. A German-American institution for nearly forty years.
Local outdoor stores: Ramsey Outdoor, 835 Rte. 17 South, Ramsey, NJ 07446; (201) 327-8141; www.ramseyoutdoor.com
Organizations: The Friends of Long Pond Ironworks, Inc., P.O. Box 809, Hewitt, NJ 07421; (973) 657-1688; www.longpondironworks.org
Native Plant Society of New Jersey, Office of Continuing Professional Education, Cook College, 102 Ryders Lane, New Brunswick, NJ 08901; www.npsnj.org
The Highlands Coalition, 520 Long St., Bethlehem, PA 18018; (610) 868-6915; www.highlandscoalition.org

Palisades Interstate Park

Walk along Millionaires Row at the top of the cliffs, retrace the steps of British invaders, and pause at the oldest house in the park, a building that served as a tavern for the maritime community that sprang up around the old dock road in the nineteenth century.

Start: At the trailhead on Closter Dock Road and US 9W
Nearest town: Alpine, NJ
Distance: 4.7-mile loop
Approximate hiking time: 2.5 to 3 hours
Difficulty: Easy to moderate, with one steep descent and a climb back up to the top of the Palisades
Trail surface: Rocky trails, dirt footpaths, and pavement
Seasons: Year-round
Other trail users: Dog walkers
Wheelchair accessibility: The Kearney House and the Alpine Boat Basin can be reached by car from Henry Hudson Drive, enabling limited wheelchair-accessible exploration of the waterfront.
Canine compatibility: Pets on leashes are permitted on the hiking trails, but not in the developed areas of the park.

Land status: Interstate park
Fees and permits: None
Schedule: Daily from dawn until dusk
Facilities: Restrooms and a picnic pavilion near the bottom of the Closter Dock Trail
Maps: USGS Yonkers, NY. Black-and-white maps of the 12-mile-long New Jersey section of the Palisades can be downloaded from the Palisades Interstate Park Commission's website (see below).
Special considerations: While rarely spotted in the park, the poisonous copperhead snake is native to the area. Watch your step—and for his safety, always keep Fido on a leash.
Trail contacts: Palisades Interstate Park Commission (New Jersey headquarters), P.O. Box 155, Alpine, NJ 07620-0155; (201) 768-1360; www.njpalisades.org

Finding the trailhead: From the western approach to the George Washington Bridge, take exit 72 onto Fletcher Avenue/US 9W. Enter Linwood Park and continue north on US 9W for 7 miles to Closter Dock Road. Do not get on the Palisades Parkway. Look for a parking lot on the right 0.2 mile beyond the light at Closter Dock Road. **By public transportation:** Coach USA's Rockland Coaches from Port Authority also travel up US 9W and stop at Closter Dock Road at the trailhead. GPS: N40 56.851′ / W73 55.369′

THE HIKE

Looming over the Hudson like stony sentinels, New Jersey's Palisades rise abruptly from the river and provide uninterrupted views of Westchester and Manhattan across the water. Increasing in size from Rahway, these massive pillars of igneous and sedimentary rock stretch all the way to Mount Ivy in Rockland County. During the American Revolution, the Continental Army constructed Fort Lee atop the cliffs to defend the waterway, but British General Cornwallis responded by ferrying 5,000 men to Huylers Landing, forcing the outnumbered colonials to retreat. In the late eighteenth century and on into the nineteenth, the durable and readily available building material offered by the cliff faces proved attractive to city planners in Manhattan, and the wood atop this prominent geologic formation fueled the steamships that began to appear after Robert Fulton's 1807 invention.

Even as natural resources were being stripped, bathing beaches were created along the Hudson below the Palisades. Large estates with names like Penlyn, Gray

A hiker studies a stone archway underneath Henry Hudson Drive.

Cliff, Falcon Lodge, and Gray Crag began to appear on the Palisades in the early twentieth century. In an effort to stop the quarrying and preserve the scenic cliffs for the public's benefit, then–New York Governor Theodore Roosevelt, New Jersey Governor Foster Voorhees, and a number of private citizens decided to establish the Palisades Interstate Park Commission.

Easily accessible by bus and possibly the single longest strip of park in the immediate metropolitan area, the Palisades are a closer, no-less-picturesque destination for day-trippers more familiar with hiking trails in western New Jersey or the Hudson Valley.

The Closter Dock Trail was once simply the Dock Road, a series of fairly steep switchbacks that enabled the transportation of goods from the Hudson below to towns on the summit. The first section of this crossover trail overlaps with the Long Path, and at times can be rather overgrown. First passing under the Palisades Interstate Parkway and then Henry Hudson Drive, the orange blazes lead down a wide, easy-to-follow gravel surface that intersects with the Shore Trail after roughly 0.6 mile. By following the white blazes to the right, you'll soon reach Closter Landing and the Alpine Boat Basin. Plump, tan harbor seals have been sighted near the dock from time to time. No signs of the general store and cereal mill that stood on the riverbank in the past remain today, but the Kearney House, built around 1761 and expanded in the 1840s to serve as a tavern, survives and can be toured on weekends from May to October.

Moving south along the water's edge, the trail rises and falls gently, dodging large rocks that have tumbled down from the steep slope on the right. Sunbeams dance across the river's surface as the day wears on, while wave after wave laps at the shore. Beyond the 2-mile mark, the jetty at Huylers Landing juts 0.3 mile out into the Hudson, and the red-blazed trail of the same name hooks back to the north before turning uphill. At the top of a moderately difficult 400-foot ascent, the flatter Long Path connects with the route used by Cornwallis and his invading force.

Guiding hikers back north, the Long Path twists and turns through the forest within earshot of the parkway, passing two stunning overlooks and the ruins of Cliff Dale, one of the mansions that was dismantled in the 1930s. Stop at any of these places, reflect on the history that has unfolded within these 2,500 acres of parkland in New Jersey, and consider another loop hike elsewhere in the Palisades.

Thomas Paine is thought to have written his famous line, "These are the times that try men's souls," while he was retreating across the Hackensack River with the American garrison from Fort Lee.

0.0 Start at the Closter Dock trailhead on US 9W, pass underneath the Palisades Interstate Parkway, and bear left (northeast) on the aqua-blazed Long Path.

0.2 Staying on the Long Path, turn right (east) downhill, make a left through a tunnel under Henry Hudson Drive, and then turn right (south) again on the Closter Dock Trail, a gravel woods road marked with orange blazes.

0.6 Turn right (south) at the T intersection onto the Shore Trail (white) and walk roughly 0.1 mile to the picnic area at the Alpine Boat Basin. Benches and picnic tables are scattered around a wide lawn, inviting hikers to linger for a few extra minutes.

0.7 Now at the water's edge, spend some time on the dock where you can study the boats moored in the marina or look up at the volcanic cliffs towering behind.

1.0 Walk past the Kearney House, cut across the parking lot, and look for a white blaze to the left of the access road that leads up to Henry Hudson Drive. Beyond the marina, the Shore Trail gently rises above the river, making its way steadily south toward Fort Lee.

1.6 The white blazes lead past a tiny beach with a floating dock, and then up a series of steps. In many places along this route, where the trail meets the water, the shoreline is strewn with rocks and shells.

2.3 Turn right (north) on the red-blazed Huylers Landing Trail and dig deep for the energy to get up the steep grade (you'll be ascending about 400 feet altogether). A jetty is visible on the left.

2.4 Turn left (southwest) onto the paved surface of Henry Hudson Drive. Look for steps leading back into the woods on the other side of the road after 0.1 mile.

2.8 The red blazes loop back to the north and the trail levels off as it approaches the Palisades Interstate Parkway.

2.9 Keep to the right as the Huylers Landing Trail merges with the Long Path.

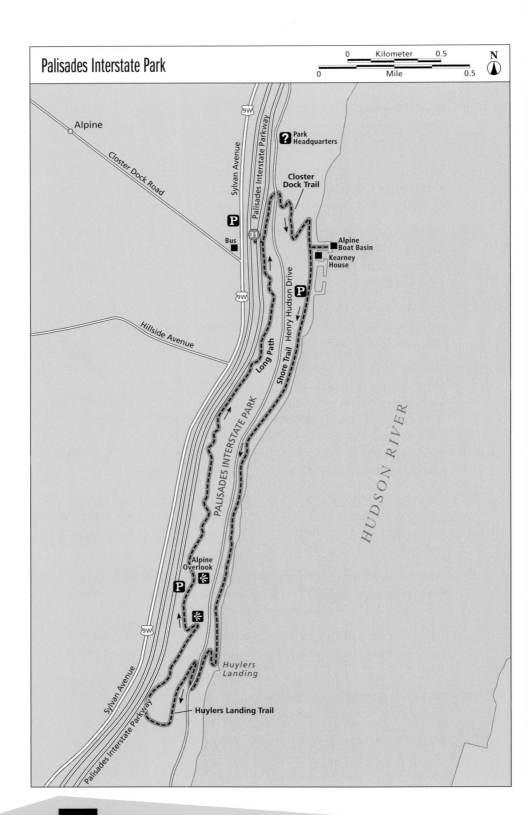

Palisades Interstate Park

Alpine

Closter Dock Road

Sylvan Avenue

Palisades Interstate Parkway

9W

Park Headquarters

Closter Dock Trail

P

Bus

31

Alpine Boat Basin

Kearney House

P

9W

Hillside Avenue

Long Path

Shore Trail

Henry Hudson Drive

PALISADES INTERSTATE PARK

HUDSON RIVER

Alpine Overlook

P

Huylers Landing

Sylvan Avenue

Palisades Interstate Parkway

9W

Huylers Landing Trail

3.2 Reach the first of two scenic overlooks. A small turret jutting out from the cliff provides a place to pull off the trail and watch barges moving freight up and down the river.

3.4 Arrive at Alpine Lookout, where a panoramic view of Yonkers warranted the construction of a pullout for drivers. Before the existence of the park, this was the location of Manuel Rionda's Rio Vista estate.

4.1 Pass by the ruins of a stone mansion—actually a palatial garage—that was once part of the estate of George Zabriskie, known as Cliff Dale.

4.7 Arrive back where the Long Trail meets the orange-blazed Closter Dock Trail. Turn left (west) to return to the trailhead on Closter Dock Road.

Option: By continuing south on the Shore Trail for another 3 miles, hikers can lengthen their trip and ascend back up to the Long Path via the Dyckman Hill Trail at the Englewood Boat Basin.

HIKE INFORMATION

Local information: New Jersey Division of Travel and Tourism, P.O. Box 460, Trenton, NJ 08625; (609) 292-2470; www.visitnj.org

Local events/attractions: Tenafly Nature Center, 313 Hudson Ave., Tenafly, NJ 07670; (201) 568-6093; www.tenaflynaturecenter.org

Fort Lee Historic Park, Hudson Terrace, Fort Lee, NJ 07024; (201) 461-1776; www.njpalisades.org. Tour the visitor center, see historical reenactments of the American Revolution, and get a closer look at the George Washington Bridge.

Steuben House, 1209 Main St., River Edge, NJ 07661; (201) 487-1739; www.state.nj.us/dep/parksandforests/historic/steuben/steuben-index.htm. Visit the sandstone house that George Washington presented to the Prussian inspector general who trained the Continental Army at Valley Forge.

Local outdoor stores: Campmor, 810 Rte. 17 North, Paramus, NJ 07652; (201) 445-5000; www.campmor.com

Ramsey Outdoor, 240 North State Rte. 17, Paramus, NJ 07652-2925; (201) 261-5000; www.ramseyoutdoor.com

Organizations: New York-New Jersey Trail Conference, 156 Ramapo Valley Rd. (Rte. 202), Mahwah, NJ 07430-1199; (201) 512-9348; www.nynjtc.org

Bergen County Audubon Society, P.O. Box 235, Paramus, NJ 07653-0235; www.bergencountyaudubon.org

Impressive sylvan views, striking rock formations, and a variety of ecological settings—including fields, forests, and wetlands—are all part of the experience during a brisk day hike through this 1,300-acre wildlife sanctuary in north-central New Jersey.

Start: Map kiosk next to the Boonton Avenue parking lot

Nearest town: Boonton, NJ

Distance: 4.4-mile lollipop

Approximate hiking time: 2.5 to 3 hours

Difficulty: Moderate, with one steep descent and several rocky stretches

Trail surface: Rocky trails and woods roads

Seasons: Year-round

Other trail users: Snowshoers and cross-country skiers (seasonally)

Wheelchair accessibility: None

Canine compatibility: Dogs permitted on leashes 6 feet or less

Land status: County park

Fees and permits: None

Schedule: Daily from dawn until dusk

Facilities: Restrooms available in the visitor center

Maps: USGS Boonton and Pompton Plains, NJ; DeLorme *New Jersey Atlas & Gazetteer,* p. 25. A map is available at the trailhead and on the Morris County Park Commission's website (see below).

Special considerations: This popular park often becomes crowded on nice weekends.

Trail contacts: Morris County Park Commission, 53 East Hanover Ave./P.O. Box 1295, Morristown, NJ 07962-1295; (973) 326-7600; http://parks.morris.nj.us

Finding the trailhead: Traveling from the north, take the U-turn at Kinnelon for Boonton Avenue (CR 511) off of Route 23. Make a right on Boonton Avenue and drive 4.3 miles to reach the Pyramid Mountain parking lot on the right. Or, from points south, take I-287 north to exit 45 (Wootton Street) in Boonton. Turn left onto Wootton Street at the stop sign. Pass under the highway, continue through the light and head up the hill to the four-way stop. Turn right on Boonton Avenue (CR 511). After approximately 2.75 miles, turn left into the Pyramid Mountain entrance. GPS: N40 56.799' / W74 23.312'

THE HIKE

Within the boundaries of this protected area, thirty species of mammals, one hundred species of birds, and more than 400 types of plant life have been recorded. And yet while bears, bobcats, and beavers all call Pyramid Mountain Natural Historic Area home, you're more likely to catch sight of other people during a visit to this park in Morris County. Longer routes can be plotted through the wilderness here, but this hike offers the greatest variety of terrain and scenery to first-time visitors.

Stash an extra granola bar in your pack and grab a free, detailed map at the trailhead before heading off into the chestnut oaks and American beech that have rooted themselves to the slopes of Pyramid Mountain. Picking up the blue-blazed Mennen Trail from the parking lot, you'll make a sharp right (northeast) onto the Yellow Trail shortly after crossing Stony Brook. The loop portion of the hike starts here. Through the trees to the right (southeast) of the trail, you'll notice playing fields, and the breeze may carry the sounds of an afternoon soccer game to your ears. Press on past the junction with the Orange Trail, which leads walkers alongside the western shore of Taylortown Reservoir. The well-compacted path becomes rockier at this point and gently climbs the back of Pyramid Mountain, skirting Little Cat Swamp.

Tripod, or Three Pillar Rock, is a glacial erratic.

After gaining about 200 feet in elevation, you'll rejoin the Mennen Trail, which first guides hikers to Lucy's Overlook and then, farther on, Tripod Rock. Also called Three Pillar Rock, this enormous, 160-ton boulder was left here during the Wisconsinan glaciation some 18,000 years ago. The blue blazes end just past this clearing, so look for White Trail blazes to the right (east). Strong ankles are needed to navigate over the rocky ground and fallen logs slowly breaking down with the help of termites, but the path around Big Cat Swamp isn't strenuous. Take a left (northwest) onto the Red Trail shortly before the 2-mile mark and weave around a shallow pond as you approach Eagle Cliff. As you proceed, listen for red-bellied and pileated woodpeckers tapping in the canopy above and notice wildflowers such as the pink lady's slipper and the tall, brilliant red cardinal flowers—a favorite food of swallowtail butterflies. At the foot of the small cliff, the red blazes lead left (west) up another incline that reaches its peak at Whale Head Rock (857 feet).

Cutting back and forth among ferns and other knee-high plants for a short distance, the trail makes a somewhat sudden descent through the rhododendron growing on the western slope of the mountain. Take a sharp right (north) after this downhill section. Once you've crossed Bear House Brook, loop back to the southwest on the Mennen Trail. A large red-and-white sign points in the direction of the visitor center at this juncture. From here, the wider, easier foot trail heads almost due south past the sizable expanse of wetland known as Bear Swamp.

As the swamp narrows, the Blue, White, and Yellow Trails intersect at Bear Rock, the other huge glacial erratic on this hike and one of the largest such rocks in the state. Continue southwest on the White Trail, paralleling Bear House Brook. A low stone wall to the west, as well as the foundation of a modest home farther on, are evidence of the farmers that settled this area in the seventeenth and eighteenth centuries.

The final stretch of the White Trail emerges from tree cover to follow the power line right-of-way. Watching for birds, such as scarlet tanagers or yellow warblers, flitting across your field of vision, follow the path as it curves left (northeast) up a small rise and then angles sharply south, back down toward the trailhead and parking lot on the blue Mennen Trail.

> 🌿 **Green Tip:**
> *If toting food, leave the packaging at home. Repack your provisions in zipper storage bags that you can reuse and that can double as garbage bags on the way out of the woods.*

Pyramid Mountain Natural Historic Area

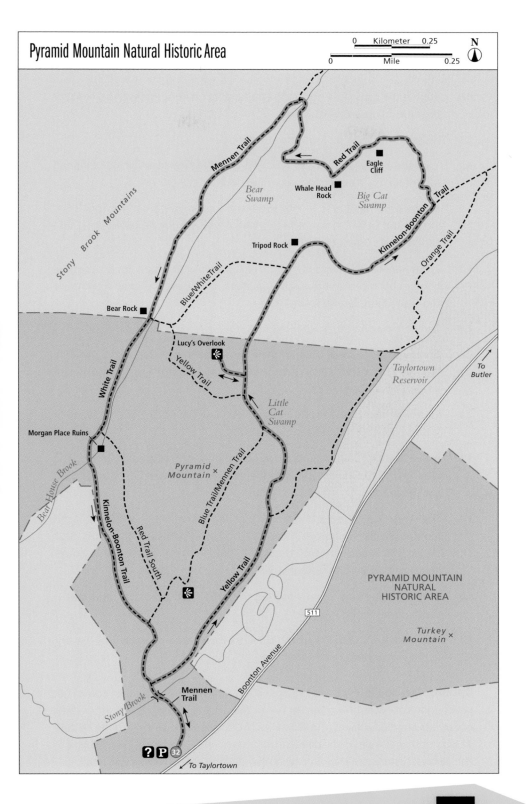

Kilometer 0.25

Mile 0.25

N

Mennen Trail

Stony Brook Mountains

Bear Swamp

Red Trail

Eagle Cliff

Whale Head Rock

Big Cat Swamp

Kinnelon-Boonton Trail

Tripod Rock

Blue/White Trail

Orange Trail

Bear Rock

Lucy's Overlook

Yellow Trail

Taylortown Reservoir

To Butler

White Trail

Little Cat Swamp

Morgan Place Ruins

Bear House Brook

Pyramid Mountain ×

Blue Trail/Mennen Trail

Kinnelon-Boonton Trail

Red Trail South

Yellow Trail

PYRAMID MOUNTAIN NATURAL HISTORIC AREA

511

Turkey Mountain ×

Boonton Avenue

Stony Brook

Mennen Trail

? P 32

To Taylortown

MILES AND DIRECTIONS

0.0 Start at the map kiosk next to the parking lot on Boonton Avenue. Look for the blue-blazed Mennen Trail.

0.1 Cross Stony Brook on a wooden footbridge.

0.2 Take the Yellow Trail at the fork and climb the eastern flank of Pyramid Mountain in a counterclockwise direction.

1.0 Merge with the Blue Trail once more and then keep right at the fork, skirting around Little Cat Swamp. For a view of the Highlands, take a short side trip to Lucy's Overlook in 0.1 mile.

1.3 Continue climbing to roughly 800 feet and arrive at Tripod Rock, a massive boulder balanced on three other smaller rocks. Leave the small clearing via the white Kinnelon-Boonton Trail.

1.9 Turn left (northwest) on the Red Trail.

2.0 Continue past a small pond to the right of the trail and ascend Eagle Cliff. Work your way west across the top of the ridge and then carefully descend a steep talus slope.

2.5 Step over Bear House Brook and turn left (southwest) on the blue Mennen Trail, which runs past a sizeable swamp.

3.1 Arrive at Bear Rock, an enormous glacial erratic. Instead of following the Blue Trail to the east, back up to the summit, proceed south (straight) on the White Trail.

3.4 The White Trail intersects the Red Trail just before the foundation of the Morgan Place, a nineteenth-century homestead. Keep right, cross Bear House Brook, and stay with the White Trail as it runs underneath a power line at the edge of the park property.

4.0 Meet the Blue Trail again, entering from the north this time, and take it south (right) to the trailhead.

4.4 Arrive back at the trailhead and the Boonton Avenue parking lot, adjacent to the visitor center.

Options: The Blue Trail continues across Boonton Avenue at the north end of the parking lot. Following this route up Turkey Mountain leads to several other hikes of varying lengths. Similarly, the Yellow Trail from Bear Rock winds through Kincaid Woods for several miles in the direction of the western boundary of Pyramid Mountain Natural Historic Area, ending at another parking area on Powerville Road.

HIKE INFORMATION

Local information: Morris County Tourism Bureau, 6 Court St., Morristown, NJ 07960; (973) 631-5151; www.morristourism.org

Local events/attractions: Boonton Historical Society and Museum, 210 Main St., Boonton, NJ 07005; (973) 402-8840; www.boonton.org/Community/HistoricalSociety.htm. Open Sat from 1 to 4 p.m., and Sun from 12 to 3 p.m. (summers); or by appointment.

Community Children's Museum, 77 East Blackwell St., Dover, NJ 07801; (973) 366-9060; www.communitychildrensmuseum.org. Open Thurs to Sat, from 10 a.m. to 5 p.m. Call for summer hours.

Good eats: Chili Willie's, 702 Main St., Boonton, NJ 07005; (973) 299-8775. Casual, affordable Mexican restaurant.

Don's Sandwich Shop, 606 Main St., Boonton, NJ 07005; (973) 263-3189

Local outdoor stores: Ramsey Outdoor Store, Inc., 281 Rte. 10, Succasunna-Kenvil, NJ 07876; (973) 584-7799; www.ramseyoutdoor.com

Organizations: New York-New Jersey Trail Conference, 156 Ramapo Valley Rd. (Rte. 202), Mahwah, NJ 07430-1199; (201) 512-9348; www.nynjtc.org

Morris Trails Partnership, P.O. Box 1295, Morristown, NJ 07962-1295; http://morris trails.org/

Wildflowers in bloom add to the enjoyment of a spring or summer hike.

Sandy Hook

Explore a landmark rich in history at the southernmost edge of New York Harbor. Admire views of Manhattan's skyline, take a dip in the Atlantic, and gain an understanding of barrier beach ecology on a fun day trip a relatively short ferry ride away from lower Manhattan.

Start: Sandy Hook Visitor Center near parking lot D in Gateway National Recreation Area
Nearest town: Highlands, NJ
Distance: 4.6-mile loop
Approximate hiking time: 2.5 to 3 hours
Difficulty: Easy
Trail surface: Sand, packed earth, and paved multiuse path
Seasons: Year-round
Other trail users: Joggers, bikers, in-line skaters
Wheelchair accessibility: The paved multiuse path is suitable for wheelchairs and motorized scooters.
Canine compatibility: No dogs on the beach; otherwise leashed dogs permitted
Land status: National recreation area
Fees and permits: No entry fee, but parking fees collected from Memorial Day to Labor Day
Schedule: Daily from dawn until dusk
Facilities: Restrooms, water fountain, and a small museum at the trailhead
Maps: USGS Sandy Hook, NJ. A black-and-white map of the Old Dune Trail is available at the visitor center.
Special considerations: It's a good idea to bring plenty of water, bug spray, and sunscreen on this hike, especially during the warmer months. Shade is intermittent and ticks are common on the Hook, as is poison ivy.
Trail contacts: Sandy Hook Visitor Center, Gateway National Recreation Area, P.O. Box 530, Fort Hancock, NJ 07732; (732) 872-5970; www.nps.gov/gate/planyourvisit/thingstodosandyhook.htm

Finding the trailhead: To reach the park by car from New York City, drive south on I-278 over the Verrazano Bridge. Continue west across Staten Island and then pick up I-95 south (the New Jersey Turnpike) on the other side of the Goethals Bridge. Merge onto the Garden State Parkway south just before signs for exit 10 on the turnpike. At Hazlet, take exit 117 onto Route 36 east, which leads to Highlands. Remain on Route 36 over the bridge, then make a left onto Ocean Avenue (becoming Hartshorne Drive) and drive 2.6 miles to the visitor center parking area. **By public transportation:** From the ferry terminal at Fort Hancock at the north end of the park, hop on one of the free shuttles to parking lot D and the visitor center. Pick up the Old Dune Trail here. By train, take New Jersey Transit's North Jersey Coast Line to Red Bank, where Bus 834 will then deliver visitors to Highlands. Buses drop off at or near the entrance to Sandy Hook. GPS: N40 25.616' / W73 59.063'

THE HIKE

When temperatures in the five boroughs start to climb during the steamy summer months, few trips seem as appealing as an escape to the seashore. Sure, wading in a creek upstate to cool off may be nice, but nothing beats a hike at the beach, where a dip in the ocean is never more than a mile away. With regular commuter rail connections as well as high-speed catamaran service from Manhattan, Sandy Hook is a maritime park that's easy to reach using public transportation.

Setting out on the Old Dune Trail from the visitor center, a former Spermaceti Cove Life-Saving Station, day hikers will discover mixed-forest communities (red maple, black cherry, shadbush), scrub-thicket residents (beach plum, bayberry, honeysuckle), and plants accustomed to the desertlike conditions of dunes (beach grass, saltwort, seaside goldenrod). A thin track leads the way north, winding around clusters of prickly pear cactus, thickets of Virginia creeper—a woody vine that can grow to be 50 feet in length—and stands of American holly, its spiky fallen leaves crunching underfoot. Most of the mammals that call this part of the Gateway National Recreation Area home won't be active during the hottest parts of the day, but you may notice their footprints in the red clay, especially those of the raccoon and less frequently, the red fox.

🌿 **Green Tip:**
Do not swim with, ride, chase, or grab marine animals.

As the trail twists and turns past pitch pine and fragrant red juniper, you'll probably hear the shrill cries of herring and ring-billed gulls, or the low buzz of an airplane towing a banner advertisement overhead. Continue through a four-way trail crossing and arrive at the southern edge of Nike Pond, a small body of water that attracts a variety of birdlife. Walk out to the end of the wood platform that extends over the surrounding marsh area to get a closer look at this freshwater oasis.

Back on the sandy path, another 0.2 mile puts walkers atop the dunes facing the Atlantic Ocean. You haven't yet traveled a mile, but this is a great opportunity for a swimming break. Stop for a while and enjoy the surf or hunt for oyster shells, skate egg cases, blue mussel shells, or tiny burrowing mole crabs. On clear afternoons, the towering skyscrapers of midtown Manhattan will be visible on the horizon.

Beach erosion can make the trail back into the forest hard to find, so instead of searching in vain for a sign or a marker, walk 0.7 mile north from Nike Pond on the sand until you see a road on the left (west), providing access to the fishing beach just ahead. Follow this road a short distance past several concrete bunkers, remnants of some of the many fortifications that were constructed to protect New York Harbor, and look for a signed entry point to your right.

After covering another 1.25 miles, passing an osprey nest, your route will cross Atlantic Drive. Make a sharp left (west) turn into a rather overgrown section of trail,

A sun-bleached snail shell on the multiuse pathway that connects the park entrance with the Fort Hancock Historic District

and then reach a stopping point where you can learn the history of coastal defense at the Nike Missile Radar Site.

The return trip south keeps to the paved multiuse pathway as it curves around Horseshoe Cove on the bay side of the Hook. Around mile 4, pause to study the 27-foot-long, 5,000-pound Nike Hercules missile ageing silently inside a fence on the left, and its smaller cousin, the Nike Ajax, on the right of the trail. Veer east around the ranger station, stroll by parking lot E, and step back into the air-conditioned visitor center to end your tour.

MILES AND DIRECTIONS

0.0   Start behind the visitor center (formerly a life-saving station) near parking lot D.

0.3   Cross the multiuse bike trail and start up a low rise, heading north into the park through a holly forest.

0.5   Reach a boardwalk leading to a bird blind overlooking Nike Pond.

0.7   The Old Dune Trail curves east first, then south, and finally east again, leading over the dunes and onto the beach. Take a dip to cool off or continue north on the sand for about 0.5 mile.

1.2   Turn left (west) onto a fishing road and leave the ocean behind. Walk by several old cement bunkers on either side of the road.

1.4   Pick up the trail again by turning right (north) off the fishing road. Farther along you'll pass an osprey nesting platform to the left of the trail.

2.1   Turn right (east) for a short detour over the dunes and a second look at the ocean, or follow the trail left (west) to continue on your loop.

2.6   Cross Atlantic Drive, then veer left with the trail through a scrub thicket and look for signs of the route heading west once more. At the intersection with the bikeway, turn right (north).

2.9   Reach the Nike Missile Radar Site and prepare to return to the start of your hike via the paved multiuse path.

3.3   The bikeway approaches Horseshoe Cove, offering sweeping views of Sandy Hook Bay. Look for two large missiles displayed near the path in another 0.75 mile.

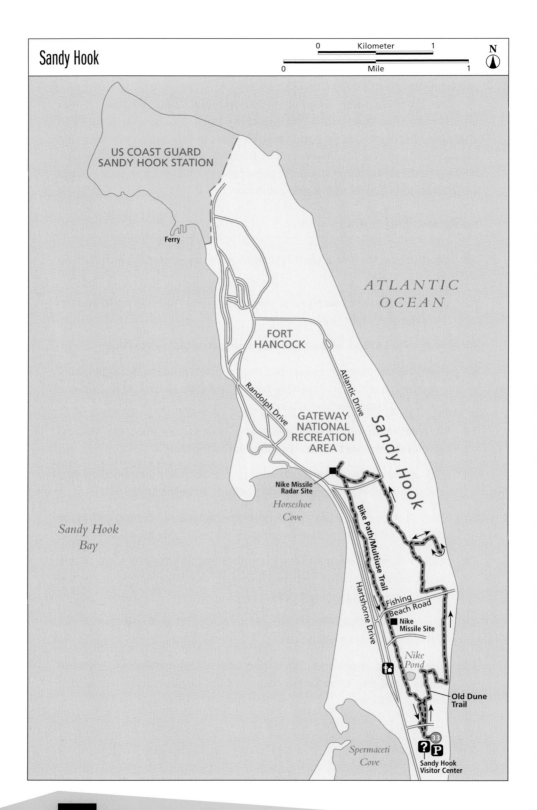

0   Kilometer   1

0   Mile   1

N

US COAST GUARD
SANDY HOOK STATION

Ferry

*ATLANTIC
OCEAN*

FORT
HANCOCK

Randolph Drive

Atlantic Drive

Sandy Hook

GATEWAY
NATIONAL
RECREATION
AREA

Nike Missile
Radar Site

*Horseshoe
Cove*

*Sandy Hook
Bay*

Bike Path/Multiuse Trail

Hartshorne Drive

Fishing
Beach Road

Nike
Missile Site

*Nike
Pond*

Old Dune
Trail

*Spermaceti
Cove*

33

Sandy Hook
Visitor Center

4.2   Follow the bikeway left as it passes the ranger station. Turn left when you see a sign for the visitor center.

4.6   Arrive back at the trailhead and the Sandy Hook Visitor Center.

HIKE INFORMATION

Local information: New Jersey Shore, 3350 Hwy. 138, Bldg. 1, Suite 214, Wall, NJ 07719; www.sandy-hook.com

Local events/attractions: The Sandy Hook Lighthouse and Keepers Quarters, as well as the Fort Hancock Museum, are both within park boundaries.

Good eats: Sea Gulls' Nest, Sandy Hook, NJ; (732) 872-0025; www.seagullsnest.info

Bahrs Landing Restaurant, 2 Bay Ave., Highlands, NJ 07732; (732) 872-1245; http://store.bahrslanding.com. Famous for seafood since 1917.

Organizations: The Sandy Hook Foundation, 84 Mercer Rd., Fort Hancock, NJ 07732; (732) 291-7733; www.sandyhookfoundationnj.org/

Friends of Gateway, 232 East 11th St., New York, NY 10003; (212) 228-3126; www.treebranch.net/friends_of_gateway.htm

Sandy Hook Bird Observatory, 20 Hartshorne Dr., Highlands, NJ 07732; (732) 872-2500; www.njaudubon.org/SectionCenters/SectionSHBO/Introduction.aspx

Four species of sea turtle (Kemp's Ridley, loggerhead, Atlantic green, and leatherback) as well as four species of seal (harbor, harp, hooded, and gray) are occasionally found in the waters around New York City.

🌱 **Green Tip:**
Keep to established trails as much as possible.
If there aren't any, stay on surfaces that will be least affected, like rock, gravel, dry grasses, or snow.

Sourland Mountain Nature Preserve

In the same hills now visited by hikers and mountain bikers, John Hart, a delegate to the Continental Congress, hid from the British troops who raided his farm in nearby Hopewell. Climb over igneous trap rock, plod through a swampy lowland between two small streams, and search for spotted salamanders, wood frogs, and gray tree frogs hiding within the boundaries of this tucked-away jewel.

Start: At the east end of the parking lot on Rileyville Road

Nearest town: Hopewell, NJ

Distance: 1.8-mile lollipop

Approximate hiking time: 1 hour

Difficulty: Easy

Trail surface: Woods road, dirt footpaths, and a few rocky sections

Seasons: Year-round

Other trail users: Mountain bikers; cross-country skiers and hunters (seasonally)

Wheelchair accessibility: None

Canine compatibility: Dogs permitted if on a leash 6 feet or less

Land status: County park

Fees and permits: None

Schedule: Daily from sunrise to sunset

Facilities: None

Maps: USGS Hopewell and Rocky Hill, NJ. A color map of the hiking trails is available at the trailhead on Rileyville Road and via the Hunterdon parks department website (see below).

Trail contacts: County of Hunterdon Department of Parks and Recreation, 1020 State Rte. 31, Lebanon, NJ 08833; (908) 782-1158; www.co.hunterdon.nj.us/depts/parks/parks.htm
D&R Greenway Land Trust at the Johnson Education Center, One Preservation Place, Princeton, NJ 08540; (609) 924-4646; www.drgreenway.org

Finding the trailhead: From I-78 west, take exit 17 onto Route 31, heading south toward Flemington (about 10 miles). Drive another 5 miles on Route 31/US 202 and exit onto Route 602/Wertsville Road. Cross US 202 and continue east for 3.3 miles to Route 607/Rileyville Road. Turn right (south) and drive 1.7 miles to the park entrance. GPS: N40 25.277' / W74 47.305'

THE HIKE

South of the Appalachian Highlands that blanket its northern counties, New Jersey's geography is characterized by piedmont and coastal plain. And although it is one of the most densely populated states in the country, with so many communities clustered near New York and Philadelphia, sizeable parts of the state still remain rural. East of the Delaware River and miles from the noisy turnpike and the Northeast Corridor, Sourland Mountain is one such area, a place that holds secrets for those who want to find them. In particular, the hilly scenery between Hopewell and Flemington is a patchwork of farmland, historic towns, and contiguous mixed forest. This is where the smaller of two preserves called Sourlands can be found.

Its name is thought to derive from the reddish- or sorrel-colored earth encountered by early settlers. The poor soil, along with limited sources of groundwater, seems to have kept it wild while the surrounding landscape has seen successive waves of development. The limited degree of intrusions or changes by people has encouraged a variety of fauna, namely migratory birds and amphibians, to seek out this parcel of unspoiled territory.

To begin the hike, follow the Service Road Trail into the preserve, crossing a streambed and passing the yellow-blazed South Loop Trail. Continuing in a northeastern direction, you may hear a northern flicker rapidly drumming out a message to its cohorts, or a black-winged scarlet tanager whistling sweetly from the canopy. May is generally the best month to hear (and see) birdlife, as these animals build nests and establish territory.

A signboard at the entrance to the Sourlands posts health warnings and rules for hikers.

Sourland Mountain Nature Preserve

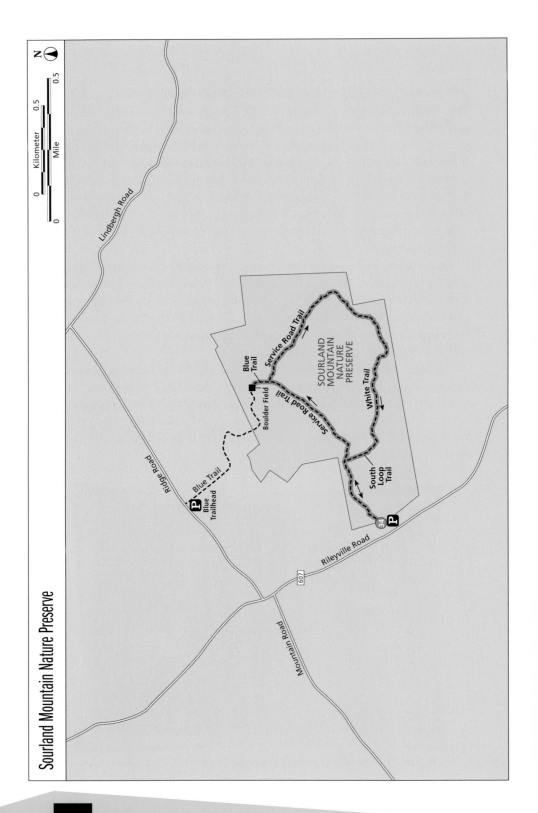

At the 0.5-mile mark, turn left (north) onto the Blue Trail and follow it a few hundred feet to a field of boulders. Scramble over hefty rocks that the elements have softened with time, and then turn around and walk back down a small rise to the Service Road Trail. Turn left and move east across another stream.

The terrain at the east end of the preserve is slightly more rugged than the land near the entrance. But that said, the elevation gain here is fairly minimal. Before the 1-mile mark, the Service Road Trail ends at a head-on junction with the White Trail. Take this narrower footpath south and try to spot the red-eyed vireo, a talkative yet infrequently seen forest dweller. You'll pass under a power line as you pick your way across the rocky trail surface in a damp, low-lying area. Frequent blazes make the route easy to find, and at 1.4 miles you'll cross a streambed (which could be empty in drier years) to join the yellow South Loop Trail.

The distance back to your vehicle is minimal once on the South Loop Trail, so if more hiking seems desirable, consider adding on the Northern Stony Brook Preserve option described below. A second option is to make the short drive to the 3,196-acre Sourland Mountain Preserve in nearby Somerset County. Several more well-maintained trails of varying lengths offer additional recreational opportunities for individuals wishing to extend their time in the Sourlands.

MILES AND DIRECTIONS

0.0　Start on the Service Road Trail, which leads northeast from the parking lot.

0.2　Continue in a clockwise direction past the start of the South Loop Trail (yellow blazes) on the right.

0.5　Turn left (north) on the Blue Trail and follow it up and around a small boulder field. Turn back from the trail's high point and pick up the Service Road Trail again, this time heading almost due east.

0.9　Join the White Trail where the Service Road Trail ends. Stay with this winding route as it heads southwest down a small slope.

1.4　Pass under a power line and then cross an intermittent stream.

1.5　Meet the South Loop Trail and follow it to the left (northwest). Make a hard left when you reach the Service Road Trail, closing the loop.

1.8　Arrive back at the trailhead and parking lot on Rileyville Road.

Option: From the parking area on Rileyville Road, turn right (north) and walk across the street to access the Northern Stony Brook Preserve, a public open space managed by the D&R Greenway Land Trust. Look for a green-blazed route heading west that will fork after roughly 0.5 mile. The trails in this part of Sourland

Mountain cover more area than those within the park boundary, can be some-what harder to follow, and may require some bushwhacking. As such they are better suited to experienced hikers. The other point of entry to Northern Stony Brook is on Mountain Road.

HIKE INFORMATION

Local information: State of New Jersey, Division of Travel and Tourism, P.O. Box 460, Trenton, NJ 08625; 1-800-VISITNJ; www.visitnj.org/lambertville

Local events/attractions: Black River Railroad Historical Trust, P.O. Box 232, Ringoes, NJ 08551; www.brrht.org. Take a weekend excursion or a holiday ride aboard a historic passenger coach.

Howell Living History Farm, 70 Wooden's Lane, Lambertville, NJ 08530; (609) 737-3299; www.howellfarm.org

Rockingham State Historic Site, P.O. Box 496, Kingston, NJ 08528; (609) 683-7132; www.rockingham.net. The second oldest house in the Millstone River valley and George Washington's temporary residence during the end of the Revolutionary War.

Good eats: The Blue Bottle, 101 East Broad St., Hopewell, NJ 08525; (609) 333-1710; www.thebluebottlecafe.com. Fresh, local ingredients add up to an inspired, reasonably priced lunch menu that includes salads, appetizers, and sandwiches.

Hillbilly Hall Tavern & Restaurant, 203 Hopewell-Wertsville Rd., Hopewell, NJ 08525; (609) 466-9856; www.hillbillyhall.com

Nomad Pizza Company, 10 East Broad St., Hopewell, NJ 08525; (609) 466-6623; www.nomadpizzaco.com. An environmentally conscientious, wood-fired brick oven pizzeria.

Local outdoor stores: Blue Ridge Mountain Sports (Princeton Shopping Center), 301 North Harrison St., Princeton, NJ 08540; (609) 921-6078; www.brmsstore.com

Eastern Mountain Sports, 3535 US Rte. 1, Space 124, Market Fair, Princeton, NJ 08540; (609) 520-8310; www.ems.com

Organizations: The Appalachian Mountain Club, New York-North Jersey Chapter, 381 Park Ave. South, Suite 809, New York, NY 10016; (212) 986-1430; www.amc-ny.org

Duke Farms, 80 Rte. 206, South Hillsborough, NJ 08844; (908) 722-3700; www.dukefarms.org. Self-guided nature trail open Fri through Sun, from 10 a.m. to 3 p.m.; classes and activities by reservation only.

Hunterdon Hiking Club; (908) 782-6428; www.hunterdonhikingclub.org. Hikes on Sat, Sun, and Wed. Indoor meetings featuring hiking-related speakers held the second Thurs of each month (except July and Aug) at the Hunterdon park office in Lebanon, New Jersey.

Sourland Planning Council, P.O. Box 72, Hopewell NJ 08525; www.sourland.org. A nonprofit organization founded in 1986 to protect the region from encroaching development.

South Mountain Reservation

The largest park in Essex Country, South Mountain Reservation encompasses over 2,000 acres of land, including 19 miles of blazed hiking trails, numerous picnic areas, a zoo, an ice rink, and sweeping views across Arthur Kill and Newark Bay to Staten Island.

Start: Locust Grove parking lot

Nearest town: Millburn, NJ

Distance: 5.7-mile loop

Approximate hiking time: 3 to 4 hours

Difficulty: Easy to moderate

Trail surface: Woodland dirt footpath, gravel, and slightly steeper, rocky terrain

Seasons: Mar through Oct

Other trail users: Joggers, mountain bikers, equestrians

Wheelchair accessibility: The River Trail, which also leaves from the Locust Grove parking lot, is a wide, well-graded bridle path suitable for disabled visitors.

Canine compatibility: Leashed dogs permitted

Land status: County park

Fees and permits: None

Schedule: Daily from dawn to dusk

Facilities: Public restrooms are available at the Millburn Public Library on Glen Avenue

Maps: USGS Roselle and Caldwell, NJ; DeLorme *New Jersey Atlas & Gazetteer*, p. 32. Maps are also available by mail for a small fee from the South Mountain Conservancy (see Hike Information).

Trail contacts: County of Essex Department of Recreation & Cultural Affairs, 115 Clifton Ave., Newark, NJ 07104; (973) 268-3500; www.essex-countynj.org/p/index .php

Finding the trailhead: From exit 50B (Maplewood/Millburn) off I-78, travel north on Vauxhall Road for 0.7 mile. At the T intersection turn left (west) onto Millburn Avenue, which jogs right after 0.6 mile and becomes Essex Street. At 0.2 mile turn right (north) onto Lackawanna Place and go 0.1 mile to the T intersection with Glen Avenue. Turn right and then make your next left into the Locust Grove parking lot, where the trailhead is located. **By public transportation:** Via New Jersey Transit, take the Morristown Line to the Millburn station, then cross Glen Avenue to reach the trailhead in the Locust Grove parking lot. GPS: N40 43.661' / W74 18.232'

THE HIKE

When early European colonists arrived in the seventeenth century, Lenape people inhabited this part of the state and the two groups maintained a peaceful relationship for many years. In 1758 they became the first tribe to receive land from the New Jersey Assembly. Brotherton, as the reservation in southeastern Burlington County was called, didn't last long however, and in 1801 the remaining Lenape sold the land, relocating first to New York, and later Wisconsin. Meanwhile, the Continental Army, led by General George Washington, used the ridges here as both an observation point and a natural defense for their encampment at Morristown. On June 23, 1780, local militia repelled an attack from Hessian mercenary troops and British regulars.

After the Revolutionary War, the Rahway River became an important site for the growing paper industry, and Samuel Campbell, a Scottish immigrant, was the first to dam the waterway in order to build a paper mill on its bank. Campbell Pond takes its name from this eighteenth-century entrepreneur. A century later, the newly established Essex County Parks Commission began purchasing the land that would become the South Mountain Reservation.

Frederick Law Olmsted, the landscape architect of Central Park fame, would make South Mountain his last public project. His stepson, John C. Olmsted, carried out much of the design work, while the Civilian Conservation Corps handled the construction of bridges, trails, and shelters. Today, visitors will still find many of the tree species the Olmsted Brothers firm reintroduced with their design, both hardwoods as well as softwoods, including hemlock, white pine, beech, tulip, and oak. Mountain laurel, dogwood, wild azalea, and rhododendron were also planted within the boundaries of the park and continue to thrive.

Leading uphill from the parking area on Glen Avenue, the Lenape Trail initially guides hikers to a picnic grove populated by weathered tables, rusted grills, and a small covered pavilion before veering into the woods, gently curving above residential lots at the base of South Mountain. Heavy footsteps might startle white-tailed deer or wild turkeys foraging in the late afternoon, while the sharp cries of blue jays and the high-pitched trilling of orange- and gray-plumed robins echo overhead. Following this short ascent, the trail intersects Crest Drive, with scenic overlooks of Chatham Township to the southwest and Staten Island and the Verrazano Bridge to the southeast.

Returning to the dirt footpath, yellow blazes lead over intermittent streams and small rises, passing by Maple Falls Cascades and Beech Brook Cascades on its route north into the reservation. Acorn shells crunch underfoot and wild blackberry bushes scrape pant legs on the climb toward Mines Point and the Overlook Trail junction. Hemlock Falls awaits hikers at the halfway point, with several benches offering a place for a short rest before beginning the trip back along the west branch of the Rahway River.

Once you leave the noisy 25-foot waterfall behind, walk along the River Trail with an eye peeled for white blazes denoting the Rahway Trail. At the fork (marked with a map kiosk), follow the Rahway Trail northwest across the river, making an immediate left (south) on the opposite bank. The way forward may be overgrown, but press on as it turns away from the shoreline back into the woods. Take care to watch for protruding roots on this narrower track. Jog left (east) on a gravel road over a stone bridge and then head back into the trees alongside the Rahway for the remainder of your journey. Resist the temptation to take the flatter River Trail just to your left, and you'll be rewarded with better views of Campbell Pond, Diamond Mill Pond, and the towering brick smokestack of an abandoned power plant.

MILES AND DIRECTIONS

0.0 Start at the north end of the Locust Grove parking lot. Take the yellow-blazed Lenape Trail right (east) through a picnic area and into the woods.

0.2 Begin a rather steep climb up a stony path that rises above the rooftops of houses on Sagamore Road.

0.5 Make a sharp left (west) and close the remaining distance to Crest Road, on top of the mountain. Follow the pavement around to the overlook.

0.7 Reach Washington Rock (elevation 483 feet). A plaque explains the events of the summer of 1780.

1.1 Twisting and turning on its northward course, the Lenape Trail passes near the Maple Falls Cascades, audible from several hundred feet away.

1.3 Jog left on a short stretch of new trail built to allow regrowth on a heavily worn section. Train your eyes on the tree trunks around you so you don't miss one of the yellow blazes.

1.6 Turn right (northeast) and climb Lilliput Knob as you venture farther into the park. Cross a small, quiet road soon thereafter.

2.8 Enter a circle of stone pillars, descend a tiny slope, and walk north across another road.

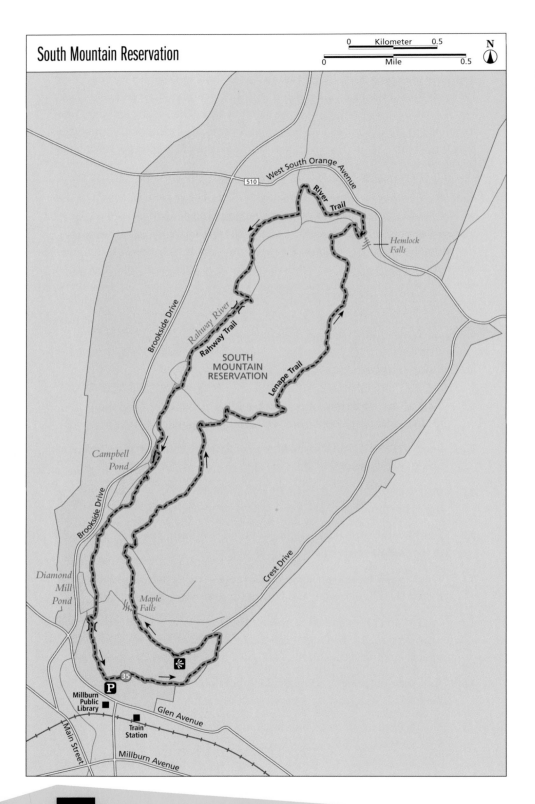

South Mountain Reservation

West South Orange Avenue

510

River Trail

Hemlock Falls

Rahway River

Rahway Trail

SOUTH MOUNTAIN RESERVATION

Lenape Trail

Brookside Drive

Campbell Pond

Brookside Drive

Diamond Mill Pond

Maple Falls

Crest Drive

35

P

Millburn Public Library

Glen Avenue

Train Station

Main Street

Millburn Avenue

3.3   Arrive at Hemlock Falls, the highlight of this hike and the apex of your loop.

3.5   Check the map kiosk at the intersection and briefly take the River Trail to the northwest, keeping left at the fork.

3.7   Leapfrog across the Rahway River and immediately turn left (south) onto the Rahway Trail on the opposite bank. This area can be overgrown.

4.2   Step over an intermittent stream as you cut across a slope above the little river valley.

4.3   Turn left (east) sharply on a gravel road that enters from the west. Cross a handsome stone bridge and then immediately turn right on the other side of the water, watching for white blazes near the edge of the river. Proceed south.

5.2   Cross a second bridge and continue walking southeast, veering east, away from Brookside Drive, the main road through the park.

5.7   Arrive back at the trailhead in the Locust Grove parking lot.

The Rahway Trail leads past millponds and an old power plant.

🍂 **Green Tip:**
Donate used gear to a nonprofit kids' organization.

HIKE INFORMATION

Local information: State of New Jersey, Division of Travel and Tourism, P.O. Box 460, Trenton, NJ 08625; 1-800-VISITNJ; www.visitnj.org/west-orange

Local events/attractions: Essex County Environmental Center, 621 Eagle Rock Ave., Roseland, NJ 07068; (973) 228-8776; www.essex-countynj.org/p/index.php?section=env/o

Turtle Back Zoo, 560 Northfield Ave., West Orange, NJ 07052; (973) 731-5800; www.turtlebackzoo.com

Good eats: Millburn Diner, 72 Essex St., Millburn, NJ 07041; (973) 376-0504; www.millburndiner.com. Burgers, wraps, pasta, pastries, and breakfast anytime.

Tinga Taqueria, 321 Millburn Ave., Millburn, NJ 07041; (973) 218-9500; www.tingausa.com. Tacos, quesadillas, salads, and inexpensive burrito specials at lunch.

Local outdoor stores: REI, 280 State Rte. 10, East Hanover, NJ 07936-2608; (973) 581-1938; www.rei.com

The Outdoor Store, 30 Church St., Montclair, NJ 07042; (973) 746-5900; http://shopoutdoor.com

Organizations: South Mountain Conservancy, P.O. Box 273, South Orange, NJ 07079; www.somocon.org

Union County Hiking Club, c/o Mary Doyle, 117 Woodward Lane, Basking Ridge, NJ 07920-2730; (908) 580-1778; http://uchc.nynjtc.org

Watchung Reservation

A longer hike through the largest property in the Union County Park System leads past a deserted village, a pair of quiet ponds, a stately evergreen forest, and an abandoned copper mine—and offers an opportunity to appreciate the numerous birds, mammals, and reptiles that make their homes within the park's 2,065 acres.

Start: At the end of New Providence Road, behind the Trailside Nature & Science Center
Nearest town: Mountainside, NJ
Distance: 7.6-mile loop
Approximate hiking time: 4 to 5 hours
Difficulty: Moderate
Trail surface: Bridle paths, dirt foot trails, and several stony sections
Seasons: Year-round
Other trail users: Joggers, dog walkers, cyclists, equestrians
Wheelchair accessibility: The nature and science center is wheelchair accessible; trails are not.
Canine compatibility: Leashed dogs permitted
Land status: County park

Fees and permits: None
Schedule: Trails open daily from dawn to dusk. Parking areas close at 9 p.m.
Facilities: Restrooms, picnic areas with grills, water fountains, stable, museum, refreshment stand (Apr–Sept), and playground
Maps: USGS Chatham and Roselle, NJ. A color map is available at the nature and science center and can be downloaded from Union County's website (see below).
Trail contacts: Union County Department of Parks and Community Renewal, 10 Elizabethtown Plaza, Elizabeth, NJ 07207; (908) 527-4000; http://ucnj .org/community/parks-community-renewal/parks-facilities

Finding the trailhead: From US 22 in Mountainside, take the Mountainside/New Provincetown Road exit. Proceed up the hill for 1 mile on Deer Path (which becomes Ackerman Street), making a right turn on Coles Avenue/Sky Top Drive to reach the parking area and trailhead, which is at the junction of Coles Avenue and New Providence Road. To reach Watchung from I-78, get off near Berkeley Heights at exit 43 and turn right at the first traffic light onto McMane Avenue. Turn left onto Glenside Avenue at the T intersection and enter the reservation at W. R. Tracy Drive after 1.2 miles. Keep to the left at the Loop and turn right at the traffic circle onto Summit Lane. Make the next right onto New Providence Road and immediately look for the parking area on the right. GPS: N40 41.052' / W74 22.326'

THE HIKE

Plunging into the woods behind the large greenhouse to the west of the Trailside Nature & Science Center, you'll pass between the First and Second Watchung Mountains at the outset of this rather long hike. Begin on the Orange Trail, which widens just beyond the trailhead, and merge onto the Blue Trail after about 0.4 mile. In another 500 feet or so the Blue Trail veers to the left—continue over the bridge (northwest), crossing Blue Brook. Head up the wide bridle path directly in front of you and look for a white blaze just on the left as the path flattens out: This is the Sierra Trail.

This route, the longest marked trail in the park, keeps to the northern side of the narrow Blue Brook waterway for more than 1 mile, swoops down to the southwestern corner of Watchung, crosses Sky Top Drive, and then levels off for the final leg back to the Trailside Center. Roughly 0.25 mile beyond the bridge, a small, fenced cemetery appears at the top of a rise, where the trail curves away from Blue Brook to the west. The burial plot is believed to contain the graves of two dozen people, including members of the Willcocks family that settled here in 1736.

The Sierra Trail jogs left onto another bridle path after the cemetery and then merges onto Cataract Hollow Road. Walk down this paved road to discover the deserted village of Feltville. Looking to expand his successful stationery business in Manhattan, David Felt purchased this land from the Willcocks in order to build a new paper factory. Between 1845 and 1847, he paid for the construction of a mill, two dams along the brook, and a town to house his workers. Nine structures and a barn, which is currently undergoing restoration, still stand today, although at its height, as many as 175 people called Feltville home. In 1882, the former mill town was converted into a summer resort called Glenside Park, and attracted seasonal residents from New York, Orange, and Newark. This property was incorporated into Watchung Reservation in the 1920s.

Skirting around the barn, the trail continues west over a carpet of pine needles and several little streams. As it approaches the park boundary and the intersection of Glenside Avenue and Valley Road, the trail turns left (east), crossing over little Seeleys Pond, and then immediately hooks to the right (south), reentering the woods. Bending around Seeleys Pond, the well-marked route ascends a bluff overlooking Green Brook and then dips below a rocky escarpment for 0.25 mile. Notice the ruins of an old mill as well as an abandoned quarry.

At mile 4.5, the trail turns left (north) and begins a steady climb of about 150 feet to an overlook. Catch your breath here and push on—at roughly 400 feet above sea level the now wider trail flattens considerably and presents no further challenges for the remainder of its length. Carefully cross Sky Top Drive and look for an unmarked trail to the right (north) of the picnic area. This short spur will link back up with the Sierra Trail. Here, in the park's interior, you will likely find yourself free of company, except the occasional frog or group of white-tailed deer.

Nearing Blue Brook again, the path becomes stonier and jogs to the left (west) before meeting the Blue Trail. Blue and white blazes guide you along the edge of a gorge that was once mined for copper, to an intersection with the Yellow Trail after 0.25 mile. Turn left (north) onto the Yellow Trail, which merges with the Orange Trail again, cross one last wooden bridge, and exit at the trailhead on New Providence Road.

MILES AND DIRECTIONS

0.0   Start behind the Trailside Nature & Science Center at the end of New Providence Road. Look for orange blazes.

0.4   Continue northwest (straight) on the Blue Trail, while the orange blazes head to the south. Cross Blue Brook and follow the dirt road uphill for a short distance until the Sierra Trail's white blazes appear on the left. Continue on the Sierra Trail.

The green frog can be distinguished from the bullfrog by the two ridges running down its back.

Watchung Reservation

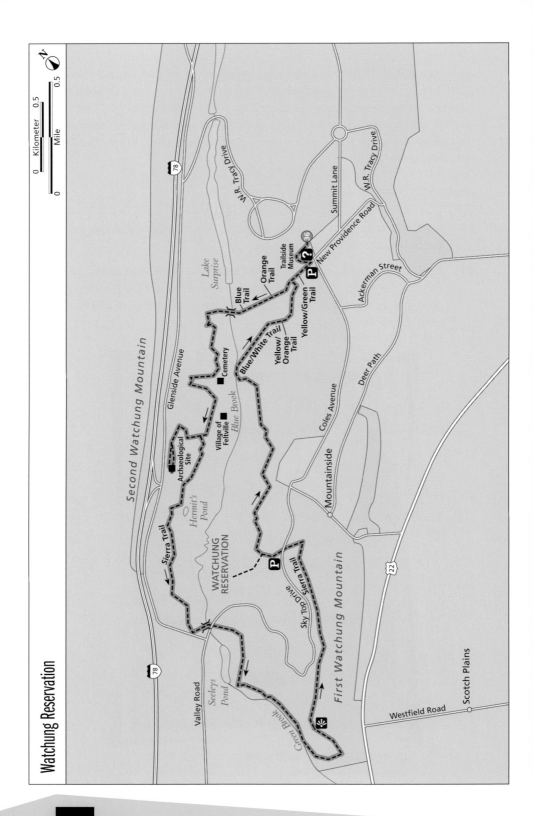

Labels on map:
- W.R. Tracy Drive
- W.R. Tracy Drive
- Summit Lane
- Trailside Museum
- 36
- New Providence Road
- Orange Trail
- Ackerman Street
- Blue Trail
- Yellow/Green Trail
- Blue/White Trail
- Yellow/Orange Trail
- Yellow/Orange Trail
- Lake Surprise
- Cemetery
- Deer Path
- Glenside Avenue
- Blue Brook
- Village of Feltville
- Coles Avenue
- Archaeological Site
- Second Watchung Mountain
- Mountainside
- Hermit's Pond
- WATCHUNG RESERVATION
- Sierra Trail
- Sky Top Drive
- Sierra Trail
- First Watchung Mountain
- Valley Road
- Seeleys Pond
- Great Brook
- Westfield Road
- Scotch Plains
- 78
- 78
- 22
- Kilometer 0.5
- Mile 0.5

0.9 The trail forks at the top of a small rise. Keep left to remain on the white-blazed trail and go by the eighteenth-century cemetery containing the headstones for two dozen early settlers.

1.1 Turn left on the pavement and walk down Cataract Hollow Road to arrive in the deserted village of Feltville. Spend some time in the small museum and wander among the houses that still stand between the museum and Masker's barn.

2.0 Arrive at the archaeology school site, where test pits form two neat rows and piles of sifted soil stand as evidence of the work that went into understanding the history of Feltville.

2.8 Stay on a westward course over an intermittent streambed at this intersection with an unmarked trail. The white blazes lead around Hermit's Pond and over a short section of boardwalk.

3.4 Emerge from the forest, briefly walk on the shoulder of Glenside Avenue, and turn left (east) over the bridge, watching for white blazes on the south side of the road once you're across Seeley's Pond.

4.5 Having followed Green Brook south from Seeleys Pond, turn left (north) and climb roughly 200 feet up a long slope to an overlook. From here the Sierra Trail levels off for approximately 0.75 mile.

5.2 Turn left (west) with the white blazes and carefully cross Sky Top Drive. Look for the trail to resume on the right (north) side of the picnic pavilion.

6.5 Curve left (northwest) on the Sierra Trail, descend a small slope toward Blue Brook, and then loop back around to the east, keeping an eye out for blue blazes. A small gorge with an abandoned copper mine is to the right.

6.9 The Blue/White Trail veers north again and meets the Yellow Trail. Turn right (east) on this path, which soon merges with the Orange Trail.

7.6 Arrive back at the trailhead after walking over a small footbridge and climbing back up to New Providence Road on a small piece of the Green Trail.

🐾 Green Tip:
*Go out of your way to avoid animals that are mating
or taking care of their young.*

Options: The Sierra Trail is the largest loop within the park. Its 10 miles lead from the riding stables off of Summit Lane in the north, along much of the length of Lake Surprise, and down to the southern boundary near Union Avenue.

HIKE INFORMATION

Local information: State of New Jersey, Division of Travel and Tourism, P.O. Box 460, Trenton, NJ 08625; 1-800-VISITNJ; www.visitnj.org/elizabeth

Local events/attractions: The Robinson Plantation, 593 Madison Hill Rd., Clark, NJ 07066; (732) 340-1571; www.clarkhistorical society.org. A seventeenth-century farmhouse built by Scottish physician and surgeon Dr. William Robinson.
Liberty Hall Museum, 1003 Morris Ave., Union, NJ 07083; (908) 527-0400; www.kean.edu/libertyhall/index.html

Good eats: Jimmy Buff's Italian Hot Dogs, 2581 US 22, Scotch Plains, NJ 07076; (908) 233-2833; www.jimmybuff.com. A hot dog cooked in soybean oil, topped with onion, peppers, and potatoes, served on a pizza roll.
Famous Dave's Bar-B-Que, 1443 Rte. 22 East, Mountainside, NJ 07092; (908) 232-5619; www.famousdaves.com/Mountainside

Local outdoor stores: Blue Ridge Mountain Sports, 23 Main St., Madison, NJ 07940; (973) 377-3301; www.brmsstore.com

Organizations: Alliance for New Jersey Environmental Education, 11 Hardscrabble Rd., Bernardsville, NJ 07924; www.anjee.net
Trailside Museum Association, 452 New Providence Rd., Mountainside, NJ 07092; (908) 789-3270

> 🍃 **Green Tip:**
> *Pass it down—the best way to instill good green habits in your children is to set a good example.*

Connecticut

Snake sightings are relatively common in Connecticut. See Hike 40.

Keep your eyes peeled as you hike in Sleeping Giant State Park. There's always the chance that a red-tailed hawk or a peregrine falcon could decide to keep you company for a moment or two. See Hike 39.

Mianus River Park

Stroll under willow trees and cottonwoods along one stretch of a river that flows to the Long Island Sound from Westchester County. Seek quietude on the Greenwich side of the park, where box turtles, eastern cottontails, and swallows are but a few species sharing more than 300 acres of woodland and wetland in suburban Connecticut.

Start: Behind the red barn on Merriebrook Lane

Nearest town: Stamford, CT

Distance: 4.0-mile loop with an out-and-back leg to start

Approximate hiking time: 1.5 to 2 hours

Difficulty: Easy to moderate

Trail surface: Primarily gravel woods road and dirt forest paths

Seasons: May through Oct

Other trail users: Mountain bikers, joggers, dog walkers, anglers

Wheelchair accessibility: None

Canine compatibility: Leashed dogs permitted

Land status: Municipal park

Fees and permits: None

Schedule: Daily from dawn to dusk

Facilities: None

Maps: USGS Stamford, CT. A detailed trail map can be downloaded from the Friends of Mianus River Park website (see Hike Information).

Trail contacts: Connecticut Department of Environmental Protection, 79 Elm St., Hartford, CT 06106; (860) 424-3000; www.ct.gov/dep

Finding the trailhead: Drive north from New York on the Hutchinson River Parkway, which becomes the Merritt Parkway when it crosses the Connecticut state line. Go about 9 miles into Connecticut and then exit the Merritt via Den Road (exit 33). Make a right on Roxbury Road and the next left onto Westover Road. Continue 1.3 miles to Merriebrook Lane. Turn right and look for the small parking area and trailhead on the right. GPS: N41 04.874' / W73 34.867'

THE HIKE

In spite of the fact that standard poodles and golden retrievers are two of the animals you're most likely to see on a trip to Mianus River Park, visitors that spend time on the trails that lead into the heart of this natural area might find themselves meeting a few other quadrupeds. Although it's tucked in between country clubs and residential developments in the middle of suburbia, Mianus River Park still manages to preserve a bit of the wilderness. Centuries ago the Algonquin-speaking Siwanoy tribe lived off the land in this part of the state—the river is actually named after Myano, the sachem, or leader, of the westernmost group of "the South people." In the seventeenth century Dutch and English colonists took control of the territory once occupied by the Siwanoy, transforming it into farms and timber lots.

Robert Goodbody, a New York financier, bought much of the property currently within the park's boundaries in 1928, stabling his horses in the large red barn that still stands on Merriebrook Lane. Some four decades later the City of Stamford purchased a small tract of land on the river for recreational use. Then, in 1972, the Goodbody estate sold Stamford and Greenwich what has become one of the most popular pieces of the Mianus River Greenway.

Winding northwest from the little parking area next to the barn, the East River Trail, the out-and-back leg of this two-part tour, is the perfect trail to introduce

The namesake feature of the Cave Trail

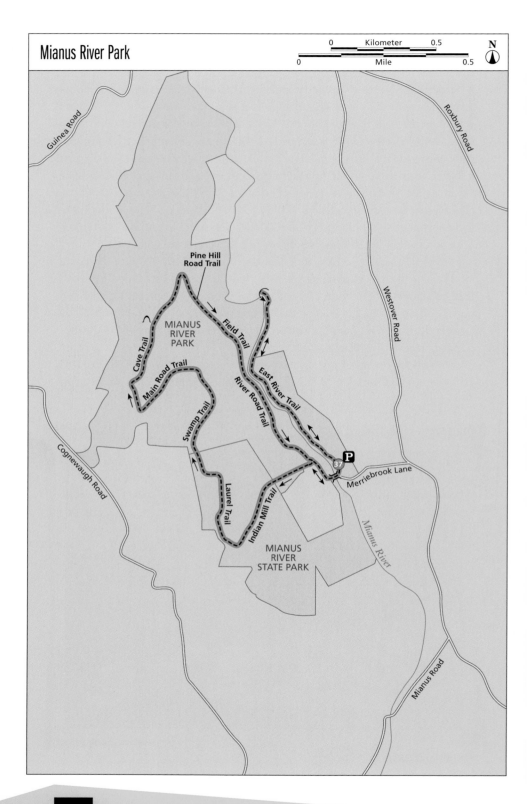

you to the park: easygoing, short, and loaded with things to see. Mallards probably won't be a surprising sight, but happening upon a regal great blue heron or even a plump muskrat might make this hike that much more memorable.

Turn around at the end of the trail and walk back through the elderberry and sycamore trees, moving past house lots abutting the preserve on the Stamford side. Now that you've warmed up your muscles, it's time to cross the Mianus and disappear for a while amidst the tupelos, sassafras, and elm on the second leg of the hike, a loop traveled in a clockwise direction. If necessary, stop to consult the sign showing the trail system before proceeding into the Greenwich portion of the park. Dog walkers frequent the River Road Trail just on the other side of the bridge, but by taking the Indian Mill Trail up and over a low ridge, you'll leave the canine commotion behind, simultaneously increasing the chances of spotting a more reclusive mammal like the red fox.

Veering right onto the Laurel Trail you'll head north for close to 1 mile, passing through uplands dominated by oak and tulip, and encountering a stone chimney that is part of a building ruin called the Creamery. A similar fireplace can be found on the East River Trail, but little is known about either.

Make a left on the Swamp Trail at mile 2, and observe the change in flora, namely an abundance of ferns drawn to the cool, moist environment. Clumps of cinnamon fern, with their extremely large fronds, are easier to recognize, but thick colonies of bracken fern and the lacy maidenhair fern also appear here. Continuing northward, the soft trail skirts around rock outcroppings and meets the Main Road Trail at a T intersection.

Turn left on the Main Road Trail, walk 0.2 mile, and turn right (northeast) on the Cave Trail. Wriggling like a serpent through the forest, this secluded corridor leads into an area populated with white pines, and does in fact arrive at a friendly-looking cave set into Pine Hill just before mile 3. Beyond the cave, turn right (south) on Pine Hill Road, which quickly runs into the Field Trail. Push on to the southeast, using the River Road with a brief detour on the Hill Trail. Resist the urge to get closer to the water on this final stretch—the Friends of Mianus have replanted native species such as spicebush, swamp rose, and serviceberry to combat erosion and help restore a riverbank damaged by flooding and heavy visitor usage.

MILES AND DIRECTIONS

0.0 Start behind the red barn on Merriebrook Lane. Follow the East River Trail northwest along the Mianus.

0.5 Arrive at a large stone fireplace and chimney standing near the damp riverbank. Continue on the narrow, level track until it fades away about 0.1 mile later. This is the turnaround point for the out-and-back leg of the hike.

1.3   Back near the barn and the small parking area, turn right (west) over the bridge spanning the Mianus. This is the start of the loop portion of the hike. Following the road, walk up a small hill and around the Tree Tops estate to the Indian Mill Trail, a path that begins as pitted, cracked, and leaf-strewn pavement.

1.5   Before reaching the chain-link fence, make a hard right (north) to remain on the Indian Mill Trail, and enter Greenwich Township.

1.8   Just past the Indian Rock Trail intersection, curve north and join the (signed) Laurel Trail.

1.9   Pass another chimney on the left.

2.0   Turn left (west) on the Swamp Trail at the signpost. Keep left on the Swamp Trail at the next junction with the short Watercan Trail.

2.4   Still staying on the Swamp Trail, walk past the Peak Trail.

2.5   Meet the broad, flat Main Road Trail and turn left (southwest). The trail surface soon shifts to gravel.

2.7   Just beyond a ridge to the right of the trail, turn sharply right (northeast) to join the Cave Trail. Don't be led off-course by the many lesser side trails that cross the Cave Trail.

2.9   Arrive at the trail's namesake—a small cave that might be 10 or 12 feet deep.

3.1   Turn right (south) on the Pine Hill Road Trail. When it forks a few hundred feet farther on, proceed southeast on the Field Trail.

3.4   Turn right (southwest) to merge with the River Road Trail. Walk through an intersection where a number of trails converge around a map kiosk.

3.6   Turn right (southwest) to take the very short Hill Trail until it meets the Laurel Trail. Make a quick left and then a right on the River Road Trail again.

3.8   Arrive back at the gate opposite the Tree Tops property where the Indian Mill Trail crosses the park. Proceed straight ahead (south) downhill on the road back to the bridge.

4.0   Cross the Mianus River to reach the trailhead.

Options: Extend your hike by adding the Second Loop Trail at the northern end of Mianus River Park, or the River Walk and Indian Rock Trails in the southern "Tree Tops" section.

Local information: Western Connecticut Convention & Visitors Bureau, P.O. Box 968, Litchfield, CT 06759; (860) 567-4506; www.visitfairfieldcountyct.com

Local events/attractions: Bartlett Arboretum & Gardens, 151 Brookdale Rd., Stamford, CT 06903; (203) 322-6971; www.bartlettarboretum.org. Open daily from 9 a.m. until sunset. Display gardens and a Silver Education Center.

Bruce Museum, 1 Museum Dr., Greenwich, CT 06830; (203) 869-0376; http://brucemuseum.org. The former home of merchant Robert Moffat Bruce is now a museum of American and Native American art, history, and culture.

Stamford Museum & Nature Center, 39 Scofieldtown Rd., Stamford, CT 06903; (203) 322-1646; www.stamfordmuseum.org. Nature trails, a working farm, an observatory and planetarium, plus a museum of art and natural history.

Local outdoor stores: Eastern Mountain Sports, 952 High Ridge Rd., Stamford, CT 06905; (203) 461-9865; www.ems.com

Outdoor Traders, 55 Arch St., Greenwich, CT 06830; (203) 862-9696; www.outdoortraders.com

Organizations: Connecticut Forest & Park Association (CFPA), 16 Meriden Rd., Rockfall, CT 06481; (860) 346-2372; www.ctwoodlands.org. A private nonprofit committed to conserving Connecticut's land, water, and wildlife. This group also established the Blue-Blazed Hiking Trail System in 1929.

Mianus River Watershed Council, P.O. Box 421, Greenwich, CT 06836; (203) 861-0077; http://mianusriver.org

Friends of Mianus River Park, www.friendsofmianusriverpark.org. A volunteer organization that seeks to foster awareness, understanding, and appreciation of the Mianus watershed.

> 🌿 **Green Tip:**
> *Consider the packaging of any products you bring with you. It's best to properly dispose of packaging at home before you hike. If you're on the trail, pack it out with you.*

Bring a GPS and leave the grind behind in an unspoiled wilderness area wedged between New Haven and Waterbury. Watch hours slip by without seeing another person, and then ascend Tobys Rock Mountain to soak up the scenery of the Naugatuck River valley.

Start: At the dirt parking lot on Cold Spring Road

Nearest town: Beacon Falls, CT

Distance: 2.9-mile lollipop

Approximate hiking time: 1.5 to 2 hours

Difficulty: Easy to moderate

Trail surface: Gravel woods road, dirt trails, and grassy footpaths

Seasons: May through Oct

Other trail users: Mountain bikers; cross-country skiers, hunters, and snowmobilers (seasonally)

Wheelchair accessibility: None

Canine compatibility: Dogs permitted if on a leash 6 feet or less

Land status: State forest

Fees and permits: None

Schedule: Daily from sunrise to sunset

Facilities: None

Maps: USGS Naugatuck, CT. A black-and-white trail map of Naugatuck's East & West Blocks can be downloaded from the Connecticut Department of Environmental Protection's website (see below).

Special considerations: Hunting is permitted in state forests. Educate yourself about the hunting season before going on a hike.

Trail contacts: Connecticut Department of Environmental Protection, 79 Elm St., Hartford, CT 06106; (860) 424-3000; www .ct.gov/dep

Finding the trailhead: By car from New York, follow I-95 north toward New Haven. Take exit 27A to merge onto Routes 25 and 8 north toward Trumbull and Waterbury. Stay on Route 8 north for 20 miles and then take exit 23 (South Main Street) toward Beacon Falls. Turn right on South Main Street/ Route 42 east and drive 1 mile to Depot Street. Cross the river, turn right on Railroad Avenue, and right again on Cold Spring/High Rock Road. Proceed 1 mile to the parking area and trailhead on the left. **By public transportation:** From Grand Central Station, take the Waterbury branch of the New Haven line to Beacon Falls on Metro North. Follow Railroad Avenue across the tracks by walking north from the station. Turn right (north) on Cold Spring/High Rock Road and walk 1.1 miles along the tracks to the trailhead. GPS: N41 27.335' / W73 03.792'

THE HIKE

Without traveling a greater distance from New York—perhaps even planning a trip to a national park—it can be difficult to find something resembling the backcountry anywhere near a major city. And yet Naugatuck State Forest, roughly 5,000 acres of secondary forest in New Haven County, doesn't contain a visitor center, campgrounds, or even many blazed trails. Generally left to its own devices, but not ignored completely, it is managed for firewood, saw timber, and habitat research. Four reservoirs are also located in the southwest corner of West Block. Follow Spruce Brook into the West Block—one of five organizational parcels of land established by the Connecticut Department of Environmental Protection (DEP)—and roam woodland trails knowing you probably won't encounter other outdoor enthusiasts.

The Metro North Railroad stops in Beacon Falls, a little town that began to take shape on the eastern side of the Naugatuck River in the late 1600s and eventually grew into a busy regional center of industry. Farming, lumbering, and other commercial activities quickly laid bare the hillsides around Beacon Falls, while businesses used the river as a source of power and waste removal for their tanneries, wool mills, and rubber companies. In 1834 this town was also responsible for introducing a small but revolutionary product to the world: the friction match invented by Thomas Sanford.

View of the Naugatuck River valley from Tobys Rock Mountain

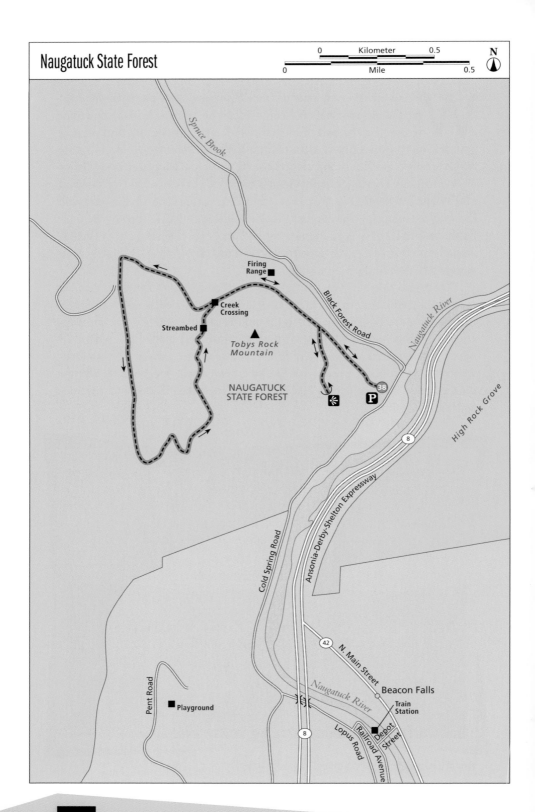

Kilometer

Mile

N

Spruce Brook

Firing Range

Creek Crossing

Streambed

Tobys Rock Mountain

NAUGATUCK STATE FOREST

Black Forest Road

Naugatuck River

38

P

8

High Rock Grove

Cold Spring Road

Ansonia-Derby-Shelton Expressway

42

N. Main Street

Beacon Falls

Train Station

Naugatuck River

Pent Road

Playground

8

Lopus Road

Railroad Avenue

Depot Street

From the train station, the walk to the forest is approximately 1 mile along a sleepy road that parallels the river and the railroad tracks for the entirety of its journey. A small DEP sign signals that you've reached the parking lot; look for a trailhead with a faint blue blaze at its northern end. Using care on the loose, slippery rocks underfoot, ascend this trail, which rises above the Spruce Brook ravine to the north. Once you've advanced 0.25 mile or more into the preserve, the buzz of cicadas and the crash of waterfalls in the ravine will replace the noise from the highway that accompanied you if you walked on Cold Spring Road. The sharp crack and pop of gunfire from the adjacent firing range will also be increasingly audible on most days.

After a few twists and turns through hemlocks and oaks that cast their shadows on the forest floor, the trail levels off and intersects several gravel roads that radiate out from a cleared area probably created by logging. Stop here and listen for some of the birds that inhabit this site, including the whistling call of the olive-sided flycatcher and the high-pitched buzzing of the blue-winged warbler (which is yellow-bodied). Goldenrod, Queen Anne's lace, and stiff aster (which look a bit like daisies) flourish in abundance. Dozens of tiny, silvery blue spring azure butterflies also flutter in the sunshine, happy for the wealth of wildflowers. Turn left and move on to the south, reentering the woods at the 1.3-mile mark.

Because the unmarked trail can be tricky to follow here, keep your map handy and consult your compass and/or GPS often. Wind your way over fallen trees, moss-covered boulders, and intermittent streams, all the while circling to the north in the direction of the main trail into the forest. When you rejoin this path, turn right (southeast) and walk back downhill to the spur trail that leads up Tobys Rock Mountain to an overlook. The 0.2 mile climb to the viewpoint is very steep and the soil can be loose; use caution. With an almost sheer drop from the rock ledges, you'll also want to watch your footing at the top. From this high point you'll be able to look up and down the river valley, watching as commuters hurry across the Constitution State on Route 8.

From the overlook, retrace your steps to the main trail, turn right, and walk back to the trailhead.

Option: With a car it's possible to drive to the town of Naugatuck, park on the north side of the state forest's East Block, and hike as many as 10.4 miles on the blue Naugatuck Trail, which reaches from Cross Street all the way to Beacon Road.

MILES AND DIRECTIONS

0.0 Start at the dirt parking lot on Cold Spring Road. Walk uphill on a blue-blazed trail.

0.2   A spur to the left leads to an overlook above the Naugatuck River; you'll visit the overlook on the return trip.

0.4   The trail briefly levels off and the big trees thin out as it curves to the west. This is the hike's closest point to the firing range, which is often audible.

0.5   Cross an intermittent stream and proceed west/northwest in a counterclockwise direction. This is the beginning of the loop.

0.9   Take the leftmost of two gravel roads, which heads south as it slopes downhill through an overgrown meadow. The other gravel road continues to the west.

1.2   Now narrower, the gravel gives way to grass. Keep to the left (east) at a fork when you reach the tree line. Make another left soon after, regaining some of the elevation you just lost.

1.6   Turn right (southeast) on another gravel road that cuts across your route. Less than 0.1 mile beyond, look for a blue blaze to the left of the trail by the burned, rusted remains of an old car.

1.8   Rising and falling with the undulating terrain, the trail dips down into a gully and then veers right. Scramble over a shoulder of rock and then bear left. Depending on the season this stretch could involve a small degree of bushwhacking.

2.0   Close the loop by rejoining the main trail that you took into the forest and turn right (southeast).

2.5   Using the spur trail you passed previously, climb a fairly steep trail to several ledges overlooking the river and the highway. Descend via the same route; turn right (southeast) at the junction to get back to your starting point.

2.9   Arrive back at the trailhead and parking lot on Cold Spring Road.

HIKE INFORMATION

Local information: Connecticut Commission on Culture & Tourism, One Constitution Plaza, Second Floor, Hartford, CT 06103; (860) 256-2800; www.ctvisit.com
Local events/attractions: Ansonia Nature & Recreation Center, 10 Deerfield Lane, Ansonia, CT 06401; (203) 736-1053; www.ansonianaturecenter.org

Mattatuck Museum Arts & History Center, 144 West Main St., Waterbury, CT 06702; (203) 753-0381; www.mattatuckmuseum.org

Good eats: Full Harvest Bar & Grill, 57 South Main St., Beacon Falls, CT 06403; (203) 672-5996; www.fullharvestbarandgrill.com

The Original Antonios, 90 North Main St., Beacon Falls, CT 06403; (203) 729-8882; www.theoriginalantonios.com

Local outdoor stores: Trailblazer, 296 Elm St., New Haven, CT 06511; (203) 865-6244; www.shoptrailblazer.com

Outdoor World Outfitters, 979 Meriden Ave., Southington, CT 06489; (860) 621-8381; www.theoutdoorworld.com

Organizations: Connecticut Forest & Park Association (CFPA), 16 Meriden Rd., Rockfall, CT 06481; (860) 346-2372; www.ctwoodlands.org. A private non-profit committed to conserving Connecticut's land, water, and wildlife. This group also established the Blue-Blazed Hiking Trail System in 1929.

Friends of Connecticut State Parks, 16 Meriden Rd., Rockfall, CT 06481; www.friendsctstateparks.org

Connecticut Botanical Society, P.O. Box 9004, New Haven, CT 06532; www.ct-botanical-society.org. This volunteer group organizes frequent plant identification field trips.

Queen Anne's lace thrives in sunny patches of the forest.

Sleeping Giant State Park

Stand atop a reclining giant and walk the first trails in Connecticut to be designated National Recreational Trails by the US Department of Interior. Wander through woods that once provided for the Quinnipiac Indians, and test your plant, animal, or fungi knowledge.

Start: Orange trailhead near the picnic area off Mount Carmel Avenue

Nearest town: Hamden, CT

Distance: 2.3-mile loop

Approximate hiking time: 1.5 hours

Difficulty: Easy to moderate

Trail surface: Gravel woods roads, dirt trails, and bare rock

Seasons: Year-round

Other trail users: Mountain bikers, equestrians, joggers; cross-country skiers (seasonally)

Wheelchair accessibility: None

Canine compatibility: Dogs permitted if on a leash 6 feet or less

Land status: State park

Fees and permits: None

Schedule: Daily from 8 a.m. until sunset

Facilities: Restrooms, water, picnic areas

Maps: USGS Mount Carmel and Wallingford, CT. A trail map/brochure is available at the main park entrance and a letter-size color version can be downloaded from www.sgpa.org or the Connecticut Department of Environmental Protection's website (see below).

Trail contacts: Connecticut Department of Environmental Protection, 79 Elm St., Hartford, CT 06106; (860) 424-3000; www.ct.gov/dep

Finding the trailhead: Take I-95 north from New York. In New Haven, head north on I-91 at exit 48. Drive 6.7 miles and then take exit 10 west on Route 40 toward Hamden. This road will merge with Route 10/Whitney Avenue after 2.8 miles. Continue north and turn right on Mount Carmel Avenue after another 1.5 miles. The entrance to the park is on the left, across from the Quinnipiac University campus. GPS: N41 25.331′W72 53.977′

THE HIKE

Stand at the base of a tremendous mass of earth and stone and one mountain can easily look like another. But take a few steps back—big ones, mind you—and they begin to assume different shapes, unique identities. From a distance of several miles, for instance, Sleeping Giant conjures memories of a well-known eighteenth-century traveler by the name of Lemuel. In the lore of the local Quinnipiac Indians, however, the anthropomorphic mountain, with its head to the west and feet to the east, is the spirit Hobbomock, sentenced to eternal sleep after he diverted the course of the Connecticut River.

Known as Mount Carmel by early settlers to the area, Hobbomock was transformed into protected land in 1933 when a group of volunteers calling themselves the Sleeping Giant Park Association (SPGA) successfully acquired the first ridge, or the "head" of the giant, after nine years of negotiating with the quarrying company that owned the lease to the property. Today eleven interconnecting trails designed by Norman Greist and Richard Elliott in the late 1950s lead hikers to numerous views and features throughout the park's 1,650 acres. The SGPA hopes to eventually expand Sleeping Giant to more than 2,000 acres.

Built in the late 1930s, the stone tower rises from the giant's left hip, near the center of the park.

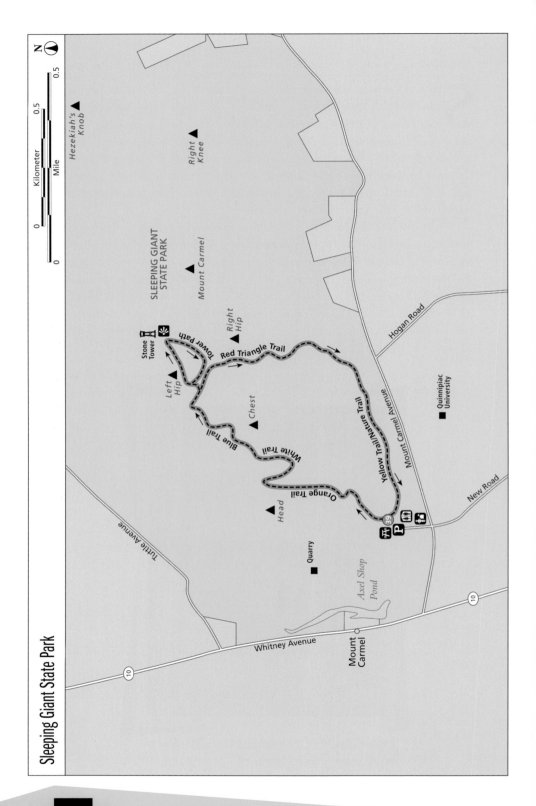

Sleeping Giant State Park

Leave the trailhead at the picnic area inside the main entrance and start up the incline in front of you on the Orange Trail. The cliff and the quarry that inspired citizens to advocate for the park's creation lie to the west. Eastern hop hornbeam (sometimes referred to as ironwood because of its durability), the hardy, aromatic eastern red cedar, and white oak are all commonly seen along the Orange Trail. Until about the 0.5-mile mark, the going is relatively easy, but on the other side of the Tower Path, the trail begins to steepen as it progresses up toward the "chest" of the Giant.

At the western end of the park, blazed trails overlap and merge into one another frequently; don't hesitate to consult your map if you get confused about which way to turn. From the chest, turn left with the blue/white blazes and follow this ridge north for a short distance. Move quietly and remain alert, and you might happen upon a long black-scaled racer or a striped garter snake warming itself on a sunny patch of bare stone. The Blue Trail heads down a small cliff en route to the "left hip" and caution should be used on this short descent.

Walk through the depression between the second and third ridges and keep going northeast on the Blue Trail toward your destination: the stone tower. Follow the ramp to the top of this four-storey structure and relish the vista you have from almost 780 feet above sea level. New Haven's tallest buildings will glisten in the sun, and across the Quinnipiac River, the low mountains to the east will appear closer than they really are. Unless it is overcast or particularly late in the day, linger here; hiking shouldn't be about rushing from place to place. There's always the chance that a red-tailed hawk or a peregrine falcon could decide to keep you company for a moment or two.

Take the Tower Path partway back down from the summit, turning left onto the Red Triangle Trail at the 1.4-mile mark. This route connects with Tuttle Avenue on the park's northern boundary, but you'll head south, staying with it for close to 0.5 mile as it passes over pebbles, small rocks, and the occasional sandstone boulder. Before you get to Mount Carmel Avenue, turn right (west) on the Yellow Trail and stick with this level footpath as it maneuvers by long-needled white pines, shrubby witch hazel, slow-growing shagbark hickory, and flowering dogwoods.

MILES AND DIRECTIONS

0.0 Start at the orange trailhead near the picnic area off Mount Carmel Avenue. Press on uphill to the north on the Orange Trail.

0.2 Turn left onto the White Trail, still heading north. The Tower Path will be on your right.

0.4 Bear right and work your way up a semisteep slope—the "chest" of the Sleeping Giant.

0.6 After ascending a stone staircase to approximately 650 feet, turn left (north) onto the blue/white-blazed trail.

0.8 Keep to the right (east) on the Blue Trail where the trail divides and then make a steep descent down a large rock outcropping.

0.9 Meet the Red Triangle Trail, running north-south across your path, and continue moving northeast on the Blue Trail.

1.1 Reach the stone tower on the Giant's left hip and climb the interior ramp for sweeping views of West Rock Ridge, New Haven's skyline, and Pistapaug and Totoket Mountains in the east. Begin to walk back down on the Tower Path.

1.4 Turn left (south) on the Red Triangle Trail in a low point between two ridges. Cross the Orange Trail and then the White Trail, but do not deviate from your southward course on the Red Triangle Trail. Watch your footing.

1.8 Back at about 280 feet of elevation, turn right (west) on the Yellow Trail. This same spot is also the farthest point on the Nature Trail loop.

2.1 Proceed around the bottom of the mountain on the Yellow Trail, crossing the Hexagon Trail, which runs north-south.

2.3 Arrive back at the trailhead and parking area on Mount Carmel Avenue.

Option: Continue hiking east from the tower on the Blue Trail to explore the other side of the park. Make your way to the "left knee," or Hezekiah's Knob, for additional views. Turn around and walk back toward the "head" on the Orange, White, or Yellow Trail.

HIKE INFORMATION

Local information: Connecticut Commission on Culture & Tourism, One Constitution Plaza, Second Floor, Hartford, CT 06103; (860) 256-2800; www.ctvisit.com
Local events/attractions: The Shore Line Trolley Museum, 17 River St., East Haven, CT 06512; (203) 467-6927; www.bera.org. Ride the oldest continuously operating suburban trolley line in the United States.
Peabody Museum of Natural History, Yale University, P.O. Box 208118, New Haven, CT 06520; (203) 432-5050; www.peabody.yale.edu. A world-class collection of over 12 million cultural and biological specimens.
Good eats: Aunt Chiladas, 3931 Whitney Ave., Hamden, CT 06518; (203) 230-4640; www.auntchilada.com. Rated best Mexican restaurant by the *New Haven Advocate*.

Eli's on Whitney, 2392 Whitney Ave., Hamden, CT 06518; (203) 287-1101; www
.elisonwhitney.com

Wentworth Old Fashioned Ice Cream, 3697 Whitney Ave., Hamden, CT 06518;
(203) 281-7429. As anyone who's been here knows, the view of Sleeping Giant is
best appreciated with a bowl of homemade ice cream.

Local outdoor stores: Trailblazer, 296 Elm St., New Haven, CT 06511; (203) 865-
6244; www.shoptrailblazer.com

Outdoor World Outfitters, 979 Meriden Ave., Southington, CT 06489; (860) 621-
8381; www.theoutdoorworld.com

Hike Tours: The Sleeping Giant Park Association leads fourteen to fifteen guided
hikes a year. See the website (below) for details.

Organizations: Connecticut Forest & Park Association (CFPA), 16 Meriden Rd.,
Rockfall, CT 06481; (860) 346-2372; www.ctwoodlands.org. A private nonprofit
committed to conserving Connecticut's land, water, and wildlife. This group also
established the Blue-Blazed Hiking Trail System in 1929.

Friends of Connecticut State Parks, 16 Meriden Rd., Rockfall, CT 06481; www
.friendsctstateparks.org

New Haven Hiking Club, 61 Eramo Terrace, Hamden, CT 06518; www.nhhc.info

The Sleeping Giant Park Association, P.O. Box 185430, Hamden, CT 06518; www
.sgpa.org

BYO Bottle

For all of its natural diversity, almost any hike near New York is guaranteed to
include a sighting of one common feature: the disposable plastic water bottle. Tossed carelessly off the side of the trail, these objects are unfortunately
far from rare in the parks and preserves of the tristate area. And yet they have
no place in the wild. According to the New York State Department of Environmental Conservation, approximately 2.5 billion bottles of water are sold
in New York every year. Nearly 90 percent of them will end up as garbage or
litter (nationally only 10 percent are recycled). What's worse is that these plas-
tics take hundreds and hundreds of years to photodegrade, or break down
into smaller compounds that can themselves be harmful to the environment.
Not to mention the fact that producing and transporting all of these bottles
uses millions of barrels of oil and generates tons of carbon dioxide that pol-
lute the air. So instead of stopping at a supermarket or a convenience store
to buy water (which is often just filtered tap water), fill up a reusable vessel
and stash it in your day pack. You'll be saving money—lots if you're a frequent
hydrator—while helping to preserve the beauty of wild places.

West Rock Ridge State Park

A crescent-shaped slice of land originally called Providence Hill, this ridge has impressed visitors since the late nineteenth century, when New Haven residents would take their carriages to the top for a view of the city and Long Island Sound. Today a relatively short hike from Wintergreen Avenue around the southern tip results in a very similar panorama—but one that's been updated for the twenty-first century.

Start: At the map kiosk just inside the park entrance

Nearest town: New Haven, CT

Distance: 4.2 miles out and back

Approximate hiking time: 2 to 3 hours

Difficulty: Easy to moderate

Trail surface: Gravel woods road, dirt trails, and paved park road

Seasons: May through Oct

Other trail users: Mountain bikers, joggers, equestrians, and anglers

Wheelchair accessibility: South Overlook can be reached by car.

Canine compatibility: Leashed dogs permitted

Land status: State park

Fees and permits: None

Schedule: Daily from 8 a.m. until sunset

Facilities: Picnic areas, composting toilets at Lake Wintergreen

Maps: USGS Mount Carmel and New Haven, CT. A two-color (and tricky to decipher) trail map is available at the park entrance and can be downloaded from the Connecticut Department of Environmental Protection's website (see below) or the West Rock Ridge Park Association's website (see Hike Information).

Trail contacts: Connecticut Department of Environmental Protection, 79 Elm St., Hartford, CT 06106; (860) 424-3000; www .ct.gov/dep

Finding the trailhead: Drive north from New York on the Hutchinson River Parkway, which becomes the Merritt Parkway/Route 15 when it crosses the Connecticut state line. At the Housatonic River, to the west of New Haven, the Merritt Parkway/Route 15 turns into the Wilbur Cross Parkway. Continue 8.8 miles northeast on Route 15, taking exit 59 onto Whalley Avenue south. At Blake Street make a left turn, and then make another left turn onto Springside Avenue after 0.3 mile. Make a final left at the four-way intersection to reach the park entrance and trailhead off Wintergreen Avenue. GPS: N41 20.689' / W72 58.077'

Sometimes a mountain is more than simply a place to go for contemplation or relaxation. High points can also make for good hiding places. At least this was the idea that two British justices, Edward Whalley and his son-in-law William Goffe, had in 1661 when they fled to West Rock to escape an arrest warrant issued by the King of England. The king was interested in their capture because they had signed the death warrant for King Charles I and then, during the Restoration, fled to New England. And while few modern criminals have probably ever contemplated evading the authorities in Judges' Cave, countless park-goers have visited this landmark during the course of a hike to one of the ridge's famous views.

For the first mile of the hike, the well-worn surface of the Red Trail runs south along the eastern side of the park, rising and falling with the terrain, but never really varying its pitch. Chipmunks emit sharp squeaks and sprint for cover as your boots kick up gravel on your southward journey, but in spite of the fact that the Connecticut Department of Environmental Protection has stated that West Rock Ridge contains more rare and endangered species than any other park in the state, many of them, like Whalley and Goffe, prefer camouflage over flashiness.

At a T intersection just beyond the 1-mile mark, the Red Trail turns right, quickly transforming from an easygoing stroll into a serious climb. Look down for a moment as you struggle up a particularly steep section. The crumbling volcanic rock that characterizes this land formation turns a rusty color with exposure to time and weather—this is due to its iron content.

When you turn your gaze back to the task of ascending West Rock, you might notice that you've reached an overlook about halfway up the trail. The Yale Golf Club, Edgewood Park, and Southern Connecticut University are all directly below

Happy to be near the top, a hiker catches his breath.

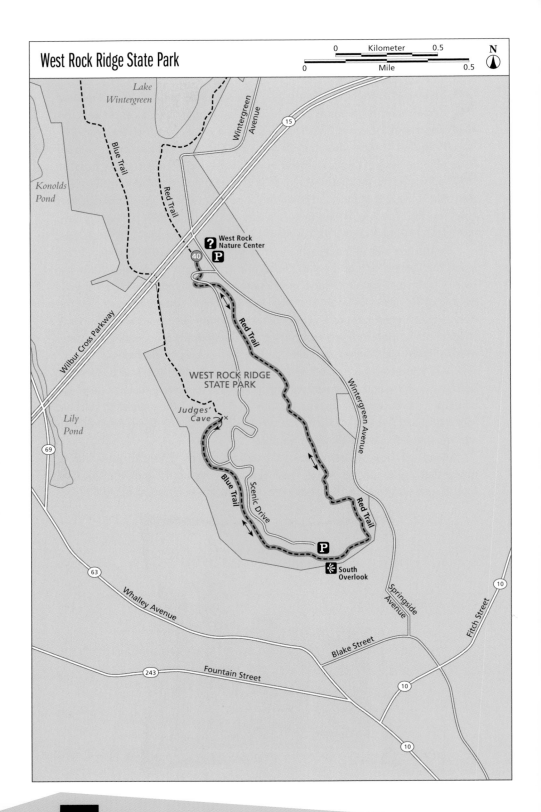

West Rock Ridge State Park

the small shelf of stone you're standing on. A more impressive view awaits, however, so continue to the northwest until mile 1.4, where the trail meets the aptly named Scenic Drive. From the southernmost tip of this fault-block mountain ridge, which runs north to the Vermont border, East Rock, New Haven, and the Long Island Sound turn the horizon into a postcard, especially early in the day and just before sunset. Consider yourself lucky if you also spot one of the few nesting peregrine falcons that have been observed in the area.

Look for blue blazes on the other side of the South Overlook's parking area and continue around the ridge to the north. Pale, almost whitish-blue chicory flowers, prickly pear cactus, and woolly hedge nettle (also known as lamb's ear) cling to the edge of the cliff just off the narrow path. To the west you'll be able to make out traffic moving on the Wilbur Cross Parkway, which tunnels underneath the park to reach Hartford.

Your own destination, a pile of stone generously labeled a cave, is considerably closer, which is fortunate, unless you're also planning to tackle the Quinnipiac Trail before heading home. Check out the cave, then retrace your steps to the trailhead.

MILES AND DIRECTIONS

0.0 Start at the map kiosk just inside the park entrance. Pick up a map and start walking south on the park road, and then dart over to the Red Trail at an opening in the trees.

0.4 The Red/White Trail enters from the west, merging with your route as it hugs the slopes of West Rock for a short distance.

0.7 A pavilion is visible down the slope to the left of the trail. Climb down a few small sets of worn stone stairs.

1.1 Turn right (southwest) on the Red Trail and prepare for a long, steady push uphill.

1.2 Arrive at a clearing that offers a view of Hamden and, farther south, New Haven.

1.3 The trails twists back to the north as it continues ascending West Rock, providing an unobstructed sightline to the Sleeping Giant.

1.4 Reach the South Overlook (elevation 406 feet), at the top of the basalt or trap rock ridge. Pick up the northbound Blue Trail on the other side of the parking lot.

1.9 Veer right (east) over jagged, angular rocks as the Yellow Trail enters from the west.

2.1 Arrive at a roundabout and Judges' Cave. Stop here for a picnic or a quick break and then return the way you came.

4.2 Arrive back at the trailhead at the park entrance.

Option: With more time, the blue-blazed Regicides Trail can be hiked from the South Overlook to the junction with the Quinnipiac Trail on York Mountain in the north. Its length in one direction is 7 miles. A 23-mile route to Cheshire, the Quinnipiac Trail is also the oldest segment of Connecticut's 800-mile Blue-Blazed Hiking Trail System.

HIKE INFORMATION

Local information: Connecticut Commission on Culture & Tourism, One Constitution Plaza, Second Floor, Hartford, CT 06103; (860) 256-2800; www.ctvisit.com

Local events/attractions: Ansonia Nature & Recreation Center, 10 Deerfield Lane, Ansonia, CT 06401; (203) 736-1053; www.ansonianaturecenter.org. Recreational opportunities and nature-oriented education programs.

Kellogg Environmental Center and Osborne Homestead Museum, 500 Hawthorne Ave., Derby, CT 06418; (203) 734-2513; www.ct.gov/dep

West Rock Nature Center, Wintergreen Avenue, New Haven, CT 06515; (203) 946-8016; www.cityofnewhaven.com/parks/parksinformation/westrockpark. asp. Explore forty-three acres of woods and fields, as well as a small animal collection. Open year-round from 10 a.m. to 4 p.m.

Good eats: Dayton Street Apizza, 60 Dayton St., New Haven, CT 06515; (203) 389-2454; http://daytonstreetapizza.com

Delaney's Restaurant & Tap Room, 882 Whalley Ave., New Haven, CT 06515; (203) 397-5494; www.delaneystaproom.com

Local outdoor stores: Trailblazer, 296 Elm St., New Haven, CT 06511; (203) 865-6244; www.shoptrailblazer.com

Outdoor World Outfitters, 979 Meriden Ave., Southington, CT 06489; (860) 621-8381; www.theoutdoorworld.com

Organizations: Connecticut Forest & Park Association (CFPA), 16 Meriden Rd., Rockfall, CT 06481; (860) 346-2372; www.ctwoodlands.org. A private non-profit committed to conserving Connecticut's land, water, and wildlife. This group also established the Blue-Blazed Hiking Trail System in 1929.

West Rock Ridge Park Association, 220 Mountain Rd., Hamden, CT 06154; http://westrockpark.wordpress.com

Connecticut Botanical Society, P.O. Box 9004, New Haven, CT 06532; www.ct-botanical-society.org. This volunteer group organizes frequent plant identification field trips.

Further Reading

Barnard, Edward Sibley. *New York City Trees: A Field Guide for the Metropolitan Area.* New York, NY: Columbia University Press, 2002.

Bryson, Bill. *A Walk in the Woods.* New York, NY: Broadway Books, 1999.

Day, Leslie. *Field Guide to the Natural World of New York City.* Baltimore, MD: Johns Hopkins University Press, 2007.

Lenik, Edward. *Iron Mine Trails: A History and Hiker's Guide to the Historic Iron Mines of the New Jersey and New York Highlands.* Mahway, NJ: New York-New Jersey Trail Conference, 1996.

Lewis, Tom. *The Hudson: A History.* New Haven, CT: Yale University Press, 2007.

Ostertag, Rhonda, and George Ostertag. *Hiking New York: A Guide to the State's Best Hiking Adventures.* 3rd ed. Guilford, CT: Globe Pequot Press, 2009.

Pritchard, Evan T. *Native New Yorkers.* San Francisco, CA: Council Oaks Books, 2007.

Shorto, Russell. *The Island at the Center of the World: The Epic Story of Dutch Manhattan and the Forgotten Colony That Shaped America.* New York, NY: Vintage, 2005.

Sibley, David Allen. *The Sibley Field Guide to Birds of Eastern North America.* New York, NY: Knopf, 2003.

Waterman, Laura. *Backwoods Ethics: A Guide to Low-Impact Camping and Hiking.* Woodstock, VT: Countryman Press, 1993.

Hike Index

About the Author

Ben Keene writes about travel, craft beer, music, and outdoor recreation for a variety of publications including *Time Out New York, DRAFT* magazine, *World Hum, Transitions Abroad, Wend, Edible East End,* and *Rails to Trails.* Formerly a touring musician and an atlas editor, he has appeared on National Public Radio, Peter Greenberg Worldwide Radio, as well as other nationally syndicated programs to discuss geographic literacy. He lives in Brooklyn, New York.

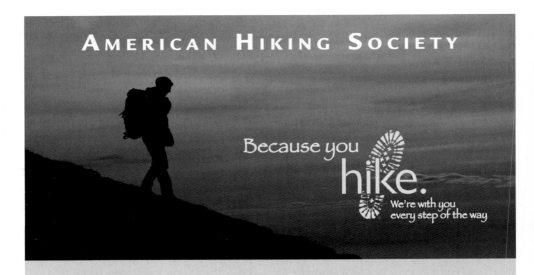
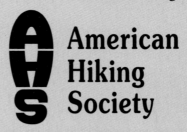